MENTAL HEALTH CARE
FOR URBAN INDIANS

MENTAL HEALTH CARE FOR URBAN INDIANS

CLINICAL INSIGHTS FROM NATIVE PRACTITIONERS

EDITED BY
TAWA M. WITKO

AMERICAN PSYCHOLOGICAL ASSOCIATION

WASHINGTON, DC

Published by
American Psychological Association
750 First Street, NE
Washington, DC 20002
www.apa.org

To order
APA Order Department
P.O. Box 92984
Washington, DC 20090-2984
Tel: (800) 374-2721; Direct: (202) 336-5510
Fax: (202) 336-5502; TDD/TTY: (202) 336-6123
Online: www.apa.org/books/
E-mail: order@apa.org

In the U.K., Europe, Africa, and the Middle East, copies may be ordered from
American Psychological Association
3 Henrietta Street
Covent Garden, London
WC2E 8LU England

Typeset in Meridien by World Composition Services, Inc., Sterling, VA

Printer: Edwards Brothers, Inc., Ann Arbor, MI
Cover Designer: Berg Design, Albany, NY
Technical/Production Editor: Harriet Kaplan

The opinions and statements published are the responsibility of the authors, and such opinions and statements do not necessarily represent the policies of the American Psychological Association.

Library of Congress Cataloging-in-Publication Data

Mental health care for urban Indians : clinical insights from Native practitioners / edited by Tawa M. Witko.— 1st ed.
    p. cm.
  ISBN 1-59147-359-4
  1. Indians of North America—Mental health services. 2. Indians of North America—Mental health. 3. Indians of North America—Counseling of. 4. City and town life—United States—Psychological aspects. 5. Indians of North America—Social conditions. 6. Cultural psychiatry—United States. I. Witko, Tawa M.

  RC451.5.I5M463 2006
  362.2089'97073—dc22   2005029125

British Library Cataloguing-in-Publication Data
A CIP record is available from the British Library.

Printed in the United States of America
First Edition

This book is dedicated to the many Indian brothers and sisters who came before me and to the many who will follow me.
Mitayke Oyasin.

Contents

Contributors

A. Mike Aragon (Pima), American Indian Clubhouse and American Indian Mental Health Project, United American Indian Involvement, Inc., Los Angeles, CA

Dolores Subia BigFoot (Caddo Nation of Oklahoma), Assistant Professor of Research Center on Child Abuse and Neglect, University of Oklahoma Health Sciences Center, Oklahoma City

Rose L. Clark (Navajo), Administrative Clinical Director, Robert Sundance Family Wellness Center, United American Indian Involvement, Inc., Los Angeles, CA

Nadine Cole (Mohawk), Clinical Psychologist, Veterans Clinic, East Los Angeles, CA

Megan Dunlap (Cherokee), graduate student, Clinical Psychology Program, Oklahoma State University, Oklahoma City

Tessa Evans-Campbell (Snohomish), Assistant Professor, School of Social Work, University of Washington, Seattle

Joseph P. Gone (Gros Ventre), Assistant Professor, University of Michigan, Ann Arbor

Carrie Lee Johnson (Dakota Sioux), Program Director, United American Indian Involvement, Inc., Seven Generations Child and Family Counseling Services, Los Angeles, CA

Rae Marie Martinez (Colville), Program Director, Native Pathways to Healing: Domestic Violence and Sexual Assault Program, United American Indian Involvement, Inc., Los Angeles, CA

Richard Milda (Crow, Lakota, and Pima), Director, Men's Reeducation Program, Cangleska, Inc., Kyle, SD

Tawa M. Witko (Sicangu Lakota), Clinical Psychologist, Heartland Psychological Services, Yankton, SD

Preface

A s I was growing up American Indian in the vast Los Angeles and San Bernardino counties, I did not understand what it meant when my father told me to be proud of my heritage but at the same time encouraged me to assimilate. In my neighborhood, there were not many Indians, and as I grew up, I began to feel the internalized hate that many of the authors in this book address. As I continued through the education system, I became even more isolated because I had little to no contact with other Indian people.

It was in college that I began to explore what it meant to "be" Indian, and as many of my friends often joked, this was my AIM (American Indian Movement) period. They were referring to the fact that I became more militant in my expressions of frustration at not feeling my people were represented in books or at my school. For example, in many classes, American Indians were not mentioned by teachers, and when I brought this up, I was often told "there is no research on Indian communities" or "that sounds like a good research study," which to this day frustrates me. Even my school, which overall was pretty culturally sensitive, often neglected to include Indian communities in events or "special" days, with the taglines, "the community is so small" or "we don't know who to contact." I suppose what bothered me the most on my educational journey was that in Los Angeles, where there is the largest concentration of urban American Indians, so many psychology students had no understanding of urban Indian needs, nor did they have any knowledge about urban relocation or boarding schools and their psychological impact on Indian communities; therefore, in their training, they did not learn to ask the questions necessary to do a thorough assessment of a client. Without my Indian mentors, the academic process I had to complete to obtain a doctorate would have been unbearable. I say this because when I was at my wits' end, frustrated with the school, with the literature, or lack thereof, and frustrated with the major problems I encountered, my mentors helped me focus and continue with the process. It was during this time that I realized how important it was to have people who understood the needs of my community, whether they were Native Americans or not. This book is a result of my desire to educate professionals and paraprofessionals about the needs of the urban Indian population, a population that is often ignored.

It is my belief that this book can serve as a bridge to further knowledge about this very important community. The chapters have been designed to give readers a basic understanding of the historical impact of colonization; the ensuing results of urban migration and boarding schools; and the effects that these events have had on the community, such as lack of cultural identity, loss of traditions, and a sense of isolation, which in turn can lead to alcoholism, violence, and other risky behaviors.

I would like to take this opportunity to thank my mentors (Joe Trimble, Teresa LaFromboise, Candace Fleming, Beth Todd-Bazemore, and Art McDonald), who taught me that I could be an Indian and a psychologist and who were always there to support me (Joe, words cannot express how much you have touched my life); my children (Jordan, Michael, Maria, Adam, and Deanna), who inspire me to make the world a better place; and my partner Rich, who has been so patient with this "relocation baby." I couldn't have asked for more. I especially thank my mother, whose unconditional love encouraged me to succeed, and my friends Margaret and Tammy, who have seen me through thick and thin with patience, friendship, and love. Thanks also to the administrative staff of the Diversity Project 2000 and Beyond (Sandy, Robin, Alberto, Bertha, and Wanda); this program encouraged me to seek my full potential through leadership and great mentoring. This book is a reflection of the skills that the program and all of you have taught me.

To the many authors who contributed to this volume, words cannot adequately express how much I appreciate your work. It has truly been an honor to work with you on this project. Your knowledge will enhance the services being provided to the community and enact change for the future. I hope that our paths will cross again some day.

MENTAL HEALTH CARE
FOR URBAN INDIANS

Tawa M. Witko

An Introduction to First Nation's People

The Indian population in the United States is growing. Numbers that were once dwindling are now increasing. Some believe this is because of the increased pride that people are taking in their heritage. The need to assimilate is diminishing, and people are actively claiming their Indian ancestry. This is evident from some of the current census data, which show an increase in the Indian population from less than 2 million in 1990 to 4 million in 2000. Many believe that even this number is vastly undercounted.

This chapter is designed to help readers understand why this book is necessary, to provide an overview of some of the significant events in tribal history that have impacted the mental health functioning of Indian people, to provide some of the background on a few traditional American Indian treatment modalities (e.g., the medicine wheel, talking circles, storytelling, and traditional healers), and to provide some current concerns (acculturation and identity issues) of urban American Indians and how these concerns may impact a psychologist's work with Indian people.

Why This Book and
Why Now?

This book is part of a work in progress. The American Indian population is growing and beginning to recapture the traditions that were forced away from them. This growing population is vastly underserved. The material presented in this volume has been developed by American Indian scholars working in Indian communities (both urban and rural) and can help both the Native and the non-Native provider or student with information that is often not taught in courses such as general psychology, psychopathology, treatment interventions, and assessment and testing.

However, this book does not address all of the issues that affect the urban Indian community. The varied impacts of HIV/AIDS, cancer, chronic and severe mental disorders, and disabilities (physical, emotional, and learning) are not addressed in this volume, yet they are clearly important issues. It is my hope that this book will serve as a beginning step in understanding the needs of urban American Indians and will inspire further research in these areas. It is also my hope that readers will develop a new understanding of the Indian people, in particular urban Indians, and with this understanding become better practitioners, researchers, and instructors who are more culturally sensitive to the needs of the Indian community.

A Historical Perspective

Before psychologists are able to help American Indian people achieve positive mental health, they must first acknowledge the impact history has had on the collective experience of Indian nations. This history is what leads us to understand more fully the multigenerational trauma cycle that has devastated many Indian people. By understanding this history, psychologists will be able to work with Indian people in a way that is culturally appropriate. The outline below is based on a format provided in F. Paniagua's (1998) *Assessing and Treating Culturally Diverse Clients*.

PRECONTACT: PRIOR TO 1492

According to Frederick E. Hoxie (1988) in *Indians in American History*, the history of Native people can be divided into pre– and post–

Christopher Columbus periods. Before the "discovery" of the New World, Native people lived on this continent working as "caretakers" of Mother Earth. They lived off the land using what it provided. Native people developed distinct and diverse ways of life depending on which geographical region they lived in. Each group had its own set of attitudes, beliefs, and postures about life, society, self, and nature. For example, the Indians of the Great Plains had a nomadic lifestyle in which they were able to move about freely. They hunted the buffalo and moved as the herds moved. They lived in homes that were mobile and portable so that following the herds was much easier. Their populations were organized into small bands, and the composition of these bands was fluid. The Indians of the Southwest, however, led a different lifestyle. These populations formed agricultural societies. They were farmers who lived off the land, their main crop being corn. Their societies were organized into cohesive groups or clans that were maintained by familial ties and ceremonial cycles. The populations in Eastern regions, which can be divided into northern and southern subregions by the Mason–Dixon line, had yet another lifestyle. The societies in the northern subregion combined hunting, gathering, and agriculture for their survival. The tribes in this area developed complex systems of government that inspired the U.S. Constitution. One of the most prominent of these was the Iroquois Confederation. The societies in the southern subregion were primarily agricultural and also developed elaborate social and political organizations. Many other regions, such as the Arctic region, the Subarctic region, the Northwest Coast, and the Far West, are not mentioned here; Indians of the Great Plains, the Southwest, and the Eastern regions are discussed as examples of different Native American populations (Hoxie, 1988). It is important to understand the differences in lifestyles, because they have implications for the generations that follow and in turn may impact the type of work a psychologist is able to do with a particular Indian client.

MANIFEST DESTINY: 1492 TO 1890

With Columbus came two concerns: (a) epidemics that cut the American Indian population in half and (b) the desire to "civilize" the "savages" who lived on this great continent. This "civilization" process took place primarily through the use of missionaries and their boarding schools (Morrissette, 1994). In addition, treaties were made and broken on a regular basis (Gone, 2004).

When Columbus arrived in the Americas, he brought with him diseases that Indian people were not accustomed to. The outbreak of smallpox, cholera, pneumonia, and syphilis produced massive deaths among the tribes of America. Not only did the number of Indians decrease, but many of these deaths were of the elders and medicine people who taught the rules of the society and helped transmit the cultural ways. Many Indian people began to give up hope and saw the only way to survive was to work with the Europeans.

The Native ways of living were further destroyed through reservations and boarding schools. The reservations were separate areas the government designated as "Indian Land." This land was not always the best land, but Indian people worked with it and saw it as a way to avoid further contact with the Europeans. This proved to be a problem, because many tribespeople who were once hunters were now required to become farmers. For some, this meant giving up their tribal ways. In addition to reservations, boarding schools were created as a way to replace the practice of "Indian language, dress, beliefs, religion, and customs with the practice of the white civilizations" (Paniagua, 1994, p. 79). This process has had devastating effects on Indian people in that Indian children were taken from their families often without parental permission and taught that being Indian was bad. The effects are still being felt by many Indian people who were raised by parents who were products of these types of schools.

Although Native people may not have fully trusted the *Wasichu* (White man), they made agreements with him in hopes of helping their tribes survive. These agreements (*treaties*), however, were made and broken. This was counter to the Native view of reciprocity. The Native people believed that if they helped the White man and worked with him, then the White man would in turn help them survive in the White man's "New World." History proved this was not the case. This betrayal is important to understand, because it has sustained effects on today's Native people. The collective past of Native people, the broken promises, the discrimination, and the cruel and oppressive treatment by mainstream systems all serve as factors that undermine the psychological well-being of Native people and their children (D'Andrea, 1994). It was toward the end of this period that U.S. policies began to shift from the physical annihilation and genocide of Indian people to what is now considered cultural genocide (Weaver, 1998).

ASSIMILATION: 1890 TO 1970

During this time period, Indians only had a few choices. They could assimilate into mainstream culture or suffer the consequences. These consequences included attempts to eliminate the relationship between the federal government and the tribes—for example, repealing acts designed to help Indian people and not following through with written treaties made with the tribes. This termination process also involved the concept of relocation, which "invited" Indian people, primarily men, to move from the reservation to cities where they were to be trained for jobs. The idea was that if Indian people moved to the cities, this would allow the reservations to be closed, and therefore, no government assistance would be needed. Unfortunately, once the Indian people reached large urban areas they found little support (Gone, 2004; Price, 1976; Witko, 2002). They were often isolated and found themselves in skid row areas. These termination measures led to increases in social and behavioral problems among Indians, most notably increased substance abuse, high suicide rates, and depression (Gone, 2004).

SELF-DETERMINATION: 1970 TO PRESENT

During this period, there began to be an increase in the number of Indians in leadership roles, and advocacy for Indian rights became common as new acts were passed to foster the growth of the Indian population. Four congressional acts are of significance to Indian people and are described here briefly. In 1975, the Indian Self-Determination Act was passed (see Walker & LaDue, 1986). It stated that Indian people had the right to control their own destiny and that tribes had control over the welfare and education of Indian people. It also protected Indian lands and resources. In 1976, the Indian Health Care Improvement Act (see Walker & LaDue, 1986) was passed, which provided for better health services to Indian communities both urban and rural, more provisions for those wishing to work with the Indian community, and more access to health services. In 1978, the Indian Child Welfare Act (see Walker & LaDue, 1986) was passed, which stated that the tribe had full jurisdiction over child custody proceedings; the tribe was to be informed and present for any court proceedings; and the tribe was to be involved in any placement or adoption proceedings. Evans-Campbell (see chap. 2, this volume) provides an in-depth look at the Indian Child Welfare Act and its impact on Indian communities. Finally, in 1978, the Indian Religious Freedom Act (see Walker & LaDue, 1986) was passed, which allowed Indian people to practice the traditional religions and ceremonies without the interference of outside sources. For example, those wishing to practice the peyote ceremonies were allowed to do so even though peyote is considered a narcotic. In addition to the passage of these acts, this time period has been notable for a unification of Indian people, especially in urban areas where there is great diversity among the represented tribes. Although Indian people can be a part of their own particular tribe, they are also learning about the ways of other tribes. This unification has led to an increase in Indian-run programs designed to help Indian people reclaim the power and pride that was once prevalent and to teach this pride to the next generation.

Understanding the history of Indian people allows psychologists to better understand the impact this history may have had on the mental health functioning of the generations that followed. This is a history that many scholars have stated has led to a series of mental health dysfunctions commonly referred to as a *multigenerational trauma cycle* that encompasses issues such as substance abuse, violence, depression, suicide, and overall poor mental health (Brave Heart & DeBruyn, 1998; Duran, 2002; Gone, 2004; Napholz, 2000; Witko, 2002; see also chaps. 5 and 6, this volume).

Traditional Treatment Modalities

Traditional Native ways of handling stress and dealing with problems were forbidden during the cultural and physical genocide that followed Columbus's arrival in America. These practices and traditions are now showing resurgence, not only on the reservations but also in urban areas. Indian people are looking back to these ways to find fulfillment and learn how to cope in today's society (see chap. 1, this volume). Some of these ways include the use of the medicine wheel, the talking circle, storytelling, and traditional healers. These areas will be briefly described to familiarize the reader with the concepts.

MEDICINE WHEEL

In traditional Native American healing practices, the medicine wheel was used for guidance and direction. It allowed for increased under-standing and spiritual guidance. The medicine wheel is divided into four parts that represent the four parts of human existence: (a) the physical, which tends to the physical aspects of the human; (b) the mental, which accounts for intellectual processes; (c) the emotional, which accounts for one's emotional responses; and (d) the spiritual, which accounts for the connection one has with the Great Spirit and the land. Each aspect is addressed through the sacred directions, which help one establish self-identity and self-confidence. Today this would be considered a holistic approach to therapy that accounts for the entire person and how one aspect of an individual can affect other aspects of being. This approach is important to effective therapy, programs, books, and classes in that it forces psychologists to look not just at the individual but at the individual, the family, and the environment. Johnson (see chap. 10, this volume) provides a closer look at the medicine wheel and its use in the healing process.

THE TALKING CIRCLE

The traditional talking circle was considered a circle of respect, part of the "sacred hoop" (a way of living in the world that involves connectedness to others). It encompassed love, understanding, respect, communication, sharing, acceptance, and strength. It was a process that allowed for discussions to take place in which specific rules governed behavior so that respect was achieved and decisions about the family or tribe could be made. Today this might look like a family therapy session or a group session. Witko (see chap. 8, this volume) and Clark and Witko (see chap. 9, this volume) provide another view of how this might look in treatment. This concept is important when working with Indian clients because it allows the psychologist to understand the importance of the family and community as part of the treatment plan. In fact, many urban Indian programs use this approach extensively, especially with Indian people in recovery (see chap. 4, this volume, for more details).

STORYTELLING

Storytelling was often used as a way to describe consequences of behaviors. Stories were used to tell how things were and why they happened. This can be an important tool for Indian people. As discussed in detail in some of the following chapters, an Indian person may not be able to describe in psychological terms the multigenerational trauma that he or she has experienced, but the person may be able to express it in some sort of narrative fashion. It also needs to be understood that a lot of urban Native people do not know the stories of their culture, so the use of storytelling may be a way to help them connect to a lost part of their heritage and in turn help them understand themselves better. This has proven to be very effective with urban Indians who are now in the process of learning the stories of their ancestors and passing them on to their children. This process has enabled Indian people to learn some of the traditional ways of handling stress and addressing problems in the home (Witko, 2002). BigFoot and Dunlap (see chap. 7, this volume) provide an excellent discussion of how this is being done in both urban and rural Indian communities.

HEALERS

Traditional healers are seen as highly respected individuals in the Indian community. Many Native people will turn to them before approaching a psychologist (Gone, 2004). For therapy, programs, classes, and books to be effective, it is important to involve healers in the process, either through consultation or by including them in the actual therapeutic group. The important thing for the psychologist is to establish a relationship with the traditional healers within the community. If these elders feel they can trust a psychologist, then they will recommend that person and that person's program, class, or book. Healers can also be used for the recruitment of individuals and families who may not otherwise attend.

Being Indian in the 21st Century

WHAT'S IN A NAME?

Before Columbus "discovered" America, Indian people referred to themselves by tribe, nation, clan, or band. In the company of other Indian people, most would use their tribal ancestry to describe themselves. For example, an Indian person today might say that he or she is an Oglala Lakota from the Pine Ridge Reservation in South Dakota. This would indicate the band (Oglala), tribe (Sioux or Lakota), reservation (Pine Ridge), and location (South Dakota). In the company of non-Indians, a person might simply say that he or she is either American Indian or Native American. There have been many discussions among Indian and non-Indian people as to which name is most appropriate or politically correct. Depending on whom one asks, one will get two very different reasons, both of which are valid.

The concept of "American Indian" came from the misidentification by Christopher Columbus. He thought he had landed in India, which would make the people he "found" Indians. Of course, he was incorrect in this identification, but the name stayed. Many Indian people prefer *American Indian* because it implies that (a) "Indian" is the primary identification, and (b) it allows for a separation between tribal governments and the United States. It acknowledges the sovereignty among Indian nations.

The concept of "Native American" came from the idea that we are all Americans and that "Native" is our cultural background. This has caused some confusion among Americans in general, because many Americans believe that anyone born and raised in the United States is "native" to America. Also, many Indians raised in urban areas prefer to call themselves "Native Americans," whereas those raised on the reservation tend to call themselves "American Indians."

The important thing to remember is that both of these terms, although acceptable, tend to gloss over the ethnic diversity among the many tribes that these terms represent (Trimble, Helms, & Root, 2002). So which is correct? The answer lies with the individual and where he or she is in the identity process. If a psychologist is unsure, he or she should ask for the individual's preference.

BLOOD QUANTUM

An interesting aspect of being Indian is that you cannot simply call yourself "Indian"; you must be able to "prove" you are Indian. This "proof" can be found on your official Indian card, known as your Certificate Degree of Indian Blood. There is no uniform criterion used to determine the level of *blood quantum* (the percentage of traceable Indian ancestry of an individual) needed to be considered American Indian. The criterion is set by each Indian nation. Some nations require an individual to be at least 50% of the specific tribe, whereas other nations require only 12% Indian blood (Weaver, 1998). In addition, some nations only trace Indian blood if the mother or father was born on the reservation. For example, a client whose mother is American Indian and father is non-Indian may not be enrolled in the tribe if the mother was not born on the reservation. These individuals are not eligible for programs or funding awarded to enrolled members of a recognized tribe even though they participate in cultural activities.

For individuals who are not enrolled in a nation, there are few to no benefits, such as the ability to participate in the political process of their particular nation and access to health care and social benefits. This lack of benefit and recognition can contribute to low self-esteem and a poor sense of identity (Weaver, 1998).

The quagmire for many urban Indians is "I look Indian, but I can't get help because I am not enrolled." This is a very real dilemma for urban Indians who have never lived on the reservation and whose parents never enrolled them in the tribe. This becomes even more complicated if they do not know who to turn to for help. This should be considered in the work practitioners do with their Indian clients, because it plays a big role in one's sense of self. Some urban Indian centers are able to offer assistance in this area, which has been beneficial to the well-being and self-esteem of their clientele.

Urban Indians

For urban Indians the impacts of boarding schools and urban migration are equally devastating. For these individuals, defining who they are becomes a key aspect of their identity and self-esteem, with the added struggle of acculturation and assimilation playing a key role.

ACCULTURATION ISSUES

Acculturation has to do with taking in another's culture, whereas assimilation involves an individual becoming part of another culture (Reber, 1985). These two concepts are an important element in the development of self-esteem and identity as an Indian person.

According to Loye and Ryan (in LaFromboise, Trimble, & Mohatt, 1993), there are five categories of "Indianness": traditional, transitional, marginal, assimilated, and bicultural. Understanding these categories is important for determining where an individual "fits" and helps in the development of treatment plans or programs that are culturally competent.

1. The *traditional* person observes the "old ways." He or she knows little or no English and speaks primarily in the Native language. This type of person is less likely to seek help from a therapist for problems he or she is having at home. This person is most likely to turn to a traditional healer like a shaman.

2. The *transitional* person speaks English and his or her Native language. He or she practices but is not embedded in the traditional beliefs and culture of his or her nation, but such a person has not fully accepted the culture of the dominant society. This person may not seek help from a therapist but may consider a traditional healer for problems he or she is having.

3. The *marginal* person is unable to live the cultural heritage of his or her tribe and is unable to live in dominant society. This person is at the most risk among these categories for social and psychological problems (Berry, 1989) because he or she does not fit in either the tribe or the dominant society, which may lead such a person to find solace with other displaced individuals in society.

4. The *assimilated* person embraces and feels accepted by the dominant society. This person feels comfortable in programs or therapy based on contemporary norms and rules. This person may not even consider incorporating his or her cultural heritage into his or her lifestyle. Such a person is seen as detached from his or her heritage and may even deny the existence of his or her Indian blood.

5. The *bicultural* person is accepted in the dominant society and in tribal society. He or she can move between both worlds.

This person may seek traditional or contemporary means to solve a problem or crisis. This is the most functional type of person in that he or she incorporates both Indian and mainstream culture. Problems can arise, however, when stress builds up trying to both serve the tribal people and succeed in the dominant society. Such individuals may not be able to determine what parts of the traditional Indian lifestyle to incorporate and what not to incorporate. These individuals are usually willing to participate in a culturally competent program or psychotherapy or counseling.

IDENTITY ISSUES

A person's level of acculturation appears to be directly linked to his or her sense of identity. For example, the primary purpose of the boarding schools and missions was to assimilate the Native people into American culture. Indian people were forced to adopt the ways of the dominant society and ignore the customs and spirit of their culture. All of the customs and ceremonies were taken away, and the culture was slowly dismantled. This dismantling had a detrimental effect on the well-being of Indian people (MacPhee, Fritz, & Miller-Heyl, 1996). Indian people today are still struggling with the development of their own sense of ethnic identity in a society that does not acknowledge that they exist (see chap. 3, this volume). This identity conflict is problematic if the individual is a parent and must in turn try to teach his or her child what it means to be Indian. If the parent is unsuccessful, this can become a serious problem as the child reaches adolescence and tries to define him- or herself (Flynn, Clark, Aragon, Stanzell, & Evans, 1998). Indian people living in urban areas are forced to establish a sense of Indianness without other Indian people around to serve as models. This can lead them to look toward the media for guidance or develop an idealized image of what being Indian means, an image most cannot fulfill.

Relational Perspective

The history of the Indian people has been devastating; use of the term *genocide* is an understatement. To effectively work with Indian people, one must be able to step out of the academic box and observe from a relational perspective. This relational perspective allows one to look at the whole picture and to understand how the collective experience of

Indian people was altered through a history that is not truly recognized. Psychologists must go from a hierarchy to a circle that values each person in the circle. In fact, the research that has been done on the use of mental health services indicates that the more a program, individual, or treatment plan incorporates traditional ways of viewing the world, the more effective that service tends to be (Chester, Mahalish, & Davis, 1999; Evaneshko, 1999; Gone, 2004).

The authors in this book seek to challenge readers to develop a new understanding of what being Indian in the 21st century really means and what practitioners can do to change it. Readers will be exposed to material that may be new and exciting and that will challenge their way of looking at the world. I encourage readers to be open to the experience and take this opportunity to learn about the historical and theoretical background of urban American Indian mental health; specific urban Indian treatment considerations such as identity development, substance abuse, issues of violence, and trauma; and, finally, new directions in treatment such as storytelling, American Indian parenting programs, working with urban Indian adolescents, and exploring new healing models.

Organization of This Book

This book is divided into three parts. Part I provides historical and theoretical background information. In Part II, authors discuss specific urban Indian treatment issues. Part III addresses new directions for providing mental health care to urban Indians, and the conclusion looks to the future, examining emerging trends.

References

Berry, J. W. (1989). Psychology of acculturation. In N. R. Goldberger & J. B. Veroff (Eds.), *The culture and psychology reader* (pp. 457–488). New York: New York University Press.

Brave Heart, M. Y. H., & DeBruyn, L. (1998). The American Indian holocaust: Healing historical unresolved grief. *American Indian and Alaska Native Mental Health Research: The Journal of the National Center*, *8*(2), 60–82.

Chester, B., Mahalish, P., & Davis, J. (1999). Mental health needs assessment of off-reservation American Indian people in northern Arizona. *American Indian and Alaska Native Mental Health Research: The Journal of the National Center, 8*(3), 25–40.

D'Andrea, M. (1994). The concerns of Native American youth. *Journal of Multicultural Counseling and Development, 22*, 173–181.

Duran, E. (2002). *Wounding seeking wounding: The psychology of internalized oppression.* Unpublished manuscript.

Evaneshko, V. (1999). Mental health needs assessment of Tucson's urban Native American population. *American Indian and Alaska Native Mental Health Research: The Journal of the National Center, 8*(3), 41–61.

Flynn, K., Clark, R., Aragon, M., Stanzell, S., & Evans, T. (1998). *The mental health status of at-risk American Indian and Alaska Native youth in Los Angeles County, 1998.* Los Angeles: United American Indian Involvement.

Gone, J. P. (2004). Mental health services for Native Americans in the 21st century United States. *Professional Psychology: Research and Practice, 35*, 10–18.

Hoxie, F. E. (1988). *Indians in American history.* Wheeling, IL: Harlan Davidson.

LaFromboise, T. D., Trimble, J. E., & Mohatt, G. V. (1993). Counseling intervention and American Indian tradition: An integrative approach. In D. R. Atkinson, G. Morten, & D. W. Sue. (Eds.), *Counseling American minorities: A cross-cultural perspective* (pp. 145–170). Dubuque, IA: Brown & Benchmark.

MacPhee, D., Fritz, J., & Miller-Heyl, J. (1996). Ethnic variations in personal social networks and parenting, *Child Development, 67*, 3278–3295.

Morrissette, P. J. (1994). The holocaust of First Nation People: Residual effects on parenting and treatment implications. *Contemporary Family Therapy, 16*, 381–392.

Napholz, L. (2000). Bicultural resynthesis: Tailoring an effectiveness trial for a group of urban American Indian women. *American Indian and Alaska Native Mental Health Research: The Journal of the National Center, 9*(3), 49–70.

Paniagua, F. (1998). *Assessing and treating culturally diverse clients.* Thousand Oaks, CA: Sage.

Price, J. A. (1976). North American Indian families. In C. H. Mindel & R. W. Habenstein (Eds.), *Ethnic families in America: Patterns and variations* (pp. 248–270). New York: Elsevier.

Reber, A. (1985). *Dictionary of psychology.* New York: Penguin Books.

Trimble, J., Helms, J., & Root, M. (2002). Social and psychological perspectives on ethnic and racial identity. In G. Bernal, J. Trimble,

K. Burlew, & F. Leong (Eds.), *Handbook of racial and ethnic psychology* (pp. 239–275). Thousand Oaks, CA: Sage.

Walker, R. D., & LaDue, R. (1986). An integrative approach to American Indian mental health. In C. B. Wilkinson (Ed.), *Ethnic psychiatry* (pp. 143–199). New York: Plenum Press.

Weaver, H. (1998). Indigenous people in a multicultural society: Unique issues for human services. *Social Work, 43,* 203–212.

Witko, T. (2002). Providing culturally competent services to American Indians. *California Psychologist, 35*(4), 25, 29.

I

Historical and Theoretical Background of Urban American Indian Mental Health

P art I of this book is aimed at providing the reader with the background necessary for understanding the urban Indian population. It is important to understand some of the historical background of Indian people because it contributes tremendously to their mental health functioning. Authors for these three chapters were selected on the basis of their extensive work with Indian people and their understanding of the phenomena of internalized oppression and racism as it pertains to the Indian Community.

Chapter 1, "A Clinical Understanding of Urban American Indians" by A. Mike Aragon, focuses on understanding the dynamics of the American Indian population and addresses ways in which mental health workers may appropriately work with this population. The author addresses the impact of American history on Indian nations, the use of alcohol as a weapon, the assimilation process, and the common issues and concerns regarding mental illness and its care. The author concludes with a discussion of efforts being made to encourage the traditional ways of being as a way to heal some of the ills within the community.

Chapter 2, "Indian Child Welfare Practice Within Urban American Indian/Native American Communities" by Tessa Evans-Campbell, focuses on the issue of Indian child welfare and how that impacts urban Indian communities. The author begins with background and historical data on the Indian Child Welfare Act and then continues with information on current practices within urban settings using case studies as examples. The author then addresses some of the clinical skills needed by those wishing to do public child welfare work within urban Indian communities. She concludes with emerging issues in child welfare practice and how these issues affect urban Indian families and children.

Chapter 3, "Mental Health, Wellness, and the Quest for an Authentic American Indian Identity" by Joseph P. Gone, focuses on identifying the historical impact of colonization and its impact on mental health and wellness. In addition the author explores new theories on American Indian identity and introduces new models for the development of an authentic American Indian identity.

A. Mike Aragon

A Clinical Understanding of Urban American Indians

1

Through colonization, American Indian people have endured one of the most systematic genocides in world history (D'Andrea, 1994). At the beginning of the colonization process in North America, prior to 1492, there were over 150 million Native American people living on the continent (Brucker & Perry, 1988). By the year 1900, there were only 250,000 (Oswalt, 1988).

Europeans forced American Indian people into reservations, removed youth to boarding schools, coerced migration to urban areas, and mandated assimilation into mainstream culture. Over time, American Indians lost their traditional means of subsistence, resources, and lifestyle while suffering from prolonged, profound, and systematic exploitation (Deloria, 1969; Zimmerman & Ramirez-Valles, 1996).

Prior to colonization by Europeans, American Indian people lived in North, Central, and South America for over 2,000 years. Loosely associated, flourishing tribal societies endorsed cultural values such as cooperation, sharing of resources, respect for nature, and family and communal welfare. American colonization has led to the current deterioration of American Indian traditional ways of life. It also led to an increase in self-hatred and drinking behavior.

Self-Hatred

During colonization, American Indian individuals and groups fell into despair, which brought on self-hatred (Duran & Duran, 1995). After years of repeated exposure to the social ills of bigotry, discrimination, and prejudice, American Indian people started to internalize their oppressors' negative and devalued caricature of themselves.

American Indians have been jeered at, pointed to, and even feared by non-Indians from the beginning of colonization to the present. Such experiences become internalized and manifest themselves in a form of self-devaluation, shame, and isolation. Turner (1982) suggested that this type of group formation resulted from the internalization of self-defining social categorizations. Once internalized, self-definitions produce stereotypic perceptions of the self and other group members, thereby increasing intragroup similarity, attraction, and shared behavior (Snyder, Decker-Tank, & Berscheid, 1977).

Despite decades of research on American Indians, there have been no studies involving the systematic investigation of the interactive effects of internalized racism. Duran and Duran (1995) have theorized that the development of self-hatred among American Indians began with colonization and has been passed down with each successive generation.

American Indian Urbanization

Only since the late 1940s, after World War II, was the urbanization of American Indians recognized as an issue of concern by social scientists. The social changes resulting from the movement of American Indian people from reservations to urban areas had an enormous impact on them.

During the 1950s and early 1960s, federal funds were generated in an effort to better assimilate Indian people into the majority society (Barse, 1994). A key component of this effort featured the relocation of American Indians to cities for jobs or job training. Half of America's Indians became enmeshed in this attempt to improve their lives. American Indians were relocated from their reservations to five major metropolitan cities in the United States by the federal government during the 1950s (Attneave, 1982).

Federal training programs and promises of a "better life" were incentives offered by the U.S. government to encourage American Indian people to assimilate into mainstream culture and urban environments. Although land, housing, and the cost of living were often cheaper on reservations, and the access to federal, Bureau of Indian Affairs, and Indian Health Service programs provided much support (LaFromboise, 1988), jobs and economic opportunity were often in short supply. Despite the pull from family networks on the reservation to remain, the push of poverty on reservations continued to propel a considerable number of American Indians to urban areas (M. T. Garrett & Pichette, 2000).

The relocation movement had some immediate consequences for American Indians (Edwards & Edwards, 1984). The urban environment was usually fraught with transitional problems and issues. American Indian migrants found it harder to get services in urban areas and were likely to be unskilled (Champagne, Goldberg-Ambrose, Machamer, Phillips, & Evans, 1996). These individuals often returned to the reservation, particularly when they had serious medical problems (Grossman, Krieger, Sugarman, & Forquera, 1994). Of those who did migrate and receive assistance from the Bureau of Indian Affairs, many fared worse economically than those who remained on their reservation (Champagne et al., 1996).

The roles that urban migration, overall community organization, poverty, unemployment, geographic isolation, lack of service resources, and racial and ethnic tensions with non-Indian communities play in relation to self-hate have been raised in the literature, but answers are few. Instead, a great deal of research has focused on the problems American Indians have presented to the greater society as they mainstreamed into urban areas from reservations. Studies on alcohol abuse and the American Indian tend to dominate the scholarly literature.

Alcohol as a Weapon

Alcohol and drugs have historically been the scourge of most Indian communities. Traders and explorers of all the colonial powers used alcohol to their advantage in dealings with naive, trusting, and inebriated Indian tribesmen.

The role of the U.S. government in relation to the development of alcoholism is an important issue. Alcohol was a powerful subversion strategy in the westward movement of American colonization. More than the rifle or the cannon, alcohol disarmed and conquered many unsuspecting and gullible Native Americans. More than a century and a half later, the specter of that history still haunts the collective cultural memory of American Indians and influences how some American Indians perceive themselves. For many Indian people cut off from the details and strengths of their heritage, there is still a vague and ill-defined yet enormous sense of loss and an image of failure and defeat that is difficult to overcome.

Of the current theories of alcohol use among American Indians, three common schools of thought emerge that incorporate the concept that history has contributed to American Indian drinking patterns. These theories propose that Indians drink to mourn the loss of tradition, to solidify their group identity or "Indianness," and to share a type of supernatural experience that differentiates their experiences from those of Whites (Weibel-Orlando, 1981).

Weibel-Orlando (1981) asserted that American Indians drink because of significant peer pressure. This group dynamic includes the belief among American Indians that intoxication is a useful expression of mutual acceptance and separateness from Whites. In the eyes of society, Indians drink because of significant peer pressure, but the roots run deep and most often go unnoticed by those who would be of help.

Tragically, alcohol has been a key to American Indian defeats of the past and has become a crutch of choice for the walking wounded of today who puzzle and frustrate bureaucrats and health providers to whom they have been assigned. Although the general etiology, biology, and dynamics of alcoholism are well-known to health care practitioners, many American Indians are likely experiencing depression, schizophrenia, and other major mental illnesses masked by rage and alcoholism.

The Indian Problem

American Indians were not recognized as citizens of the United States until 1926. Since that time, researchers have been striving to find new methods to unify the identity and describe the needs in Indian communities. "Let's make them all farmers" was a government program. "Let's send their children away to boarding schools to help them assimilate" was another. In retrospect, it is clear that under the U.S. policy of forced acculturation, federal authorities completely disregarded both the desires and the psychological development of American Indians.

American Indians were also stripped of their lands, traditions, dress, religion, language, and children as a result of what we now consider ethnic genocide. For many generations, American Indians have likely experienced what today is called posttraumatic stress disorder. It is the result of a history of wars, violence, incarceration, forced relocation, self-hate, and all the rest of the litany of woes that make up our history since White Americans of European origin moved west and Indians were subjugated, bypassed, or eliminated under the banner of "manifest destiny."

Once a group of people has been assaulted in a genocidal fashion, psychological ramifications tend to occur (Krell, 1990; Shosan, 1989). In only one generation before the effects of the Jewish holocaust were studied, American Indian people were suddenly separated from loved ones, their culture, and their homes. Many of the dynamics from the Jewish experience are similar to those of the American Indian experience, with the exception that the world has not acknowledged or studied the holocaust of Native American people in this hemisphere. Cole (see chap. 6, this volume) provides additional discussion of this connection.

The impact of the American historical relationship with Indian nations remains part of an almost hopelessly complex parcel of issues that must somehow be understood to provide appropriate services to American Indians. In reality, the diversity of the American Indian population cannot be overstated. American Indians are different from the dominant culture, and even distinctly different from one another; however, the government often persists in creating one-size-fits-all simple solutions that most often do not work (Weibel-Orlando, 1989).

Predictably, after 25 years of "relocation" to the cities, American Indians have joined the crush of unwanted "newcomers." Many young Indian families live dead-end lives in urban poverty. Many Indian women raise their children in impoverished circumstances that breed depression, crime, and disillusionment. Indian infants have over a 50% greater chance of dying at birth than do non-Indian babies (Grossman et al., 1994). In addition, they grow up in homes that are 3 times more likely to be substandard than those of other city dwellers (M. T. Garrett & Pichette, 2000). Nearly three out of every four Indian students drop out before finishing high school (May & Moran, 1995). Concluding the urban experience are alcoholism, infectious disease, and poverty that too often coalesce into early death.

All Indian peoples were impacted by the conquest of this land. However, to many people, American Indians are invisible members of contemporary society. To others they are an incorrigible socioeconomic, welfare, and law and order problem.

What About Mental Illness Care?

The treatment of severe mental illness problems within Indian communities, whether urban or reservation, is complicated by the ever-present abuse of alcohol and drugs. It becomes further confused because both legal medication prescriptions and illicit street drugs often do not have the same impact on Indians as they do on members of other ethnic groups (Reed, 1985). There are also psychological differences between Indians and other population group members (Renfry, 1992). Common medications often have affects on the patient that are not anticipated, and the impact varies depending on the degree of Indian blood of the individual. As a result, American Indian people are over- and under-medicated, creating additional concerns about compliance.

Studies on the mental health conditions of urban American Indians remain virtually nonexistent. Most published studies on the general health of American Indians have been based on data from clinics and hospitals that cannot be generalized to an entire American Indian and Alaska Native population. Furthermore, the Indian Health Service does not collect or publish vital statistics or population characteristics from urban programs except when these data are included with national-level data on the reservation states (LaFromboise, 1988). Many of the studies that do exist are within unpublished dissertations or outdated manuscripts, representing a body of work that is not readily accessible. Of the studies on mental health care of various different ethnic groups, the data suggest that American Indians tend to underuse services and have a high dropout rate (Sue, Allen, & Conaway, 1978; Trimble & Hayes, 1984).

Recently, psychology interns in a doctoral program encountered great resistance while working with Indian clients in Denver, Colorado. They had difficulty securing regular appointments and establishing rapport with these clients. The interns reacted by intellectualizing, devaluing, or expressing hostility toward the Indian clients who often failed to return for their second appointments. They referred to the clients as unmotivated, unreliable, substance abusing, language challenged, and developmentally slow. What was missed and misread about their clients was found in the interns' own overwhelming frustrations driven by dominant-group values and perceived differences between themselves and their Indian clients (Aragon, 1999). Perhaps a greater understanding of the specific needs of Indian people would have helped these interns better understand how to work effectively with their Indian clients.

Apparently, even the sophisticated next generation of mental health professionals is not being provided with the appropriate training to enable them not to fall prey to some of the common stereotypes of American Indians as silent, angry, and lost victims in our society. This is an area that must be rectified if the needs of Indian people are to be met in culturally competent ways.

The Clinical Approach to American Indian Clients

There is no single best method to approach American Indian clients in the clinical milieu; however, a seasoned practitioner generally follows the path of unconditional positive regard in the establishment of a relationship. LaFromboise, Trimble, and Mohatt (1990) asserted that considerable evidence supports the view that counseling services designed around conventional individual therapy regimes are inappropriate for service delivery in Indian communities. However, because of client diversity within urban environments, assumptions about the strength of Indian identity and affiliation cannot be made.

One of the first and most important elements in working with a client is to complete a thorough intake. A standard psychosocial assessment, in addition to the legal forms for treatment consent and confidentiality, is an appropriate instrument for American Indian clients. A robust psychosocial instrument will serve to structure the session and help the client to focus his or her responses. Additional dimensions of the interview should include items regarding a client's level of tribal and cultural affiliation with respect to bicultural competence and assimilation.

The use of a genogram during preliminary sessions appears to greatly enhance the understanding of the client's history, relative position within the family, and strength of relationships. A genogram can highlight relevant family medical history, substance abuse patterns, tribal connections, early living arrangements, employment patterns, and other concerns.

Another relevant tool is a time line diagram. Drawing a time line with distinct demarcations that represent the dates of significant events in the client's history can help identify the major milestones and setbacks in his or her life. The use of a time line can also be helpful in concretizing any significant developments or patterns that may have contributed to the presenting problem. Sensitivity to a client's level of reading ability should always be present.

Anecdotal reports suggest that American Indian clients disclose only what they want you to know and no more. A modest degree of guardedness is an appropriate response when any individual is asked to confide in a stranger. American Indian clients, however, may have had negative social experiences that have deepened their feelings of powerlessness and mistrust, particularly toward non-Indians and others outside of their family (Cooley, Ostendorf, & Bickerton, 1979; Dukepoo, 1980). Recognition of the power differential between patient and practitioner is an important clinical element to monitor. In addition, transference and countertransference issues may also arise, particularly when the counselor–client nonverbal interaction is not understood. For example, American Indians usually speak softly and take ample time to reflect before speaking, which can easily be misread by clinicians unaware of cultural norms.

It is particularly important for the practitioner to demonstrate respect for the American Indian client through active listening and not interrupting. Reflective responding and use of descriptive statements rather than questioning (J. T. Garrett & Garrett, 1994) can help to engage the client in the description of his or her concerns. Periodic comments by the practitioner about the counseling process and modeling self-disclosure through anecdotes or short stories may also comfort the client and demystify the counseling experience, which to many is new. Furthermore, assistance with associated case management needs, such as linkage to American Indian services when appropriate, may also facilitate the development of the clinical relationship. The aim is to establish a partnership with the American Indian client in the movement toward self-empowerment, whereby the client becomes an active participant in the understanding of his or her presenting problem.

The use of psychoeducation can be a valuable tool with American Indian clients. For example, psychoeducational material of common clinical conditions may reduce a client's anxiety related to his or her presenting concerns. Some conditions can be better accepted when the Indian client understands and perceives his or her concerns as solvable or manageable problems in relation to daily living. Active alcohol use or abuse should be stabilized prior to addressing the deeper issues of personality development. Finally, the stigma that many urban American Indians feel about using mental health services can be reduced when confidentiality, a positive clinical relationship, and an understanding of basic American Indian values have been established.

Exhibit 1.1 compares traditional American Indian values with mainstream American culture values and can be used as a beginning guide for clinicians working with American Indian clients. It lists some

EXHIBIT 1.1

A Comparison of American Indian and Mainstream American Values

American Indian values	Mainstream American values
Group life is primary	The individual is primary
Extended family is important	Nuclear family is usual focus
Respect elders and those with spiritual powers	Respect youth and success
Orientation toward the present and past	Orientation to the future
Personal character is the primary source of status	Educational degrees are source of status
Cooperation, generosity, sharing	Competition, saving, individual ownership
Personal caution: indirect criticism	Personal openness: direct criticism
Modesty, humility, patience, calmness	Less modesty, impatience, activity
Time is always with us	Time is negotiable; every minute should be used
Introverted—avoid ridicule or criticism of others, if possible	Extroverted—seek analysis and criticism of situations
Pragmatic, accept "what is"	Must change or fix problems
Emphasis on responsibility for family and personal sphere	Emphasis on authority and responsibility over a wide area of social life
Emphasis on how others behave, not on what they say; listening and observation skills valued	Eager to relate to others; emphasis on how they feel or think; verbal skills valued
Work to meet needs; nonmaterialistic	Work for work's sake; materialistic
Incorporate helpers in family network	Keep network of family, friends, and acquaintances separate
Seek harmony	Seek progress
Religion and spirituality pervade life	Religion is a segment of life
Holistic approach to health; illness is a result of a mental, spiritual, and physical imbalance	Attention to physical ailments; illness is seen as primarily a physical imbalance
Lack of or limited eye-to-eye contact is a sign of respect	Eye-to-eye contact demonstrates interest, involvement, and respect
Self-exploratory child-rearing practices	Directive-oriented child-rearing practices

Note. Adapted from *American Indian Perspectives on Disability* (Native American Research and Training Center Monograph Series No. 3, p. 4), by J. R. Joe and D. L. Miller, 1987, Tucson: Native American Research and Training Center, University of Arizona. Copyright 1987 by the Native American Research and Training Center. Adapted with permission.

of the inherent differences that can impact how Native and non-Native clients interact with one another.

A Rebirth of Hope

With all the ills in urban American Indian communities, where will hope come from? That is a question one hears over and over in meeting after meeting about the plight of American Indian people. What we are seeing now is American Indians in their respective urban communities beginning to demonstrate that they are again in a period of transition, except that this time it appears to be self-started and moving away from self-hatred and self-medication. Currently, there is a national movement among urban leaders to teach Indian youth traditional ways. In addition, many urban American Indian adults who are far removed from tribal connections are rediscovering their unique cultural heritage. The hope is to instill positive attitudes about Indian identity without alcohol as part of the behavior. There is an eminent need for this identification of a culturally positive role model. Unfortunately, many urban Indian youth have been heavily exposed to negative adult role models in whom substance abuse patterns are commonly visible (Mail, 1995).

Parents, relatives, community teachers, and elders are all joining to strengthen and empower young people through their Indian culture. The belief is that a return to core traditional Indian values will prove to be a path that relieves the stressors that lead to depression and the resulting destructive substance abuse that continue to be salient issues in the urban American Indian environment.

The information that is being introduced to the urban American Indian community is at once new, old, and different. It represents a contrast to mainstream culture by a value system that respects and embraces both family and community and which, in turn, is directly linked to a culturally sanctioned spiritual path.

Members of many American Indian tribes are sharing their emotional frustration in the presence of sanctioned medicine people, traditional healers, or elders during sweat lodge, kiva ceremonies, or Native American church meetings in urban centers throughout America. Prayer, sage and sweetgrass, and song are being used to further the validation of experiences by the urban American Indian patient who is, at times, far removed from a home reservation. By establishing such tribal practices in rapidly growing urban Indian communities, American

Indians can ascribe failures and successes to internal or external causes and redefine them by their own culture.

Conclusion

Will old and new Indian solutions have an impact on urban American Indians and reduce self-medication through alcohol abuse? Can bridges be built between the family and the community at large? Will young people learn to cope with the non-Indian world and rid themselves at long last of that cultural shame that too often identifies Indianness as a negative attribute? New economic opportunities, such as gaming and the change in federal policies, have begun to encourage a resurgence of Indian tribal life within urban areas, and there is great anticipation that hope for American Indians will appear with the start of the new century. The resurgence of traditional practices of the past just might be what is needed to lead to better lives in the future, including more effective, timely, and culturally relevant mental health care.

References

Aragon, A. M. (1999). Getting beyond self-hate and self-medication: New hope for American Indians. *Journal of the California Alliance for the Mentally Ill, 10*, 17– 20.

Attneave, C. (1982). American Indian and Alaska Native families: Emigrants in their own homeland. In M. McGoldrick, J. K. Pearce, & J. Giordano (Eds.), *Ethnicity and family therapy* (pp. 55–83). New York: Guilford Press.

Barse, H. (1994). American Indian veterans and families. *American Indian and Alaska Native Mental Health Research, 6*(1), 39–47.

Brucker, P. S., & Perry, B. J. (1988). American Indians: Presenting concerns and considerations for family therapists. *American Journal of Family Therapy, 26*, 307–319.

Champagne, D., Goldberg-Ambrose, J. D., Machamer, A., Phillips, B., & Evans, T. (1996). *Service delivery for Native American children in Los Angeles County, 1996.* Los Angeles: University of California, American Indian Studies Center.

Cooley, R. C., Ostendorf, D., & Bickerton, D. (1979). Outreach services for elderly Native Americans. *Social Work, 29*, 151–153.

D'Andrea, M. (1994). The concerns of Native American youth. *Journal of Multicultural Counseling and Development, 22,* 173–181.

Deloria, V., Jr. (1969). *Custer died for your sins: An Indian manifesto.* New York: Macmillan.

Dukepoo, P. C. (1980*). The elder American Indian.* San Diego, CA: Campanile.

Duran, E., & Duran, B. (1995). Community intervention. In R. D. Mann (Series Ed.), *Native American postcolonial psychology* (pp. 185–200). Albany: State University of New York Press.

Edwards, D. E., & Edwards, M. E. (1984). Group work practice with American Indians. *Social Work With Groups, 7,* 7–21.

Garrett, J. T., & Garrett, M. W. (1994). The path of good medicine: Understanding and counseling Native American Indians. *Journal of Multicultural Counseling and Development, 22,* 134–144.

Garrett, M. T., & Pichette, E. F. (2000). Red as an apple: Native American acculturation and counseling with or without reservation. *Journal of Counseling and Development, 78,* 3–13.

Grossman, D. C., Krieger, J. W., Sugarman, J. R., & Forquera, R. A. (1994). Health status of urban American Indians and Alaska Natives. *Journal of the American Medical Association, 271,* 845–850.

Joe, J. R., & Miller, D. L. (1987). *American Indian perspectives on disability* (Native American Research and Training Center Monograph No. 3). Tucson: University of Arizona.

Krell, R. (1990). Holocaust survivors: A clinical perspective. *Psychiatric Journal of the University of Ottawa, 15,* 18–21.

LaFromboise, T. D. (1988). American Indian mental health policy. *American Psychologist, 43,* 388–397.

LaFromboise, T. D., Trimble, J. E., & Mohatt, J. V. (1990). Counseling intervention and American Indian tradition: An integrative approach. *The Counseling Psychologist, 18,* 628–654.

Mail, P. D. (1995). Early modeling of drinking behavior by Native American elementary school children playing drunk. *International Journal of the Addictions, 30,* 1187–1197.

May, P. A., & Moran, J. R. (1995). Prevention of alcohol misuse: A review of health promotion efforts among American Indians. *American Journal of Health Promotion, 9,* 288–299.

Oswalt, W. H. (1988). *This land was theirs: A study of North American Indians* (4th ed.). Mountain View, CA: Mayfield.

Reed, T. (1985). Ethnic differences in alcohol use, abuse, and sensitivity: A review with genetic interpretation. *Social Biology, 32,* 195–209.

Renfry, G. S. (1992). Cognitive–behavior therapy and the Native American client. *Behavior Therapy, 23,* 321–340.

Shosan, T. (1989). Mourning and longing from generation to generation. *American Journal of Psychotherapy, 43,* 193–207.

Snyder, M., Decker-Tank, E., & Berscheid, E. (1977). Social perception and interpersonal behavior: On the self-fulfilling nature of social stereotypes. *Journal of Personality and Social Psychology, 35,* 656–666.

Sue, S., Allen, D. B., & Conaway, L. (1978). The responsiveness and equality of mental care to Chicanos and Native Americans. *American Journal of Community Psychology, 6,* 137–146.

Trimble, J. E., & Hayes, S. A. (1984). Mental health intervention in the psychosocial contexts of American Indian communities. In W. A. O'Connor & B. Lubin (Eds.), *Ecological approaches to clinical and community psychology* (pp. 293–321). New York: Wiley.

Turner, J. C. (1982). Towards a cognitive redefinition of the minimal group paradigm. In H. Tajfel (Ed.), *Social identity and intergroup relations* (pp. 15–40). Cambridge, England: Cambridge University Press.

Weibel-Orlando, J. C. (1981). There's a place for everything and everything in its place: Environmental influences of urban Indian drinking patterns. In T. C. Harford & L. S. Gaines (Eds.), *Social drinking contexts* (NIAAA Research Monograph No. 7, pp. 206–227). Washington, DC: National Library of Medicine.

Weibel-Orlando, J.C. (1989). Hooked on healing: Anthropologists, alcohol and intervention. *Human Organization, 48,* 148–154.

Zimmerman, M. A., & Ramirez-Valles, J. (1996). The development of a measure of enculturation for Native American youth. *American Journal of Community Psychology, 24,* 295–310.

Tessa Evans-Campbell

Indian Child Welfare Practice Within Urban American Indian/ Native American Communities

2

C hildren are the future of any community. Through them, tradition and culture remain alive and are passed on to new generations. At a time when many American Indian/Native American (hereafter referred to as AIAN or Native) communities are determined to protect their cultural inheritance, the role of children as the sustainers of tribal survival is essential. Without them, Native communities are literally in danger of losing themselves, and when children are mistreated or are taken from Native communities, the future of the entire community is put at risk. This may be especially true in urban Native communities where efforts to preserve Native culture and family norms can be especially challenging.

One of the biggest challenges Native communities face today is the struggle to keep Native children in their communities. Too many tribal children are involved in the child welfare system, and reports of child maltreatment among Native families, already high, continue to rise. The statistics are dramatic:

- Child maltreatment rates for American Indian children are the second highest in the country (21.3 cases per 1,000), higher than those for Asian children (2.7 cases per 1,000), Hispanic children (9.9 cases per 1,000),

White children (11.0 cases per 1,000), and African American children (20.4 cases per 1,000); they are lower only than those for Pacific Islander children (21.4 cases per 1,000; U.S. Department of Health and Human Services [DHHS], Administration on Children, Youth, and Families, 2003). Although Native children make up only 1% of the total U.S. population of children, they account for 3% of all children entering the child welfare system (U.S. DHHS, 2003).

- During the mid-1990s, American Indians and Asian Americans were the only two groups in the United States to see a rise in Child Protective Services (CPS) documented cases of child maltreatment, and the rise for American Indians was 3 times that of Asian Americans (18% compared with 6%; U.S. DHHS, Administration on Children, Youth, and Families, 2001). Moreover, much of this rise occurred despite stricter federal policies regulating the determination of child maltreatment and the development of numerous Native child welfare programs.

- In many states, Native children are highly overrepresented in the child welfare system relative to the population. In South Dakota, for example, although Native children make up 14% of the child population, they represent 64% of the children in foster care. In Minnesota, Native children make up 1.8% of the child population but represent 13% of children in foster care. In Washington State, Native children represent 2% of the child population and 9% of children in foster care (U.S. DHHS, 2003).

- Native children in substitute care tend to be younger than the national average (9 years 11 months compared with 12 years 7 months) and tend to stay in care longer than other children (Plantz, Hubbell, Barrett, & Dobrec, 1999).

- Finally, though there are few statistics regarding urban American Indian children specifically, the few that are available present an equally grim picture. In Los Angeles County, which has the largest child welfare system in the country, for example, there were over 400 Native children living in out-of-home care in 2000. About half of these children were placed with relatives, but almost one third were living in non-

Native foster or group homes. In 2,000, the county had only three county-licensed and eight privately licensed American Indian foster homes to serve Native children (Los Angeles City/County Native American Indian Commission, 2000).

Despite these statistics, what researchers know about child maltreatment in Native communities, especially urban Native communities, is incomplete. It is clear that within the child welfare system, cases of child neglect in Native communities are far more common than cases of abuse (DeBruyn, Lujan, & May, 1992; U.S. DHHS, 2003). The consequences of child neglect are not fully understood, but some researchers contend that the harm resulting from neglect is equal to or more serious than that resulting from physical abuse (White & Cornely, 1981).

Explaining High Rates of Child Maltreatment in Native Communities

Although it is well documented that American Indian children are overrepresented in the CPS system across the country, a great deal of speculation exists about why this may be the case. The speculation exists partly because there have been relatively few studies looking specifically at child maltreatment in Native populations, so researchers know relatively little about the causes and consequences of child abuse and neglect in these communities, and partly because there is still considerable debate within the field over how the problem of high rates of maltreatment should be defined. Should these rates be seen as accurately reflecting real practices, or are they indicative of deeper cultural differences in parenting and ongoing historical divisions between Native communities and the child welfare practitioners who assess them? What does seem clear is that a full explanation for the high rate of child maltreatment cases must take into account several interrelated factors, including socioeconomic conditions; the effects of long-term historical patterns of oppression and social disruption; and broader cultural differences in defining abuse, neglect, and appropriate parenting.

SOCIOECONOMIC FACTORS RELATED TO CHILD MALTREATMENT

Ample evidence associates child neglect and abuse with several inter-related socioeconomic factors. The most frequently associated factor contributing to child maltreatment across a wide range of cultures is substance abuse (Berlin, 1987; DeBruyn et al., 1992; Gelles, 1987; Hauswald, 1987; Lujan, DeBruyn, & May, 1989; Piasecki et al., 1989). Scholars have also found an association between rates of maltreatment and certain types of family structure, including higher divorce rates, teenage births, births out of wedlock, and single parenthood (Giovannoni & Billingsley, 1970; Polansky, Chalmers, Williams, & Butten-wieser, 1981). An association between maltreatment and poverty has also been shown (Giovannoni & Billingsley, 1970; Wolock & Horowitz, 1984), although poverty itself is associated with a number of other factors correlated with child maltreatment, such as unemployment and low educational attainment. In addition, child maltreatment has also been associated with high levels of family stress (Polansky, Gaudin, Ammons, & Davis, 1985; Zuravin, 1988) and social isolation (Polansky et al., 1985).

Although few of the studies on which these findings are based include Native communities in their samples, the Native-specific studies suggest that the general trends found in wider populations are also true for AIANs. Several researchers, for example, have found that high rates of child neglect in Native communities are related to high levels of poverty, poor health, substance abuse, and mental health indicators (Berlin, 1987; Earle & Cross, 2001; Miller, Hoffman, & Turner, 1988). In their study of 77 Native families from three areas of the country, Nelson, Saunders, and Landsman (1993), for example, found that 43% of the families in their sample had been reported for child neglect and 36% of the children in these families had been placed outside the home by authorities. Parents reported for child neglect were more likely than others to be divorced, separated, or single mothers. Parents reported for neglect were also more likely to have had their first child as a teenager, had children born out of wedlock, and had one more child on average compared with parents who had not been reported for neglect. In addition, those reported for neglect had more stress-related problems than other parents. Two thirds had a history of substance abuse, criminal arrest, or psychiatric treatment and more than three fourths (78%) had been convicted of a crime.

Many of these trends are found in rural or reservation-based as well as urban-based communities. However, in addition to the problems of substance abuse, poverty, and family disruption, research suggests that urban families also suffer from feelings of social isolation and lack many of the informal support systems found in reservation-based communities (Evans-Campbell & Walters, 2006; Flynn, Clark, Aragon, Stanzell, & Evans-Campbell, 1998). Without these informal supports, urban AIAN parents are often left with few role models for parenting and may lack people to turn to for parenting assistance. Moreover, the formal tribally run child welfare and parenting programs developed in many reservation communities are unavailable to urban Native families, and although other formal child welfare services may be available in urban environments, they are often inaccessible or not Native-specific in their approach. To further complicate this issue, urban American Indian parents may be wary of using non-Native formal support systems because of the historic legacy of mistrust engendered by child welfare policies directed at AIAN families.

HISTORICAL–CULTURAL FACTORS RELATED TO CHILD MALTREATMENT

Indian child welfare scholars have suggested that several historical–cultural factors specific to Native populations contribute to high rates of child maltreatment. For example, Cross, Earle, and Simmons (2000) have argued that the effects of forced acculturation and the stress that accompanies it must be considered precursors to child maltreatment. Along similar lines, several scholars have asserted that an erosion of traditional parenting norms and practices is a contributing factor (De-Bruyn et al., 1992; Lujan et al., 1989; Mannes, 1993). These losses have been attributed to the fact that many of today's Native parents grew up outside the family home in boarding schools or foster care. In out-of-home care, these children were deprived of the chance to learn positive parenting practices from parental role models (Cross et al., 2000) and often were exposed to new negative behaviors (e.g., neglect by adult caretakers) in their stead (Horejsi, Craig, & Pablo, 1992). Although the majority of former boarding school attendees go on to parent with success, emerging research has shown that Native parents who attended boarding school as children are more likely than others to feel overwhelmed and inadequate in their parental roles (Brave Heart, 1999b; Spicer, 1998).

Scholars have also asserted that Native parents may have stresses around parenting related to the historical trauma they and their communities have endured (Brave Heart, 1999b; Duran, Duran, Brave Heart, & Yellow Horse-Davis, 1998). *Historical trauma* is defined as trauma resulting from successive, compounding traumatic events perpetrated on a community over generations (Brave Heart, 1999a).

Although the trauma is based on events shared by a collective, it need not be directly experienced for it to have a profound impact on future generations. Indeed, the suffering may accumulate over generations as community members retain the trauma of their ancestors while they continue to experience current traumatic events and life stressors. Examples of historically traumatic events include forced attendance at Indian boarding schools, forcibly removing and relocating Indians away from traditional lands, and disproportionately removing Indian children and placing them into non-Indian homes. Although all Natives share a history of historically traumatic events, only some develop what Brave Heart (1999a) termed a "historical trauma response" (see also Duran et al., 1998). Such a response may include depression, numbness, unresolved grief and mourning, and anxiety, all of which can have an adverse effect on parenting practices.

DEFINITIONAL DISPARITIES

Clearly, there are several sociodemographic and historical–cultural factors that put urban Native families at high risk for child maltreatment, and it is likely that many reports of child neglect are related to these factors. However, many Indian child welfare experts have also argued that the high rate of child neglect in Native communities may be linked to another phenomenon, one that has less to do with the conditions related to neglect and more to do with its definition. They have asserted that much of the rise in reports of child maltreatment in Native communities can be explained by ethnocentric views on child rearing and by a misunderstanding of Indian culture on the part of outsiders (Brown, Limb, Munoz, & Clifford, 2001; Hollinger, 1992). As a consequence, some non-Native welfare workers may interpret typical Native parenting practices as neglectful or abusive.

There is good reason to consider this argument. Historically, American Indian children have been removed from their homes at substantially higher rates than non-Native children, a trend that continues today. It is notable that the majority of these children are removed for neglect (Earle & Cross, 2001), and this neglect is determined for the most part by non-Native social workers who have little familiarity with traditional Native child-rearing practices or cultural norms (Cross, 1986). Many social workers, for example, being unaware of the ways of Native extended family life, view the common Native practice of leaving a child with non–nuclear family members for more than a few hours as neglectful. Yet sharing child-care responsibilities among extended family and community members is common in many Native cultures (Cross et al., 2000; Earle & Cross, 2001; Locust, 1990). This suggests that Native people may have culturally specific views on appropriate child rearing.

Cultural norms, values, experiences of discrimination and racism, and life experiences as a member of an ethnic minority group all impact how a person views the world, including how he or she defines appropriate child rearing practices. Research shows, for example, that people from different ethnic groups hold significantly different perceptions and definitions of child abuse and neglect (Evans-Campbell, in press; Giovannoni & Becerra, 1979; Hong & Hong, 1991; Rose & Meezan, 1993; Song, 1986). Evidence also suggests that parents from diverse ethnic groups, including Natives, may have unique ideas about what constitutes appropriate parenting. For example, scholars have suggested that Native parents are less apt to intervene and direct their children than parents from other ethnic groups, preferring instead to allow children to learn by example (Earle & Cross, 2001). It is important to note that these culturally specific parenting practices may be misunderstood by non-Natives.

Within-group differences in perceptions of child maltreatment may also be significant, and individual perceptions among members of the same ethnic group often vary greatly. Several studies have explored intragroup differences in perceptions of child maltreatment, and findings suggest that people within the same ethnic or cultural group differ in their attitudes according to social class and gender (Giovannoni & Becerra, 1979; Hong & Hong, 1991; Rose & Meezan, 1995). In a study of urban American Indian parents, Evans-Campbell (2000) found that perceptions of child neglect differed significantly according to gender, level of education, marital status, and experience with the public child welfare system.

Child Welfare Policy in the United States: A Historical Perspective

It is important to recognize that the current plight of Native children and families is not new. It has roots that lie deep within U.S. policy toward Native populations, and it has been nourished by the predominantly destructive relationships between Native communities and the U.S. government that characterize this country's history. For centuries, governmental policies created to eradicate or forcibly assimilate Native people have left many Native families and communities struggling to maintain their traditional culture and ways of life. Child welfare policies have played a prominent role in these governmental attempts at assimilation and have left a legacy of mistrust regarding any outside interference in the lives of American Indian children.

Attempts to assimilate Native children began with the first European settlers who were encouraged to adopt or care for Native children (Earle, 2000). In 1819, the federal government established the Civilization Fund Act created to fund private agencies developing programs to "civilize" young Native people (Earle, 2000). Toward this end, private organizations developed Indian boarding schools with the purpose of assimilating American Indian children into Western culture, and by the mid-1800s, thousands of AIAN children were attending such institutions (Adams, 1995; George, 1997). Soon after, the assimilation of Native children became a federal goal, and the government took control of many Indian boarding schools. Within these schools, children were not allowed to practice any of their traditional ways of life and, instead, were forced to learn Western mannerisms and speak English. Many children died in these institutions, and many more were mistreated (Adams, 1995). Child abuse and neglect were commonplace, and children were often punished by physical means or neglect (Hauswald, 1987). Countless others were sexually abused in the schools (Smith, 2003). Abuse suffered in the schools has profoundly influenced how Native people view policies directed at Native children and families.

After the Indian Reorganization Act of 1934, the government began to close many of the boarding schools. However, relief efforts directed at AIAN communities were still premised on the assumption that assimilation was in the best interest of Native children (Cross et al., 2000). The phenomenon of trying to assimilate Native children is clearly apparent, for example, in the foster care and adoption policies directed at Native families during this time. Before the 1940s, the child welfare system had generally advocated matching children with families of the same ethnic and cultural group as the child. In the late 1940s, however, this stance changed and child welfare agencies began to actively encourage transracial placement (George, 1997). Throughout the 1950s and 1960s, transracial adoptions were widespread, and in 1959, the Child Welfare League of America, in cooperation with the Bureau of Indian Affairs, initiated the Indian Adoption Project, which led to the adoption of thousands of Indian children into non-Native families in urban areas (Mannes, 1995).

By the 1960s and 1970s, the crisis in Indian child welfare had reached epidemic proportions. Federally funded studies conducted in 1969 and 1974 by the Association on American Indian Affairs (AAIA) showed that Native children were being placed in substitute care at a rate between 5 and 25 times higher (varying by state) than non-Native children (Byler, 1977). In states with large Native populations, the rates were particularly disturbing. For example, Minnesota's rate of out-of-home placement for Native children was 16 times that of non-Native children, and Washington State's adoption rate for Native children was 19 times that of non-Native children (Byler, 1977; Fischler, 1985). Tribes responded to these alarming conditions by demanding more power over the right to raise their own children and began to advocate for federal policy to support their mission.

The Indian Child Welfare Act

In the late 1960s, after decades of having their children taken away, the Devil's Lake Sioux Tribe of North Dakota requested assistance from the AAIA. In response, the association conducted a study of child welfare conditions in Native communities and found that in the states with the largest Native populations, between 25% and 35% of all Native children had been removed from their homes and placed in out-of-home care (Byler, 1977; Fischler, 1985). The vast majority of these children (99%) were removed from their homes on the basis of child neglect, and 85% of them had been placed in non-Native homes (Byler, 1977). The study results highlighted the enormity of the problem and gave Native child welfare advocates hard evidence regarding the number of Native children in the child welfare system. The first Congressional hearings on the matter took place in 1974 and led, in 1976, to 130 tribes unanimously supporting a draft of major Indian child welfare provisions that provided the basis for the Indian Child Welfare Act of 1978 (ICWA; Weaver & White, 1999).

The ICWA became law on November 8, 1978, and was implemented in May 1979 (H.R. Rep. No. 1386, 1978). The ICWA sets forth strict new requirements in child welfare cases involving Indian children and places authority for Native children within the tribes. The central premise behind the ICWA is the belief that protecting the cultural identity of Native children is fundamental to their mental health and to the cultural integrity of their communities (Weaver & White, 1999). Toward these ends, the ICWA outlines eight major provisions regarding custody proceedings involving Native children:

1. Tribes have exclusive jurisdiction over children who live on reservations except in cases in which federal law already has designated jurisdiction to the state.
2. Native nations have the right to petition for previously lost jurisdiction.

3. Parents as well as their tribes have the right to intervene in state proceedings involving Native children.
4. Higher standards of proof are applied to state initiated custody proceedings involving American Indian children.
5. For Native children in substitute care, there is a preference for placement with family members, tribal members, or other Native families.
6. In placement or adoption proceedings, Native parents must demonstrate informed consent and have an extended period of time to revoke such consent.
7. Native tribes and parents must have access to state records regarding their cases (Barsh, 1996; Weaver & White, 1999).
8. Agencies that place children must provide culturally appropriate services to Native families before placement occurs.

The ICWA has led to a number of positive changes, including an increase in tribal and other Native child welfare programs, more thorough training around child welfare work with Native children and families, and the formation of numerous state–tribal agreements that support working toward the best care for Native children in the child welfare system. In addition, there has been a significant increase in the awareness that Native people have about child welfare issues. A study of urban American Indian parents in Los Angeles, for example, found that 89% of those interviewed were familiar with the basic tenets of the ICWA (Evans-Campbell, 2000).

Limitations of the Indian Child Welfare Act

Despite the many improvements that the ICWA has brought to Indian child welfare, findings from several surveys conducted to assess its impact indicate that there are also a number of serious problems with its implementation that have led to ambiguous outcomes for Native children and families (Brown, Limb, Munoz, & Clifford, 2001; Earle, 2000; Mannes, 1995). For example, although placements of Native children increasingly are under the jurisdiction of tribal courts and Indian child welfare agencies, Native children are still placed in care almost 4 times more often than non-Indian children (U.S. Administration for Children and Families, 2005). Problems in implementation have been especially profound in urban settings (Mindell, de Haymes, & Francisco, 2003), putting urban American Indian families at particular risk.

One reason that the overall success of the ICWA has been mixed may stem from its uneven implementation across the country. In some states, for instance, the ICWA has been implemented successfully, and social service agencies have worked intensively with tribes to serve Native families. In other states, however, there is no infrastructure to support the ICWA, and a tremendous burden has been placed on tribal and urban Native communities to provide comprehensive social and legal services for Native families. Indeed, even within the same state, implementation may vary dramatically from county to county.

Another factor affecting the implementation of the ICWA is the fact that most off-reservation child welfare workers have limited knowledge of the ICWA and its provisions. The ICWA can only be truly effective if all social service workers are aware of its tenets and abide by them. Yet in most cases, only limited training has been offered on the ICWA, and many child welfare professionals find the law confusing and burdensome (Weaver & White, 1999). This may be especially true in urban areas where workers may have only a few cases involving Native children and families and consequently lack experience with the ICWA's provisions. Urban child welfare workers may also have less familiarity with Native culture and history. With limited understanding of urban Native communities or the history of Indian child welfare, workers may discount the historical significance of the ICWA to urban Native communities and resist applying it in their work.

Partly as a result of the lack of training around the ICWA in urban areas, urban American Indian children are often misidentified by workers who may rely on phenotype, name, or language to make decisions about ethnicity instead of asking directly about tribal affiliation. This is particularly true when children are members of more than one ethnic group, a common occurrence in metropolitan areas. As a consequence, some misidentified urban American Indian children never benefit from the ICWA. In other cases, American Indian children in urban areas are identified as Native at a later point in their case history, a development that can lead to serious problems, including the disruption of placements and adoption proceedings (Evans-Campbell, 2000).

One of the most serious obstacles to the successful implementation of the ICWA has been persistently inadequate funding. Indeed, the lack of resources overall for Indian child welfare has forced some tribes to decline jurisdiction of ICWA cases. Wares, Wedel, Rosenthal, and Dobrec (1994) conducted a study of Indian Child Welfare programs and found that most programs are small, with 30% employing only one staff member and 35% employing two to five staff members. These few individuals are often expected to handle all the Native cases in their area, and about half of respondents reported that they were in charge of both caseworker and administrator duties in their job (Wares et al., 1994). Resources have been critically low in urban settings because federal funding for all off-reservation Native child welfare programs was cut in 1997 (Weaver & White, 1999), and many urban social service agencies have been forced to cut back or even eliminate their Native child welfare programs.

Finally, it is important to note that since its inception, there have been numerous attempts to reduce the scope of the ICWA through proposed amendments that limit its applicability, particularly as it applies to families living off-reservation. A number of states have adopted the "Existing Family Exception" and require that Indian children receiving ICWA services be born in Indian homes or communities (Brown et al., 2001). This can create obstacles in child welfare cases in which non-Indian parents or relatives are the primary caregivers of Indian children or when non-Indian mothers give up their Indian children for adoption. Some states have refused to apply the ICWA if parents were not enrolled members of their tribes at the time of CPS involvement, even if parents were eligible for enrollment. In California, some state judges have claimed the right to determine if a family was an existing Indian family, even in cases in which household family members were enrolled in a tribe (Champagne, Goldberg-Ambrose, Machamer, Phillips, & Evans-Campbell, 1996). To make this determination, some judges have relied on parameters based on Western stereotypes of "Indianness," including religion, phenotype, the number of powwows a family attends, how often a family visits their reservation, and how many other Native people a family interacts with. Another attempt to limit the ICWA was Title III of the Adoption Promotion and Stability Act of 1996, which sought to limit the ICWA in cases in which parents did not maintain tribal affiliation. These attempts by nontribal entities to determine Native status are a serious threat to Native sovereignty.

Recommendations for Child Welfare Work With Urban American Indian Families

Numerous changes in attitudes and behaviors might result in improvements in child welfare services for urban American Indian families.

USING A CULTURALLY RELEVANT FRAMEWORK FOR PRACTICE

Native cultures have been devalued for centuries, and child welfare professionals have relied primarily on a Western framework for practice with Native families. It is imperative that professionals recognize that work with urban American Indian families requires familiarity with Native norms and values as well as an understanding of the history of colonization that impacts all indigenous communities. At the same time, practitioners must recognize the diversity among and within Native communities. Although there are some generally shared norms and values among Native people, each tribe has its own culture, and professionals working with Native families should not simply assume that Native clients will display stereotypical American Indian behaviors such as avoiding eye contact or being less talkative than others. Moreover, urban American Indian families represent many tribes and cultures, and each family should be viewed as unique.

Urban American Indian families are also diverse in their levels of acculturation and enculturation. Many in the helping professionals continue to assume that acculturation falls along a continuum and that Native people are either traditional, highly acculturated, or somewhere in between. It is more helpful, however, to consider acculturation as a fluid phenomenon, one in which a person who is highly acculturated to Western culture may also be highly enculturated to his or her tribal culture. Practitioners should also recognize that a person can acculturate to any number of cultures—European American, African American, Latino, and so on. An urban Native adolescent boy in Los Angeles, for example, may be acculturated to his tribal culture, European American culture, and Latino culture.

It is also important to note that some urban Native parents and children may feel alienated from their tribal culture, which may be exhibited in depression, low self-esteem, and violent behavior. To help urban Native families suffering from feelings of alienation, child welfare professionals can connect families with urban Native cultural and social programs in the area. In many cities, there are Native organizations that run programs specifically targeted to Native children and families, including parenting classes, Native-specific support groups, talking circles for parents, and sports programs. In urban areas with reservations close by, tribes often offer their services to Native families who are not tribal members. Workers should become familiar with these programs and the services they offer.

FOCUSING ON RESILIENCE AND STRENGTH

Practitioners must also strive to focus on strengths and resiliencies when working with urban Native families. Despite the significant losses and traumas they have experienced, Native families remain strong and vital today. In many Native communities, recognition of Native resistance in the face of oppression has instilled a strong sense of pride and the motivation to help others. Yet survival stories are often not clearly identified within Native family histories. Practitioners can play a major role in helping illuminate personal and ancestral survival strategies and identifying how these strategies are currently manifested in the family system.

RESPECTING CULTURALLY APPROPRIATE CHILD-REARING BELIEFS AMONG URBAN AMERICAN INDIANS

Beliefs about child rearing are defined by cultural norms and values, and evidence suggests that Native parents have unique cultural beliefs about what constitutes appropriate child rearing. Historically, the child welfare system in this country has assumed a framework for working with families that is based on Western notions and beliefs instead of exploring the ways in which Native communities have traditionally dealt with parental neglect and child abuse. To minimize cultural misunderstandings, there must be an acknowledgment that what is deemed appropriate in one community may be considered inappropriate in another and that urban Native parents and communities sometimes deal with children in culturally specific ways. To this end, all child welfare workers should have training around cultural differences in child rearing, and administrators must encourage a respect for diverse child rearing practices among their workers.

In many Native communities, children are seen as equal beings central to the entire community and are treated accordingly (Blanchard & Barsh, 1980; Green, 1983). Native parents often encourage their children from an early age to be independent and to develop a strong sense of responsibility (Green, 1983). For example, Gray and Cosgrove (1985) found that Blackfeet parents gave little overt guidance to their children. Indeed, direct intervention is viewed in many Native cultures as rude and disrespectful. Rather than stopping an unwanted behavior, a Native parent may instead role model a desired behavior and expect his or her children to emulate it.

Native families are also known for their tendency to share child rearing duties among extended family and community members. This spreads the responsibility of child rearing among several persons and keeps any single person from becoming overburdened (Cross et al., 2000). In a sense then, each child is the community's, and there is an expectation that everyone has a stake in that child's rearing. In such circumstances, the importance of including the extended family and community in case plans for urban American Indian families cannot be overstated. Indeed, extended families and community members are often a family's most important resource.

DEALING WITH MISTRUST OF THE CHILD WELFARE SYSTEM

American Indian parents may also have culturally specific attitudes toward the child welfare system. One common attitude is a deep mistrust of CPS agencies and staff among Native communities that is born out of their long and troubled history with federal child welfare policies. High levels of mistrust among Native parents toward CPS have been documented in several studies and appear to impair the ability of Native parents to work effectively with CPS agencies and staff (Evans-Campbell, 2000; Horejsi et al., 1992). Sadly, many Native parents believe that once a child goes into the foster care system, he or she will remain there (Horejsi et al., 1992). Champagne et al. (1996) found that urban American Indian parents continue to be deeply critical of the way Native Americans are treated at every level of the child welfare system, from encounters with individual social workers, to dealings with the Department of Children and Family Services, to experiences within the court system that handles dependency cases.

Given the long history of CPS intervention in Native families and the continuing problems Natives face, such views are understandable and should be expected. It is likely, for instance, that urban American Indian clients will at least initially distrust child welfare workers, particularly those who are non-Native. They may appear uncooperative or angry to practitioners who lack a historical context for work with Native families. Child welfare professionals should anticipate mistrust in early work with families and reframe it as a normal reaction to child welfare intervention.

TRAINING ON THE INDIAN CHILD WELFARE ACT

The ICWA is critical to the well-being of Indian families and communities, yet many child welfare professionals are still unaware of or unfamiliar with it. This is particularly true in urban areas where child welfare professionals may have few Native clients and consequently little experience with the ICWA implemented to its full potential. To address this problem, ICWA training for all workers in urban areas is a necessity. Such training would help demystify the ICWA's provisions as well as engender a climate of respect for the ICWA and its tenets. Urban child welfare practitioners also need to have training on the history of Indian child welfare in this country to give them a context for the ICWA as well as an appreciation for its importance to the survival of American Indian communities.

Lawyers, judges, and child advocates who work in urban children's courts must also be familiar with the ICWA. In some areas (e.g., Los Angeles County), specific courtrooms are designated to handle all of the ICWA cases. This allows the judges, lawyers, and social workers working in this court to be intimately familiar with the ICWA. Court systems might also consider developing ICWA advisory boards made up of tribal leaders, elders, Native parents, and community members to assist with cases involving Native families.

Finally, it is useful to note several encouraging trends in ICWA training. Many schools of social work have developed Indian child welfare curricula for child welfare workers, and training manuals have been developed in some urban areas for judges and lawyers. In addition, Indian child welfare conferences are held at the local, state, and national level across the nation each year, and the National Indian Child Welfare Association offers a wealth of training materials for child welfare workers and educators. All of these sources can provide training models and materials and can be adapted to be locally relevant.

INCREASING RESOURCES IN INDIAN CHILD WELFARE ACT PROGRAMS

As noted previously, one of the most serious obstacles to the successful implementation of the ICWA has been a persistent and profound lack of resources. Of all Indian child welfare administrators surveyed, 82% indicated that their programs were underfunded (Wares et al., 1994). In particular, funds provided through the ICWA to urban programs have been cut off in past years, forcing many urban agencies to cut or eliminate critical programs. Yet as these programs are being reduced, the number of Natives moving to urban areas is increasing. Approximately 70% of all American Indian people now live in urban centers (U.S. Census Bureau, 2000), and it is imperative that Indian child welfare programs are available to families in these areas. Indeed, although virtually all Indian child welfare programs, on or off the reservation, need additional funding, the need to fund urban programs is especially urgent.

American Indian foster homes are another resource in desperately short supply in urban settings. Although this resource may be more difficult to increase than others, it should be noted that many potential Indian foster homes exist but are often not granted licensure on the basis of family income levels of the owners and the physical features of the home (Weaver & White, 1999). It is important to note that these licensure reviews tend to be conducted by non-Natives who may have limited knowledge of Native norms and values. To increase the number of Indian foster homes, particularly in urban areas, it will be necessary to review the certification guidelines for foster homes and consider rewriting them to reflect the cultural conditions of American Indian families.

Conclusion

The historical relationship between American Indian communities and the American child welfare system has been long and profoundly damaging, a relationship characterized by the systematic attempt to eliminate Native cultures and societies rather than by an honest concern for the well-being of Native children. Today, conditions have improved with the passage of the ICWA and other measures taken at the state and local levels to increase training, access, and appropriate responses to child maltreatment in all Native communities, including urban communities. Nonetheless, work needs to continue. Native communities suffer from some of the highest levels of poverty, substance abuse, and family breakdown of any population in the country. Child welfare officials, on the other hand, continue to be misinformed or uninformed about Native practices, cultural values, and tribal law. As a result, Native children remain heavily overrepresented in the child welfare system. They enter younger, stay longer, and all too often are placed in non-Native facilities that remove them from their cultural heritage and identity.

The passage of ICWA in 1978 was an important step toward alleviating some of these conditions, but the ICWA's effectiveness has been reduced by uneven implementation, a lack of training among urban child care professionals, and a chronic shortage of funds, particularly for programs in cities. Tribes may be supportive but are likely to struggle with limited resources themselves. Nevertheless, there is a great need for all urban child welfare administrators to work closely with tribes and community groups and for non-Native child welfare agencies to develop and implement appropriate child welfare services for urban American Indian children and families. Urban areas should have Indian child welfare advisory boards to assist in these collaborations. To reflect the diversity of urban American Indian communities, these boards should be made up of staff from local Indian child welfare agencies, Native community members, parents, elders, and community leaders. With effort and intention, dedicated urban child welfare professionals workers can help to promote the successful implementation of the ICWA. Indeed they must, both for the Native children they are pledged to protect and for the survival of Native communities.

References

Adams, D. W. (1995). *Education for extinction: American Indians and the boarding school experience*. Lawrence: University Press of Kansas.

Adoption Promotion and Stability Act of 1996, H.R. 3286. 104th Cong. (1996).

Barsh, R. L. (1996). The Indian Child Welfare Act of 1978: A critical analysis. In J. R. Wunder (Ed.), *Recent legal issues for American Indians, 1968 to the present* (pp. 219–268). New York: Garland.

Berlin, I. (1987). Effects of changing Native American cultures on child development. *Journal of Community Psychology, 15,* 299–306.

Blanchard, E., & Barsh, R. (1980). What is best for tribal children: A response to Fischler. *Social Work, 25,* 350–357.

Brave Heart, M. Y. H. (1999a). Gender differences in the historical trauma response among the Lakota. *Journal of Health and Social Policy, 10*(4), 1–21.

Brave Heart, M. Y. H. (1999b). Oyate Ptayela: Rebuilding the Lakota Nation through addressing historical trauma among Lakota parents. *Journal of Human Behavior in the Social Environment, 2,* 109–126.

Brown, E. F., Limb, G. E., Munoz, R., & Clifford, C. A. (2001). *Title IV-B child and family services plans: An evaluations of specific measures taken by states to comply with the Indian Child Welfare Act.* Seattle, WA: Casey Family Programs.

Byler, W. (1977). The destruction of the American Indian family. In W. Byler (Ed.), *The destruction of the American Indian family* (pp. 1–11). New York: Association of American Indian Affairs.

Champagne, D., Goldberg-Ambrose, C., Machamer, A., Phillips, B., & Evans-Campbell, T. (1996). *Service delivery for American Indian children in Los Angeles, 1996* (Report No. RC021766). Los Angeles: UCLA American Indian Studies Center. (ERIC Document Reproduction Service No. ED426827)

Cross, T. L. (1986). Drawing on cultural traditions in Indian child welfare practice. *Social Casework, 67,* 283–289.

Cross, T. L., Earle, K., & Simmons, D. (2000). Child abuse and neglect in Indian country: Policy issues. *Families in Society, 81,* 49–58.

DeBruyn, L., Lujan, C., & May, P. (1992). A comparative study of abused and neglected American Indian children in the southwest. *Social Sciences and Medicine, 35,* 305–315.

Duran, E., Duran, B., Brave Heart, M. Y. H, Yellow Horse-Davis, S. (1998). Healing the American Indian soul wound. In Y. Danieli (Ed.), *International handbook of multigenerational legacies of trauma* (pp. 341–354). New York: Plenum Press.

Earle, K. (2000). *Child abuse and neglect: An examination of the American Indian data.* Seattle, WA: Casey Family Programs.

Earle, K., & Cross, A. (2001). *Child abuse and neglect among American Indian/Alaska Native children: An analysis of existing data* (Report for the National Indian Child Welfare Association). Seattle, WA: Casey Family Programs.

Evans-Campbell, T. (2000). *Perceptions of and attitudes towards child neglect among urban American Indian parents in Los Angeles.* Unpublished doctoral dissertation, University of California, Los Angeles.

Evans-Campbell, T. (in press). Perceptions of child neglect among urban American Indian/Alaska Native parents. *Child Welfare.*

Evans-Campbell, T., & Walters, K. L. (2006). Indigenist practice competencies in child welfare practice: A decolonization framework to address family violence and substance abuse among First Nations peoples. In R. Fong, R. McRoy, & C. Ortiz Hendricks (Eds.), *Intersecting child welfare, substance abuse, and family violence: Culturally competent approaches.* Alexandria, VA: CSWE Press.

Fischler, R. (1985). Child abuse and neglect in American Indian communities. *Child Neglect, 9,* 95–106.

Flynn, K., Clark, R., Aragon, M., Stanzell, S., & Evans-Campbell, T. (1998). *The mental health status of at-risk American Indian and Alaska Native youth in Los Angeles County.* Los Angeles: Indian Health Services.

Gelles, R. J. (1987). What to learn from cross-cultural and historical research on child abuse and neglect: An overview. In R. J. Gelles & J. B. Lancaster (Eds.), *Child abuse and neglect: Biosocial dimensions* (pp. 15–30). New York: Aldine.

Giovannoni, J., & Becerra, R. (1979). *Defining child abuse.* New York: Free Press.

Giovannoni, J., & Billingsley, A. (1970). Child neglect among the poor: A study of parental adequacy in families of three ethnic groups. *Child Welfare, 49,* 196–204.

George, L. J. (1997). Why the need for the ICWA? *Journal of Multicultural Social Work, 5,* 165–175.

Gray, E., & Cosgrove, J. (1985). Ethnocentric perception of child rearing practices in protective services. *Child Abuse and Neglect, 9,* 389–396.

Green, H. (1983). Risks and attitudes associated with extra-cultural placement of American Indian children: A critical review. *Journal of the American Academy of Child Psychiatry, 22,* 63–67.

Hauswald, E. (1987). External pressure/internal change: Child neglect on the Navajo reservation. In N. Schepter-Hughes (Ed.), *Child survival* (pp. 145–164). Boston: Reidel.

Hollinger, J. H. (1992). *Adoption law and practice: October 1992 supplement.* New York: M. Bender.

Hong, G., & Hong, L. (1991). Comparative perspectives on child abuse and neglect: Chinese versus Hispanics and Whites. *Child Welfare, 70,* 463–475.

Horejsi, C., Craig, B. H. R., & Pablo, J. (1992). Reactions by Native American parents to child protection agencies: cultural and community factors. *Child Welfare, 62,* 329–342.

H.R. Rep. No. 1386, 95th Cong., 25 U.S.C. 1901 *et seq.* (1978) (enacted).

Locust, C. (1990, February–March). Discrimination against American Indian families in child abuse cases. *Indian Child Welfare Digest,* 7–9.

Los Angeles City/County Native American Indian Commission. (2000). *Urban American Indian policy position paper.* Los Angeles: Los Angeles City/County Native American Indian Commission Policy Sub-Committee.

Lujan, C. C., DeBruyn, L. M., & May, P. A. (1989). Profile of abused and neglected American Indian children in the Southwest. *Child Abuse & Neglect, 13,* 449–461.

Mannes, M. (1993). Seeking the balance between child protection and family preservation in Indian child welfare. *Child Welfare, 72,* 141–152.

Mannes, M. (1995). Factors and events leading to the passage of the Indian Child Welfare Act. *Child Welfare, 74,* 264–282.

Miller, D., Hoffman, F., & Turner, D. (1988). A perspective on the Indian Child Welfare Act. *Journal of Contemporary Social Work, 61,* 468–471.

Mindell, R., de Haymes, M. V., & Francisco, D. (2003). A culturally responsive practice model for urban Indian child welfare services. *Child Welfare, March–April,* 201–217.

Nelson, K., Saunders, E., & Landsman, M. (1993). Chronic child neglect in perspective. *Social Work, 38,* 661–671.

Piasecki, J., Manson, S., Biernoff, M., Hiat, A., Taylor, S., & Bechtold, D. (1989). Abuse and neglect of American Indian children: Findings from a survey of federal providers. *American Indian and Alaska Native Mental Health Research, 3,* 43–62.

Plantz, M., Hubbell, R., Barrett, B., & Dobrec, A. (1999). Indian child welfare: A status report. *Children Today, 18,* 24–29.

Polansky, N. A., Chalmers, M. A., Williams, D. P., & Buttenwieser, E. W. (1981). *Damaged parents: An anatomy of child neglect.* Chicago: University of Chicago Press.

Polansky, N. A., Gaudin, J. M., Ammons, P. W., & Davis, K. B. (1985). The psychological ecology of the neglectful mother. *Child Abuse & Neglect, 9,* 265–275.

Rose, S., & Meezan, W. (1993). Defining child neglect: Evolution, influences, and issues. *Social Service Review, 67,* 279–293.

Rose, S., & Meezan, W. (1995). Child neglect: A study of the perceptions of mothers and child welfare workers. *Children and Youth Services Review, 17,* 471–486.

Smith, A. (2003, Summer). Soul wound: the legacy of Native American schools. *Amnesty Now,* 14–17.

Song, K. (1986). *Defining child abuse: Korean American study.* Unpublished doctoral dissertation. University of California, Los Angeles.

Spicer, P. (1998). Drinking, foster care, and the intergenerational continuity of parenting in an urban Indian community. *American Indian Culture and Research Journal, 22,* 335–360.

U.S. Administration for Children and Families. (2005). *National Survey of Child and Adolescent Well-Being, 1997–2005.* Washington, DC: U.S. Government Printing Office.

U.S. Census Bureau. (2000). *Census of population and housing 2000: Public use microdata sample.* Washington, DC: Author.

U.S. Department of Health and Human Services, Administration on Children, Youth, and Families. (2001). *Child maltreatment: 1999.* Washington, DC: U.S. Government Printing Office.

U.S. Department of Heath and Human Services, Administration on Children, Youth, and Families. (2003). *Child maltreatment: 2003.* Washington, DC: U.S. Government Printing Office.

Wares, D., Wedel, K., Rosenthal, J., & Dobrec, A. (1994). Indian Child welfare: A multicultural challenge. *Journal of Multicultural Social Work, 3*(3), 1–15.

Weaver, H., & White, B. (1999). Protecting the future of indigenous children and nations: An examination of the Indian Child Welfare Act. *Journal of Health and Social Policy, 10*(4), 35–50.

White, R., & Cornely, D. (1981). Navajo child abuse and neglect study: A comparison group examination of abuse and neglect of Navajo children. *Child Abuse & Neglect, 5,* 9–17.

Wolock, I., & Horowitz, B. (1984). Child maltreatment as a social problem: The neglect of neglect. *American Journal of Orthopsychiatry, 59,* 377–389.

Zuravin, S. (1988). Child maltreatment and teenage first births: A relationship mediated by chronic sociodemographic stress? *American Journal of Orthopsychiatry, 58,* 91–103.

Joseph P. Gone

Mental Health, Wellness, and the Quest for an Authentic American Indian Identity

3

When I first arrived on the Fort Belknap Indian reservation in north central Montana to live and work following my graduation from college, I began systematically asking some of the more respected members of my community what it means to be American Indian (or, more precisely, what it means to be "Ind'in"—very few reservation community members used the term *Native American* at that time). I soon discovered that they too had devoted much thought and energy to the question despite their close and enduring ties to the reservation. It was during these conversations that I first encountered some of the surprising complexities that characterize the politics of identity in Indian country.

One particularly memorable conversation involved a former chairman of the Fort Belknap Community Council, the elected head of our tribal government. This quiet, middle-aged man was born and raised at Fort Belknap to a Gros Ventre parent and an Assiniboine parent. His Certificate Degree of Indian Blood—the U.S. Bureau of Indian Affairs' (BIA's) official record of an Indian person's degree of Native ancestry—attested to his "full-blood" status, a designation somewhat uncommon for his generation at Fort Belknap. He described a time in his life when he had just completed a successful reelection campaign, having previously been the youngest tribal chairman in Fort Belknap history. Once the new council was sworn in, the first order of business was to determine which of their members should be made the new chairman. Naturally, some of the council members nominated this accomplished former chairman for a second term on the basis of his experience and success in the position. A debate ensued, however, in which the former chairman's fitness for the office was challenged by a faction of dissenters. More specifically, these individuals complained that the former chairman was not "Indian enough" to continue representing the people of Fort Belknap in the highest elected office of the tribal government. Supporters of the former chairman immediately countered with a detailed presentation of his credentials: He was a full-blood, born and raised on the reservation, of good character, with an established record of proven efficacy as a tribal leader, and the like. In short, these supporters attested to the authenticity of the former chairman's "Indianness" relative to the cultural identities of the challengers by recounting a laundry list of characteristics that were understood locally to capture the very essence of Indian identity. A heated exchange ensued in which the former chairman's opponents ultimately grounded their challenges on the fact that he had not been raised in an alcoholic home and had not himself become an alcoholic. Fortunately, these arguments were ultimately dismissed as ridiculous by a majority of the council, and the former chairman was reelected to a second consecutive term, an extremely rare occurrence at Fort Belknap.

This example is instructive in several regards. First, it exemplifies the tumultuous interpersonal arena in which American Indian identity is alternately contested and established in complex ways. In fact, very few American Indian people would be unfamiliar with the kind of heated exchange described above, and most have participated in such discourse and contributed to (or endured) its force and function at one time or another.

Second, this example reveals the operative mechanism of Indian identity discourse along with several of its most familiar constituents: The assertion or refutation of an authentic Indian "essence" as evidenced usually by blood quantum, duration of reservation residence, language fluency, ceremonial practice, and the like. This is not to suggest, of course, that "essentialism" is actually viable as a conceptual framework for understanding the complexities of American Indian identity; rather, such essentialism is characteristic in practice of Indian identity discourse.

Third, this example illustrates the often implicit deficits, disorders, or pathologies that an authentic American Indian identity is assumed to entail, sometimes even among Indian people themselves. In this instance, elected tribal leaders contested the authenticity of one of their own to govern the community on the grounds that neither he nor his parents had habitually abused alcohol. More typically, of course, such implicit deficits are more subtle: Authentic or "real" Indians (it is supposed) cannot sustain happy marriages, raise terrific children, excel in their academic work, pursue successful careers, manage money well, thrive in the big city, and so on. Indeed, these subtle assumptions regarding an authentic Indian identity are most directly concerned with mental health or wellness insofar as they hobble the aspirations and expectations of contemporary Indian people who harbor them.

Fourth and finally, this example underscores that the implicit deficits, disorders, and pathologies that too often suffuse notions of an authentic Indian identity were cemented in the context of a brutal Euro-American colonialism. Although this observation may seem too obvious to mention, it is absolutely crucial to this chapter and this book because the colonial project known as the United States of America sought to shatter the cultural foundations on which the mental health and well-being of entire communities of Indian people depended, inaugurating a sometimes desperate pursuit of (post)colonial[1] alternatives for grounding personal and communal meaning-making. It is this nearly frantic pursuit of a viable (post)colonial source of coherence, connectedness, and continuity that renders concerns about American Indian mental health and contemporary American Indian identity utterly inextricable.

Given the centrality of identity to wellness among American Indian people, it is the purpose of this chapter to provide a conceptual overview of Native identity that will enable mental health professionals, practitioners, and researchers to more effectively address the mental health needs of American Indians in urban settings. This chapter thus

---

[1] In considering the colonial experience of the indigenous peoples of the United States, the issue of appropriate terminology becomes significant. Despite its currency in contemporary literary circles, the term *postcolonial* seems inappropriate to the contemporary indigenous circumstance because the colonizers (or their descendants) still retain dominance over the domestic, political, and economic affairs of tribal communities. Indeed, the U.S. Congress might well exercise its plenary power to terminate tribal communities at any time. At the same time, the term *colonial* also seems inappropriate because U.S. policies of military conquest, occupation, and outright resource theft ended a few short generations ago. In fact, since the era of self-determination commenced in the 1970s, when tribal governments began to exercise a degree of authority and autonomy uncharacteristic of colonial subjects in other parts of the world, the term *colonial* seems even less appropriate. Furthermore, for several generations now, many American Indian peoples have found innovative sources of meaning and coherence within established Euro-American symbols and institutions (e.g., sovereignty, literacy, legal claims, military service, blood quantum, Christianity, star quilting, cattle ranching, casino operation, and tribal college administration), effectively rendering them distinctively our own (in the postcolonial sense). To capture this extremely complex state of affairs, I have chosen to adopt the ambiguous term *(post)colonial* from Chadwick Allen (2002), albeit with different connotations.

summarizes and evaluates a range of approaches that psychologists and other social scientists have used to conceptualize Indian identity, with an emphasis on the ability of variant models to effectively capture the complexities of lived American Indian experience. Finally, this chapter draws out the implications of such complexities (and the conceptualizations that best describe them) for the mental health professional or practitioner engaged in serving Native people or communities in urban settings.

Theorizing American Indian Identities: Conceptual Alternatives

When it came to cultural identity, I was often instructed by the behavior of my youngest siblings who were born and raised at Fort Belknap. On more than one occasion during their childhoods, I observed them engaging in a make-believe activity or donning an article of traditional dress, only then to declare, "Look, I'm an Indian!" Sometimes it was explained to them that they were Indian regardless of how they dressed or the activities in which they engaged. Nevertheless, my siblings had some difficulty accepting the explanation that Indianness involves something one is, not something one does. I attribute this confusion to two sources. First, portrayals of American Indians are so stereotyped in (post)colonial America that it remains difficult even for Indian young people not to think of authentic or real Indians as stoic figures in feathers and paint who dance, ride horses, and hunt with bows and arrows. Second, these young siblings had difficulty recognizing their Indianness because their lives had unfolded in the insular routines of a fairly remote Indian community. Like fish in water, then, they simply had yet to recognize the distinctive features of the culturally saturated environment that nurtured them from birth (rendered suddenly salient once they later attended the nearby off-reservation public schools). Naturally, as they came of age, my siblings quite easily embraced the notion that being Indian involves intrinsic rather than enacted qualities. Reality, of course, is more complicated than superficial attributions of the *intrinsic* (what one is) versus the *enacted* (what one does), and so the range of ways that Indian identity has been conceptualized in theoretical terms (primarily within the social scientific disciplines of psychology, sociology, and cultural anthropology) has proliferated.

Most formal models of Indian identity were developed by White researchers to describe the variations in orientation and experience of Indian people in the rarified terms of the Western academy. These conceptualizations usually reflect a mix of intrinsic and enacted explanations in their efforts to classify American Indian identities for analytic purposes. To discuss these models in detail, however, it is imperative to consider briefly the colonial legacy that colors all conceptualizations of American Indian identity, whether in the research of social scientists or the routine interpersonal interactions of Native people. More specifically, the most influential conceptualization of Indian identity throughout the colonial era depended on a distinctively American ideology of race (Omi & Winant, 1994).

Sovereignty and Identity: The Influence of Racial Ideology

For a century or more, U.S. Indian policy has rested on the twin pillars of collective tribal sovereignty and individual political identity. The sovereign right of the various tribal communities that comprise Native North America to govern their own affairs is the unlikely result of Western conceptions of international law: As historical parties to treaties with the United States, for example, Indian groups inherited the legal status of nationhood. Of course, the federal government could not allow Indian tribes full status as truly independent nations given the larger American colonial project. Thus, the sovereignty of Indian "nations" has been tailored legally to the colonial interests of America insofar as the "external" powers of sovereignty (e.g., rights to make treaties, regulate immigration, and print money) have been extinguished by Congressional fiat, although the "internal" powers of sovereignty (e.g., rights to determine citizenship, regulate elections, and tax) remain. As a result, all federally recognized Indian tribes in the United States continue to enjoy their rather idiosyncratic status as domestic, dependent nations, albeit always at the "pleasure" of Congress (for a thorough and accessible overview, see Pevar, 2004).

One consequence of nationhood—even a domestic, dependent nationhood—is the right and responsibility to establish criteria for citizenship in the greater polity. Thus, tribal sovereignty is necessarily concerned with the status of individual Indians who compose the nation in question. No matter which criteria a federally recognized tribe adopts to define its citizenry (or its enrolled membership), the endorsement of such criteria is a statement about Indianness, a delineation of Indian identity. As a result, even the casual inspection of the citizenship criteria for diverse tribal nations could in principle reveal those aspects of tribal identity that particular Native communities have thoughtfully considered with regard to inclusion in the body politic. Unfortunately, such determinations were shaped by colonial relations in which the U.S. government effectively enforced its vested interest in defining Indians for the purposes of controlling Native people, lands, and resources. One consequence of this legacy is that instead of carefully considered and creatively selected citizenship criteria (which themselves are constructed through Western discourses of sovereignty, nationhood, and international law), most tribes continue to endorse a variant of the standard colonial theme: blood quantum or racial purity.

In the context, then, of American racial ideology, an Indian was simply someone who shared the biological or genetic heritage of the American Indian "race" to some specified degree. As such, this approach was the quintessential intrinsic explanation of Indian identity. Racial ideology afforded a potentially stable classification of Indianness (so long as a consensus regarding the particular specification endured), insofar as an individual evidencing the requisite racial characteristics was understood to be Indian for life, independent of the shifting tableau of experience. Difficulties arose, however, once an Indian, so determined, married a non-Indian: Were the descendants also Indian (and therefore subject to federal supervision and regulation) or not? Anthropologists and legal specialists debated this weighty question with reference primarily to biological attributes, including hair texture, cranial features, and the like (Beaulieu, 1984). It is this school of thought—born essentially of American capitalist concerns with the property status of African slaves and "reserved" Indian lands held in "trust" on behalf of tribal communities by the U.S. government—that gave rise to the influence of blood quantum as the most salient metonym of Indian identity.

Contemporary examinations of racial ideology in America have compellingly demonstrated that ascendant notions of race and racial purity are historically contingent social constructions, fictions (albeit with serious real-world consequences) developed in the American colonial context for the promulgation of Euro-American supremacy in this hemisphere (Jaimes, 1992; Jordan, 1974; Morgan, 1975; see Miller, 2005). The purported biological bases for the classification of race and racial purity have been completely debunked in scientific circles (Cartmill, 1998; Templeton, 1998). In fact, many phenotypical racial characteristics (e.g., skin color, facial features, and hair texture) are now recognized as fairly arbitrary collections of biological features with no socially meaningful correlates in terms of human ability or character (Appiah, 1996). Hypothetically speaking, any society could invent a nearly infinite array of racial groupings using completely arbitrary constellations of biological qualities. Finally, even if the concept of racial purity were firmly grounded in biology, modern Americans—American Indians included—could make little claim to such purity given the extensive (but often suppressed) history of intermarriage and reproduction between Indians, Blacks, and Whites (Forbes, 1993; Williamson, 1995).

Nevertheless, degree of ancestry, racial purity, or blood quantum remains an influential vestige of this history, one that distills the essence of Indian identity to degree of biological heritage. The BIA still issues Certificate Degree of Indian Blood documents to Indian people that subdivide their Native ancestry by tribe to an astonishing degree (e.g., 1/256 quantum Nez Perce). It persists in almost every modern tribal community's criteria for citizenship (with one-quarter degree of Indian blood being the most common) and plays an important semiotic function in Indian identity discourse, both within urban and reservation Indian communities. In fact, so pervasive and entrenched is this racial ideology in America's conceptions of Indian authenticity that it is not at all uncommon for Native people in urban settings to be asked by enthusiastic White interlocutors the intrusive question, "So, are you a full-blood?" One relative of mine who worked for the BIA reported occasional telephone requests by White people for a blood test to determine whether they had sufficient Indian ancestry to qualify for federal benefits.

Given the dominant influence of so widespread an ideology in America, it should not be surprising that social scientists have embraced this kind of essentialism in much of their early research as well. In more recent work, however, blood quantum and racial purity have retreated in the face of new strategies for conceptualizing American Indian identity. These strategies vary widely in terms of their essentialist commitments. I describe several of these strategies in turn, reviewing them on the basis of certain shared features as the *dimensional* models and the *discursive* models. As an aside, I should note briefly that social scientists have also conceptualized ethnic identity in terms of developmental stages that individuals are presumed to negotiate at key junctures during the lifespan (for an example of such a stage model, see Phinney, 1989; also, for a more general review of approaches to studying ethnic identity, see Phinney, 1990). These developmental models have not been adapted for use with American Indians, however, with the exception of the urban American Indian identity model currently under revision by its creator Karina Walters (1996, 1999).

The Dimensional
Models

One approach to conceptualizing American Indian identity arose when anthropologists and other social science researchers began to study the consequences for Indians of the intersection of Native and Euro-American cultures in the everyday lives of Native people. The study of assimilation or acculturation recognized that many Native people were participating with greater frequency and regularity in the practices of Euro-American society while simultaneously forgoing participation in Native ritual and practice. For example, one obvious marker of this shift in practice is the frequency of an individual's use of his or her tribal language versus his or her use of English. This conceptualization of Indian identity has been modeled as a linear dimension or continuum in which opposite end points represent traditional and assimilated identities. Thus, one needs only to determine which criteria are indicative of traditional or assimilated identities—anthropologists have used standards like blood quantum, language fluency, employment status, and ownership of a television (Graves, 1967)—to position an Indian person along the identity continuum. Such criteria clearly exhibit the familiar essentialist logic of inferring authenticity (i.e., a "traditional" identity) on the basis of a short list of basic or fundamental characteristics. This positioning requires the dramatic distillation of potentially complex experience into a single parameter that is then assigned to a unidimensional continuum. Furthermore, an individual's position along this continuum is relatively stable—it is unlikely that someone would move from the traditional end of the continuum to the assimilated end even in the course of an entire lifetime. Still, in contrast to the supposedly impermeable categories provided by racial ideology, the linear model can in fact account for some shift along the continuum during the life span.

With regard to this unidimensional modeling of American Indian identity, survey researchers have developed many variations on this methodological strategy, quite sensibly augmenting the list of presumably relevant criteria to include self-reported identity attributions and affiliations by Native respondents (Oetting & Beauvais, 1990–1991). Furthermore, these researchers have expanded such models to accommodate bi- or even triculturalism. For example, the cultural identifications of a particular individual can now be modeled simultaneously along two (or more) continua representing a respondent's self-reported comfort and competency with both Indian and Euro-American beliefs and practices (Moran, Fleming, & Somervell, 1999; Oetting & Beauvais,

1990–1991). Such models suggest that one's facility with Indian cultural practices need not conflict with or compromise one's facility with Euro-American practices—dual or bicultural identities are possible for single individuals who routinely "code-switch" between divergent cultural practices (LaFromboise, Coleman, & Gerton, 1993). This recognition of an individual's capacity for multiple cultural identities undoubtedly adds further complexity to the model but retains a fairly static quality—even lifetime shifts along the various continua are unlikely. In addition, these multidimensional models still require the distillation of complex information to a few points along the continua. Nevertheless, given their propensity for dimensional models, survey researchers will no doubt continue to generate variations of this kind.

Such conceptualizations represent an alternative to the untenable ideology of racial purity (which locates identity in blood and genes), merging a fluid combination of intrinsic explanations (e.g., blood quantum) and enacted explanations (e.g., speaking one's tribal language). One limitation of these models, of course, is that they fix American Indian identity through the simplistic distillation of complex life experience into the a priori criteria and categories deemed important by social scientists. In this regard, they remain rather distant from the richness and complexity of actual lived identities. More important, though, these simplistic representations posit Indianness as largely independent of the immediate and unfolding social contexts in which Native persons live and act. That is, they locate Indian identity primarily in the predictable and durable habits of thought and behavior of the individual in question, with little attention to the communicative processes, interactive environments, social structures, and institutional relations that might give rise to (or constitute) such identities. In essence, then, these constructs remain fundamentally psychological in nature, privileging the agentic intentions, reflexive attributions, and durable dispositions of the individual actor.

The inability of these models to render a satisfying account of lived cultural identities becomes obvious if one simply returns to the example from the beginning of this chapter in which the dimensional models seem ineffectual in representing (much less explaining) the heated exchange surrounding the selection of a new tribal chairman. This is because the dimensional models posit a core or essence of Indianness, usually a laundry list of certain qualities that a person either does or does not evidence, independent of the social processes through which Indian identity is regularly asserted and contested. And yet, the prevalence of what my friend Patrita "Ime" Salazar casually has referred to as "MITT contests" ("More Indian Than Thou"; personal communication) in Indian country suggests an important consideration in the conceptualization of Indian identity: Claims to kinds of Indian identity are routinely asserted and contested in concrete social interactions for particular rhetorical and pragmatic purposes. Thus, to represent more accurately the actual give and take of Indian identity that is so evident in everyday social interactions among Native people, a more prominent emphasis on dynamic social process is necessary. Instead of theorizing Indian identity as a relatively static personal attribute evidenced in the ordered and enduring thoughts and behaviors of individual Indian people, attention to social process suggests that Indian identity is more appropriately viewed as the creative product of two or more persons engaged in unfolding interaction within the context of available and preexisting discursive practices.

The Discursive Models

My informal inquiries at Fort Belknap regarding cultural identity were my first concrete opportunities to grasp the significance of dynamic social process for understanding American Indian identity. Perhaps the most significant contradiction I encountered in my early days on the reservation was a subtle one. I had taken to routinely asking members of my extended family what they thought it meant to be Gros Ventre in today's society. I vividly remember my uncle's response to my question: "There are no more Gros Ventres today." I was unprepared for this assertion, especially from someone like my uncle, who (like the chairman described in the opening of this chapter) was born and raised on the reservation, avidly participated in traditional ceremonial practices, and was listed (for all intents and purposes) as a full-blood Gros Ventre in the enrollment records. What could my Gros Ventre uncle possibly have meant by asserting to his Gros Ventre nephew that there are no Gros Ventres left today?

I had ample opportunity to explore this startling assertion with older Gros Ventres in research I undertook as a doctoral candidate at the University of Illinois (Gone, 1996). Designated the Gros Ventre Cultural Identity Project, this research involved loosely structured interviews with members of the elder generation of Gros Ventres at Fort Belknap. Not surprisingly, I discovered that many of our elders also firmly believed that a legitimate modern Gros Ventre identity was impossible because "Gros Ventre ways are gone." Although I visited with about 30 of our elders, I decided to focus my thesis on the identity interviews I conducted with my grandmother. She too insisted that Gros Ventre ways were gone, despite clear evidence that a host of uniquely Gros Ventre cultural ideals and concerns had shaped and ordered her life. In other words, from my perspective, my grandmother's beliefs and behavior seemed to directly contradict her own self-professed ideas about Gros Ventre identity. The dimensional models of Indian identity were fairly useless here—how could I reconcile these seemingly contradictory phenomena, and what did all of this imply about contemporary Indian identity?

THE GONE MODEL

On the basis of these investigations, two colleagues and I (Gone, Miller, & Rappaport, 1999) have proposed a conceptualization of cultural identity that is distinctive in at least two ways. First, this approach acknowledges that American Indian people actively construct cultural identities, drawing on the rich cultural resources in their own unique communities. Thus, Indian identities are intentional constructions by individual agents engaged in making sense of their experiences. At the same time, the possibilities for constructing such identities are channeled by the particular cultural histories, community traditions, and institutional relations that affect the tribal community in question, and such possibilities are not infinite, but limited. Thus, Indian identities are historical products of enduring social structures that are both powerful and pervasive. In short, the construction of cultural identity emerges at the confluence of intention and convention, agency and structure, individual and community, and mind and world. Rather than arbitrarily privileging either side of these analytic dichotomies, our model situates cultural identity within the reemerging discipline of cultural psychology (Shweder, 1991; Shweder & Sullivan, 1990) by asserting that culture and identity coconstitute one another (i.e., make each other up). The implications of this approach are distinctive on several counts. For one, it recognizes that the construction of Indian identity is simultaneously facilitated and constrained by the forces of history, power, and tradition. Additionally, in view of the local character of history, power, and tradition, it may not make much sense to talk about Indian identity in generic terms. Finally, such identities vary in remarkable ways even within a single community, depending on the multiple ways that creative individuals might draw on existing cultural meanings and practices to make sense of their own personal experiences.

Through engagement with established notions within cultural anthropology, we understood this fusion of agency and structure, mind and world, to occur through action, praxis, or practice (i.e., human activity in life context; see Ortner, 1984). The practices we encountered in the study of Gros Ventre cultural identity were primarily communicative and interactive. Thus, a second contribution of our approach is that American Indian identities are understood to emerge as products of dialogic interaction with others. That is, instead of being evidenced simply in the ordered and enduring thought and behavior of individuals, Indian identities are understood to emerge from the creative use of language in social interaction. More specifically, we have argued that the kind of communicative interaction best suited to the construction of cultural identity is the recounting of past personal narratives to particular audiences for intentional purposes. For example, in the identity interviews with my grandmother (Gone, 1996), she offered numerous accounts of her own personal experiences to instruct me on the meaning of being Gros Ventre in the modern world. Closer examination of these narratives revealed a richly textured local moral world (i.e., an interpreted environment that provides the context for meaningful action; see Kleinman, 1995) evoked through and comprised by her identity discourse, demonstrating how her culturally grounded understandings of spiritual matters informed and made possible her assertion that Gros Ventre ways were gone.

I have already noted that my grandmother's astonishing assertion that a legitimate Gros Ventre identity was no longer possible plainly contradicted her routine transactions in the world in which distinctive Gros Ventre ideals and values continually informed and guided her behavior. It was only through careful narrative analysis, however, that I came to understand that her conception of Gros Ventre identity depended heavily on her equating Gros Ventre ways with sacred Gros Ventre ritual tradition. Because my grandmother also reasoned that the Supreme Being must have intended for Catholicism to replace this ancestral ceremonial tradition, and because such tradition had not been properly observed in over a century (and indeed is no longer available for appropriate use), my grandmother concluded definitively that real Gros Ventres had ceased to exist. This fuller understanding of the cultural context that informed my grandmother's sophisticated worldview (her local moral world) resolves the mystery of the apparent contradiction in words and behavior: Her anguish over the colonial annihilation of Gros Ventre ceremonial tradition (and all that this implies) required the renunciation of an authentic contemporary Gros Ventre identity. The irony of my grandmother's position is that her adamant denial of the possibility for a legitimate modern Gros Ventre identity was itself a legitimate modern Gros Ventre identity. Only a discursive model can adequately represent this paradoxical state of affairs, and narrative analysis becomes the central analytic tool for disentangling such complexity (for a detailed example of narrative analysis and Gros Ventre cultural identity, see Gone, 1999).

It should now be clear that our conceptualization of Indian identity attempts to circumvent the age-old tension between agency and structure, focusing on specific social contexts in which the complicated meanings of cultural traditions and community events furnish the materials for the intentional construction of individual identities through narrative practice. Furthermore, it recognizes that Indian identities emerge through dialogic social practice, especially communicative interaction with others. As an alternative to previous conceptualizations of Indian identity, then, our proposal is neither especially simplistic nor necessarily static. That is, serious attention to social context allows for the mobility of individuals to transition in and out of particular cultural identities depending on their interpretations of shifting social contexts, including unfolding historical events (e.g., U.S. Congressional termination of one's tribal sovereignty) or changing relationships with others (e.g., sudden responsibility for raising a grandchild). In addition, it shifts the balance away from an intrinsic explanation to an enacted explanation insofar as the communicative interpretation of one's role or place within existing social contexts is a subtle yet powerful creative activity in itself.

Yet, our conceptualization of Indian identity still implies a fairly stable construct in the sense that an individual's local moral world (i.e., richly interpreted social context) is unlikely to shift so dramatically that sudden identity transformations ever seem routine (though Indians, too, sometimes experience extraordinary religious conversions). In fact, most Gros Ventre elders I know have maintained a strict and lifelong adherence to the interpretation of community life that asserts that Gros Ventre ways are gone despite the rejection of this idea by several younger tribal members today (Fowler, 1987). It is important to acknowledge, therefore, that at least some significant aspects of Indian identity seem to defy even this level of stability or regularity in everyday practice. For example, a middle-aged Indian man might portray himself as a "Seventies SuperSkin" (i.e., a Red power militant) to an uninformed White female admirer in the afternoon, only to admit rather sheepishly to a community elder at a ceremony later that evening that he does not speak his tribal language and should not be considered culturally competent for ritual purposes. To explain this kind of ephemeral versatility, Indian identity must also be theorized as a series of dynamic and rhetorical constructions that may shift dramatically in a person's interactions with others precisely because the identities individuals construct in given situations are highly sensitive to the immediate social context. In short, such a conceptualization greatly emphasizes an enacted explanation over an intrinsic explanation in which the acting in question is the attempt to influence others through communication.

THE O'NELL MODEL

One sophisticated attempt to represent American Indian identity as a series of versatile, dynamic, and rhetorical constructions that might fluctuate dramatically in a person's immediate interactions with others was developed by anthropologist Theresa O'Nell (1996) during her fieldwork among the Flathead people in Montana. This conceptualization of Indian identity was O'Nell's effort to carefully describe the ongoing negotiation of identity as it actually occurs in an Indian community. For reasons explained below, she labeled this perspective on Indianness as the "empty center" rhetoric of Indian identity. To understand this model, the reader should imagine a target diagram consisting of the usual rings of concentric circles surrounding a bull's-eye at its core. This bull's-eye can be seen to represent for any particular individual the conceptual realm occupied by genuine, legitimate, authentic, or real Indians whose identities as Flathead people (in cultural terms) are absolutely beyond question. Given the nature of identity politics in contemporary Flathead life, this inner sphere of real Indianness is unlikely to contain even a single living person in the eyes of most contemporary Flathead individuals—hence, the term *empty center*. Rings closest to the bull's-eye, however, represent for Flathead individuals those spaces occupied by living people who most closely approximate the characteristics and traits of the real Indians, whereas rings farther toward the outer edge of the target represent spaces occupied by people whose cultural identity is deemed less authentic or in question. Thus, according to O'Nell, most negotiation and conflict concerning Indian identity within the Flathead community may be conceptualized in terms of which of the concentric rings between the bull's-eye and the outermost edge of the target various community members are seen to occupy.

The power of this empty center model of Indian identity is threefold. First, the model allows for a diversity of identity assessments or attributions for a given individual depending on the social status of that individual within the community. For example, a tribal elder widely recognized in the community as most closely approximating what it means to be a real Indian would probably deny that he or she is in fact a real Indian and would thus invoke the empty center within discussions of his or her own identity. In contrast, a younger person positioned more marginally to the central realm of the real Indians might actually assign this particular elder to the bull's-eye as a genuinely real Indian in his or her own discussions of Flathead identity. For this individual, then, the center is sparsely populated but not quite empty. Thus, the "empty center" conceptualization of Indian identity allows for tremendous variability in terms of how any given individual makes sense of his or her own cultural identity as well as the cultural identities of other members of the community. Multiple individuals, then, construct multiple identities, each invoking an identity status for him- or herself as well as for all of the other people in the community in such a way that different people might disagree as to the specific placement of a given community member (i.e., closer to or further from the realm of the real Indians) in their own individual identity conceptions.

Second, the model allows for a shifting historical reformulation of Indian identity in which passing generations of Indian people consistently move toward the empty center, always redefining what it means to be a real Indian for new generations. For example, in today's Plains Indian communities, the last buffalo-hunting generation might occupy the empty center for most tribal members, although for the buffalo-hunting generation, their ancestors (who perhaps were less dependent on the White man's trade goods) must have defined what it meant to be a real Indian. Thus, rather than imagining a single universal target diagram, one can imagine a series of telescoping diagrams in which cohorts of individuals pass successively into the center as the community endures throughout history. As a result, the model captures the ever-evolving nature of Indianness within the endless cultural shifts that have characterized Indian life throughout time immemorial.

Finally, the empty center conceptualization can easily accommodate the rhetorical posturing so characteristic of the MITT contests described earlier. More specifically, individual Indian persons can represent themselves as occupying different rings of the target diagram depending on the immediate social context of the interaction. For example, when making a case before a relatively ignorant White authority figure, an individual might position him- or herself relatively close to the empty center to lend pragmatic force to his or her arguments (perhaps emphasizing his or her impressive lineage, cultural knowledge, or facility with the language). In contrast, the same individual might distance him- or herself from the empty center when engaged rhetorically with other Indian people who are in a position to effectively challenge his or her claims to authentic Indianness (perhaps humbly acknowledging that he or she spent years away from the community for educational purposes or that one of his or her grandparents was White). Thus, this model can effectively represent the routine communicative acts of rhetorically constructing an Indian identity tailored to the instrumental purposes at hand in any given interaction. For these various reasons, I find this sophisticated and dynamic theory of Indian identity both potent and elegant.

As one final example of the explanatory power of the empty center rhetoric model of American Indian identity, I return briefly to the words of my grandmother. In her complex assertion that a modern Gros

Ventre identity is impossible, she actively invoked an empty center through her identity discourse: All of the real Gros Ventres are gone. The power of O'Nell's particular discursive model is that it can adequately account for the empty center invoked by my grandmother while simultaneously allowing that, for me, the center is not quite empty: My grandmother embodies nearly all that it means to me to be Gros Ventre today.

Comparison and Evaluation

In concluding this discussion, it is important to note that both the dimensional and the discursive models of American Indian identity represent progress beyond the corroded foundation of American racial ideology. In fact, both kinds of models have been used productively in research by social scientists. Nevertheless, one clear advantage of the discursive models seems readily apparent. Such models can accurately represent the fundamentally essentialist practices that characterize Indian identity discourse—and indeed, if they could not, a central facet of the phenomenon would be obscured—without actually reifying such essentialism in the analytic process itself. They do so by privileging open-ended, open-minded investigations of American Indian identity that are attuned to the emergent social and interactive processes by which such identities are negotiated and contested. In contrast, the dimensional models involve the assessment of American Indian identity on a priori grounds, specifying the relevant characteristics or criteria for authenticity in advance of conducting the research. Rather than discover the locally relevant terms of essentialist discourse, they risk creating an authoritative alternative that retains little meaningful cultural validity—whether such practices are justifiable in principle is a question of empirical as well as political significance.

Improving Urban Indian Lives: Professional Recommendations

In this chapter, I have reviewed a variety of approaches to theorizing American Indian identity. The contrasting approaches described here are meant to illustrate the complexities of cultural identity in Indian communities so as to prepare the mental health professional or practitioner to serve Native people more effectively (Gone, 2003, 2004a, 2004b). More specifically, I hope that a general familiarity with the nuances of cultural identification—especially those that involve dynamic social process—will alert practitioners to the dangers of overly simplistic clinical or community formulations in consultation or treatment with American Indians.

If conceptualizing Indian identity is complicated in general, nowhere is that complexity more daunting than within Indian communities in urban settings. Other chapters in this book detail the history and significance of the BIA Relocation program and other sources of 20th century urban migration for Indian people (Fixico, 1986). The arrival of sizable numbers of tribal members in many of America's largest cities—nearly two thirds of Native American households in the United States are currently located in urban areas (U.S. Census Bureau, 2003)—confronted these individuals with the intimidating problem of how to forge social relations across preexisting tribal allegiances, divergent cultural practices, and (for the most part) diffuse neighborhood residency. Some Native critics have charged that the American diaspora of Native peoples to the big city signaled the end of distinctive and authentic communal affiliations in exchange for new identities as ethnic Indians who embrace a questionable pan-Indianism that remains divorced from reservation cultural routines and ritual space. Nevertheless, Indian people have demonstrated tremendous resilience in the face of such challenges, creating vibrant urban communities, establishing enduring urban institutions, and forging novel urban traditions (Buff, 2001; Fixico, 2000; Jackson, 2002; LaGrand, 2002; Lobo & Peters, 2001; Weibel-Orlando, 1999).

With regard to the mental health needs of these urban populations, too little is known. As of this writing, I could identify no contemporary, inclusive, and authoritative studies of psychiatric epidemiology published for adult Native Americans in general (but for a description of pending findings, see Beals, Manson, Mitchell, Spicer, & the AI-SUPERPFP Team, 2003), much less for those in urban areas. Nevertheless, clinical observations regarding the centrality of cultural identity for the mental health status of urban Indians have been documented for decades (for an early example, see Olson, 1971), usually emphasizing the psychological dangers of cultural disorientation, assimilation pressures, and anomie. Certainly, Indians in America's cities who interact with non-Indians routinely and evidence high rates of intertribal and interracial intermarriage (Gonzales, 2001) must navigate and negotiate innovative contexts for constructing cultural identity in comparison to their reservation kin. One result, for example, is that urban

Indians seem to value an individual's faithful participation in the "community" much more than blood quantum or tribal enrollment as a marker of Indian identity (Gonzales, 2001; Lobo, 2001; Straus & Valentino, 2001). The point here is simply that urban life is likely to inflect, refract, or convolute the fundamentally intricate phenomenon of American Indian identity in particular ways. Appropriate professional appraisal of such complexity would seem especially pressing in the context of increasing commitments to cultural competency in clinical training and practice.

Conventional approaches to cultural competency in mental health service delivery have been both limited and limiting. The typical means to cultural sensitivity in clinical contexts have included (a) cursory familiarity with respective ethnic group characterizations (usually dependent on the abstract description of ethnic prototypes or cultural generalities), (b) offhand generalizations from firsthand professional experience with clients of color, (c) reflexive awareness by majority-culture clinicians regarding the assumptions and privileges inherent to socialization into the dominant culture vis-à-vis the cultural experiences of people of color, and (d) obliged inclusion of people of color in clinically relevant research protocols (often using self-identified race or ethnicity as proxies for presumed cultural participation). In fact, none of these methods adequately prepares the mental health professional or practitioner to flexibly and dynamically engage any particular American Indian client who may bring a host of distinctive cultural practices— thereby constituting and embodying cultural identity—into the therapeutic or consultative relationship.

Unfortunately, the empirical literature documenting the processes and outcomes of psychological services delivered to Native clients and communities is virtually nonexistent (for an authoritative overview attesting to this fact, see U.S. Department of Health and Human Services, 2001; see also Gone & Alcantara, in press). In light of so scant an empirical record, I tentatively recommend the following for mental health professionals and practitioners committed to serving urban American Indian people and communities.

1. *Consider that psychological difficulties experienced by urban Indian clients are existential in origin and expressive of conflicts in cultural identity.* The Euro-American conquest of Native America resulted in the sweeping disruption or destruction of almost every facet of pre-Colonial Indian existence. Whether resulting from warfare, disease, relocation, containment, impoverishment, or deliberate policies of cultural eradication, the American holocaust heralded an unprecedented existential crisis for the vast majority of Native communities. The psychic shock of these depredations reverberates throughout contemporary Indian life in ways both subtle and profound, including distortions in what have become

normative experiences of spirituality, personhood, social relations, wellness, and of course, cultural identity. In the challenging historical project of reconstructing our communal ways of life, it has become difficult even for Indian people to authoritatively identify which of our contemporary cultural differences represent colonial distortions of indigenous tradition and which represent potentially desirable alterations or adaptations in tribal practice.

The challenge for clinicians is to engage urban Indian recipients of mental health services with this history in mind, attending to indications that presenting problems might be productively viewed as existential in origin. That is, clinicians should consider that the distress and dysfunction encountered with their urban Indian clients are symptomatic of unresolved intergenerational grief and historical trauma (Duran, Duran, Brave Heart, & Yellow Horse-Davis, 1998) that have rendered these clients bereft of the spiritual, psychological, and emotional resources for a robust cultural identity and fertile personal meaning-making. Framing client difficulties in the context of the enduring colonial legacy may help to avoid the withering implications of person-centered explanations that blame the victim (Ryan, 1976) for his or her problems, thereby preserving trust and motivation for change. In short, clinicians must be prepared to augment their explanatory models of psychological distress and disorder (i.e., theoretical orientations) to include collective, historical, and intergenerational understandings of the roots of personal dysfunction that imply interventions targeted at the therapeutic (re)integration of clients into their cultural, communal, and familial contexts.

2. *Continuously assess and (re)formulate the cultural identity status of urban Indian clients in the context of therapeutic goals.* If the psychological problems of urban Indian clients are to be viewed as existential in origin, then the quest to (re)imagine an authentic Indian identity in (post)colonial America is likewise entangled with Native ideas and ideals concerning wholeness, wellness, and robust mental health (Gone, 2005). One consequence of this relationship is that Indian identity discourse—including the ways and means by which individual Indians participate in such discourse—remains an informative venue through which to ascertain the often implicit ideas and concepts about wholeness and wellness that Native people embrace, especially those that either facilitate or constrain therapeutic progress. As such, professional attention to identity discourse represents an underused point of access for clinical and consultative assessment and understanding. Thus, to properly contextualize psychological difficulties within histories of colonization and conquest, and subsequent crises in personal and communal meaning-making, the clinical assessment of cultural identity as an individual instantiation of these constituting influences seems essential.

The challenge for clinicians is to engage urban Indian recipients of mental health services in sensitive, ongoing, and therapeutically relevant assessments of cultural identity that appreciate the complexities and perspectives reviewed in this chapter. Obviously, cursory identification of urban Indian clients as full-blood or mixed-blood, assimilated or traditional, and bicultural or anomic is not enough, because such labels may stereotype client experiences in ways that preclude proper therapeutic understanding of the thorny issues at stake. Instead, clinicians should pursue a more thorough and open-ended formulation of the cultural identity of urban Indian clients, especially as it pertains to therapeutic goals. The outline for cultural formulation specified in the *Diagnostic and Statistical Manual of Mental Disorders* (4th ed., text rev.; American Psychiatric Association, 2000) remains a useful clinical tool for assessing a range of cultural information, including cultural identity, in relationship to client problems (independent of clinician attitudes toward the *Diagnostic and Statistical Manual* classification scheme in general). In many instances, however, initial assessment must be augmented with ongoing clinical explorations, with sensitive inquiry into the meanings and practices associated with cultural identity in the context of therapeutic goals. Open-ended questions, such as "What does it mean to you to be Indian?"; "Who do you consider to be an authentic Indian person and why?"; "Who in your family has most taught you how to be Indian?"; and "In what ways does your community see you as Indian?" can evoke in-session examples of Indian identity discourse that become immediately available for discussion, reflection, and interpretation. Over time, intermittent clinician entry into the identity discourse of urban Indian clients can yield successive reformulations of earlier understandings that should enhance therapeutic progress.

3. *Harness the social process of the therapeutic relationship to support distressed urban Indian clients in reconstituting cultural identity as a path to wellness.* The discursive approaches to theorizing American Indian identity reviewed in this chapter recognize that cultural identity plays out in the context of unfolding social process. It seems reasonable, then, for clinicians to acknowledge that engagement in the therapeutic or consultative function is itself a form of social process, one that is unfamiliar to most Americans (the majority of whom do not obtain psychotherapeutic services even when they require them; see Kessler et al., 1994). Given American Indians' disproportionately limited access to mental health services (Gone, 2003, 2004b; U.S. Department of Health and Human Services, 2001), American Indian people are even less likely to encounter psychological assessment and treatment firsthand. As a result, the precise contours of the therapeutic relationship merit careful and reflexive attention by clinicians to effectively monitor the negotiated meanings of the therapeutic encounter for urban Indian

clients. For it is in the unusual therapeutic context that particular cultural identities will be constructed "online" through the immediate and unfolding discursive practices that characterize psychological service delivery. In addition to facilitating therapeutic progress, such reflexive awareness and attention also has the potential to preclude instances in which the legacy of U.S. colonialism might continue to imprint the relationships between Euro-American clinicians and urban Indian clients in nearly invisible but counterproductive ways (Gone, 2003, 2004a). Careful attention to the standoffs and breakdowns in the therapeutic relationship may provide opportunity to avoid or overcome these dangers.

The challenge for clinicians is to engage urban Indian recipients of mental health services through the unusual social processes of the clinic toward the reconstitution of cultural identity as a path to wellness in the context of therapeutic goals. This reconstitution of cultural identity, when warranted, may result in the rethinking of long-standing but unhealthy assumptions embraced by urban Indian clients that inherently pathologize Indian identity (such as in the incident portrayed at the beginning of this chapter). In addition, such reconstitution may relieve or resolve distress related to identity confusion or contestation that emerges from urban Indian client interactions with others. To accomplish such effects, however, clinicians probably need to guide and support urban Indian clients in processes of discovery and innovative meaning-making that far surpass their own clinical expertise or professional experience. Collaborations with and referrals to Native elders, community leaders, and spiritual advisors could ensure a productive journey for urban Indian clients, with clinicians providing motivational encouragement, empathic support, and compassionate feedback along the way. As in all clinical work, however, such efforts must be integrated within and tailored to explicitly defined therapeutic goals.

4. *Recognize the limitations of the conventional therapeutic or consultative relationship, and venture out of the clinic into urban Indian communities that you desire to serve.* As the first sections of this chapter detailed, American Indian identity is fashioned in the give and take of social process and community interaction. As a result, nothing can provide a more thorough understanding of these discursive processes than witnessing them firsthand. Thus, in addition to the potential for fruitful collaborations with community members as described above, participation in the routines of an urban Indian community should afford powerful insights into the public rhetorics and pragmatics entailed in the construction of cultural identity. Most important, however, the clinician with commitments to better serving urban Indian people has few alternatives other than to venture forth from the therapy office or consulting room, because the vast majority of Native people—even those who might

conceivably benefit from mental health services—will never cross the threshold of the mental health clinic for a host of legitimate reasons. As an alternative approach to reaching the underserved, community psychologists have been advocating a shift in professional priorities and practices for decades. Established as a critical alternative to conventional clinical psychology in the 1960s, community psychology (Rappaport, 1977) has integrated its professional commitments to progressive political activity, human resource development, and rigorous psychological science in the context of an approach that explicitly embraces ecology, diversity, and cultural relativity. In regard to the practices of conventional mental health service delivery, community psychologists have undertaken community-based consultation and education (instead of clinic-based psychotherapeutic services) that emphasize collaborative and empowering role relationships with community members (instead of expert–client relationships with patients) toward the cultivation of strength-focused (instead of deficit-focused) and preventive (instead of rehabilitative) interventions (Rappaport & Seidman, 1983). In applying the principles of community psychology, then, mental health professionals might embark on collaborative and empowering projects undertaken in partnership with urban Indian communities to facilitate the cultivation and development of healthy cultural identities among urban "at-risk" youth in their own settings. The possibilities are truly limitless, and at the same time, such efforts promise to counter— perhaps even to redress—the shattering colonial legacy in which Euro-American experts implement "West is best" solutions to Indian problems (for more details, see Gone, 2003, 2004a, 2004b).

Conclusion

I hope that this review of American Indian identity and its implications for mental health service delivery will inspire professionals and practitioners committed to serving urban Indian people and communities to a more fruitful engagement in their therapeutic and consultative relationships with Native clients. In addition, I hope that together, knowledgeable and sensitive professionals in service to resilient Indian communities can bind up the wounds of colonialism and chart the course for a new era of wellness and self-determined authenticity in the lived identities of urban American Indians.

References

Allen, C. (2002). *Blood narrative: Indigenous identity in American Indian and Maori literary and activist texts.* Durham, NC: Duke University Press.

American Psychiatric Association. (2000). *Diagnostic and statistical manual of mental disorders* (4th ed., text rev.). Washington, DC: Author.

Appiah, K. A. (1996). Race, culture, identity: Misunderstood connections. In K. A. Appiah & A. Gutman (Eds.), *Color conscious: The political morality of race* (pp. 30–105). Princeton, NJ: Princeton University Press.

Beals, J., Manson, S. M., Mitchell, C. M., Spicer, P., & the AI-SUPERPFP Team. (2003). Cultural specificity and comparison in psychiatric epidemiology: Walking the tightrope in American Indian research. *Culture, Medicine, and Psychiatry, 27,* 259–289.

Beaulieu, D. L. (1984). Curly hair and big feet: Physical anthropology and the implementation of land allotment on the White Earth Chippewa reservation. *American Indian Quarterly, 8,* 281–314.

Buff, R. (2001). *Immigration and the political economy of home: West Indian Brooklyn and American Indian Minneapolis, 1945–1992.* Berkeley: University of California Press.

Cartmill, M. (1998). The status of the race concept in physical anthropology. *American Anthropologist, 100,* 651–660.

Duran, E., Duran, B., Brave Heart, M. Y. H., & Yellow Horse-Davis, S. (1998). Healing the American Indian soul wound. In Y. Danieli (Ed.), *International handbook of multigenerational legacies of trauma* (pp. 341–354). New York: Plenum Press.

Fixico, D. L. (1986). *Termination and relocation: Federal Indian policy, 1945–1960.* Albuquerque: University of New Mexico.

Fixico, D. L. (2000). *The urban Indian experience in America.* Albuquerque: University of New Mexico.

Forbes, J. (1993). *Africans and Native Americans: The language of race and the evolution of Red–Black peoples.* Urbana: University of Illinois Press.

Fowler, L. (1987). *Shared symbols, contested meanings: Gros Ventre culture and history, 1778–1984.* Ithaca, NY: Cornell University.

Gone, J. P. (1996). *Gros Ventre cultural identity as normative self: A case study.* Unpublished master's thesis, University of Illinois at Urbana–Champaign.

Gone, J. P. (1999). "We were through as keepers of it": The "missing pipe" narrative and Gros Ventre cultural identity. *Ethos, 27,* 415–440.

Gone, J. P. (2003). American Indian mental health service delivery: Persistent challenges and future prospects. In J. S. Mio & G. Y. Iwamasa (Eds.), *Culturally diverse mental health: The challenges of research and resistance* (pp. 211–229). New York: Brunner-Routledge.

Gone, J. P. (2004a). Keeping culture in mind: Transforming academic training in professional psychology for Indian country. In D. Mihesuah & A. Cavender-Wilson (Eds.), *Indigenizing the academy: Transforming scholarship and empowering communities* (pp. 124–142). Lincoln: University of Nebraska Press.

Gone, J. P. (2004b). Mental health services for Native Americans in the 21st century United States. *Professional Psychology: Research and Practice, 35,* 10–18.

Gone, J. P. (2005). *"We never was happy living like a Whiteman": Cultural divergences and American Indian mental health disparities.* Manuscript submitted for publication.

Gone, J. P., & Alcantara, C. (in press). Practice makes perfect? Identifying effective psychological treatments for mental health problems in Indian country. In E. H. Hawkins & R. D. Walker (Eds.), *Best practices in behavioral health services for American Indians and Alaska Natives.* Portland, OR: One Sky National Resource Center for American Indian and Alaska Native Substance Abuse Prevention and Treatment Services.

Gone, J. P., Miller, P. J., & Rappaport, J. (1999). Conceptual self as normatively oriented: The suitability of past personal narrative for the study of cultural identity. *Culture & Psychology, 5,* 371–398.

Gonzales, A. A. (2001). Urban (trans)formations: Changes in the meaning and use of American Indian identity. In S. Lobo & K. Peters (Eds.), *American Indians and the urban experience* (pp. 169–185). Walnut Creek, CA: Altamira.

Graves, T. D. (1967). Acculturation, access, and alcohol in a tri-ethnic community. *American Anthropologist, 69,* 306–321.

Jackson, D. D. (2002). *Our elders lived it: American Indian identity in the city.* DeKalb: Northern Illinois University.

Jaimes, M. A. (1992). Federal Indian identification policy: A usurpation of indigenous sovereignty in North America. In M. A. Jaimes (Ed.), *The state of Native America* (pp. 123–138). Boston: South End Press.

Jordan, W. (1974). *The White man's burden: Historical origins of racism in the United States.* London: Oxford University Press.

Kessler, R. C., McGonagle, K. A., Zhao, S., Nelson, C. B., Hughes, M., Eshleman, S., et al. (1994). Lifetime and twelve-month prevalence of *DSM–III–R* psychiatric disorders in the United States. *Archives of General Psychiatry, 51,* 8–19.

Kleinman, A. (1995) *Writing at the margin: Discourse between anthropology and medicine.* Berkeley: University of California Press.

LaFromboise, T., Coleman, H. L. K., & Gerton, J. (1993). Psychological impact of biculturalism: Evidence and theory. *Psychological Bulletin, 114*, 395–412.

LaGrand, J. B. (2002). *Indian metropolis: Native Americans in Chicago, 1945–75*. Chicago: University of Illinois.

Lobo, S. (2001). Is urban a person or a place? Characteristics of urban Indian country. In S. Lobo & K. Peters (Eds.), *American Indians and the urban experience* (pp. 73–84). Walnut Creek, CA: Altamira.

Lobo, S., & Peters, K. (Eds.). (2001). *American Indians and the urban experience*. Walnut Creek, CA: Altamira.

Miller, J. (Ed.). (2005). *Daedalus, 134*(1).

Moran, J. R., Fleming, C. M., & Somervell, P. (1999). Measuring bicultural ethnic identity among American Indian adolescents: A factor analysis study. *Journal of Adolescent Research, 14*, 405–426.

Morgan, E. (1975). *American slavery, American freedom: The ordeal of colonial Virginia*. New York: Norton.

Oetting, E. R., & Beauvais, F. (1990–1991). Orthogonal cultural identification theory: The cultural identification of minority adolescents. *International Journal of the Addictions, 25*, 655–685.

Olson, J. W. (1971). Epilogue: The urban Indian as viewed by an Indian caseworker. In J. O. Waddell & O. M. Watson (Eds.), *The American Indian in urban society* (pp. 398–408). Boston: Little, Brown.

Omi, M., & Winant, H. (1994). *Racial formation in the United States: From the 1960s to the 1990s* (2nd ed.). New York: Routledge.

O'Nell, T. D. (1996). *Disciplined hearts: History, identity and depression in an American Indian community*. Los Angeles: University of California Press.

Ortner, S. B. (1984). Theory in anthropology since the sixties. *Comparative Studies in Society and History, 26*, 126–66.

Pevar, S. L. (2004). *The rights of Indians and tribes: The authoritative ACLU guide to Indian and tribal rights* (3rd ed.). New York: New York University.

Phinney, J. S. (1989). Stages of ethnic identity development in minority group adolescents. *Journal of Early Adolescence, 9*, 34–49.

Phinney, J. S. (1990). Ethnic identity in adolescents and adults: Review of research. *Psychological Bulletin, 108*, 499–514.

Rappaport, J. (1977). *Community psychology: Values, research, and action*. Fort Worth, TX: Holt.

Rappaport, J., & Seidman, E. (1983). Social and community interventions. In C. E. Walker (Ed.), *The handbook of clinical psychology: Theory, research, and practice* (pp. 1089–1123). Homewood, IL: Dow Jones-Irvin.

Ryan, W. (1976). *Blaming the victim* (Rev. ed.). New York: Vintage Books.

Shweder, R. A. (1991). *Thinking through cultures: Expeditions in cultural psychology*. Cambridge, MA: Harvard University Press.

Shweder, R. A., & Sullivan, M. A. (1990). The semiotic subject of cultural psychology. In L. A. Pervin (Ed.), *Handbook of personality: Theory and research* (pp. 399–416). New York: Guilford Press.

Straus, T., & Valentino, D. (2001). Retribalization in urban Indian communities. In S. Lobo & K. Peters (Eds.), *American Indians and the urban experience* (pp. 85–94). Walnut Creek, CA: Altamira.

Templeton, A. R. (1998). Human races: A genetic and evolutionary perspective. *American Anthropologist, 100*, 632–650.

U.S. Census Bureau. (2003). *American housing survey for the United States: 1999*. Washington, DC: U.S. Government Printing Office.

U.S. Department of Health and Human Services. (2001). *Mental health: Culture, race, and ethnicity—A supplement to mental health: A report of the surgeon general*. Rockville, MD: U.S. Department of Health and Human Services, Substance Abuse and Mental Health Services Administration, Center for Mental Health Services.

Walters, K. L. (1996). *Urban American Indian identity and psychological wellness*. Unpublished doctoral dissertation, University of California, Los Angeles.

Walters, K. L. (1999). Urban American Indian identity attitudes and acculturation styles. *Journal of Human Behavior in the Social Environment, 2*, 163–178.

Weibel-Orlando, J. (1999). *Indian country, L.A.: Maintaining ethnic community in complex society* (Rev. ed.). Chicago: University of Illinois.

Williamson, J. (1995). *The new people: Miscegenation and mulattoes in the United States*. Baton Rouge: Louisiana University Press.

II

Specific Urban American Indian Treatment Considerations

This part of the book addresses specific urban Indian treatment needs. The three chapters in this part are geared toward providing information about common issues affecting the urban Indian population. Authors explore issues related to alcohol and drug rehabilitation, violence against women, and the effects of trauma within the urban Indian community.

Chapter 4, "Healing the Generations: Urban American Indians in Recovery" by Rose L. Clark, provides a historical overview of the effects of alcohol and drug addiction within the urban Indian community, emphasizing the effects of historical factors and posttraumatic stress. The author addresses some of the treatment considerations involved with this population, including family dynamics, assessment and diagnosis, prevention and treatment, and homelessness. The author then addresses current treatment outcome research, including the efforts to heal the generations through traditional ceremonies. The author concludes with recommendations based on her own contextual experience working with American Indians for ways in which therapists can begin healing the generations.

Chapter 5, "Understanding Domestic Violence Within the Urban Indian Community" by Tawa M. Witko, Rae Marie Martinez, and Richard Milda, focuses on some of the current research on issues of violence within the urban Indian community, paying special attention to its effect on urban Indian women. The authors explore the impact history has had on the evolution of violence in Indian communities and the connection between internalized oppression and violence. They also address ways in which practitioners can help break the cycle of violence. The authors conclude with recommendations for research and practice.

Chapter 6, "Trauma and the American Indian" by Nadine Cole, focuses on the effects of trauma on the urban Indian community. The author begins by looking at some of the historical trauma experienced by Native people and how this trauma is affecting the individual, family, and tribe today. She addresses areas for treatment such as substance abuse, shame and self-defeating behaviors, and perpetuation of trauma patterns. She concludes with a culturally appropriate model that addresses the psychological, physical, and spiritual essence of the client.

Rose L. Clark

Healing the Generations: Urban American Indians in Recovery

4

A lcohol and drug use have had a devastating effect on American Indian people. The situation is even more difficult for those American Indians and Alaska Natives (AIs/ANs) who are already experiencing co-occurring disorders and who are living in urban environments. Those individuals and families living in the urban environment find themselves facing their problems, including oppression and discrimination, with relatively limited coping mechanisms, no economic security, and no social support network provided by their tribal community. Families who have always relied on the availability of family, kin, and clan networks suddenly find themselves alienated, disempowered, and overwhelmed by a sense of hopelessness. There are also those families who have lived most, if not all, of their lives in an urban environment disconnected from their tribal identity and communities. As a consequence, AIs/ANs living in urban environments are at increased risk for mental health problems, which may cause them to turn in desperation to a broad range of self-destructive behaviors, including substance abuse, suicide attempts, and high-risk behaviors (e.g., defying death through dangerous driving or taking major chances without regard for the consequences).

Over the past 3 decades, studies have indicated that there are high rates of alcohol and drug abuse among

AIs/ANs, although there is tremendous variation over time, by tribe, and by reservation (May, 1996). Additional factors such as urbanization, level of acculturation, and multiethnic background can also contribute to the variation in alcohol and drug use among AIs/ANs. The prevalence of alcoholism among AIs/ANs has been observed to have reached epidemic proportions and has been described as a major health problem in these cultural groups (Hodge, 1997). Of the leading causes of death for AIs/ANs, 4 out of 10 are alcohol related. Mortality from illicit drugs is 18% higher for these groups than for other ethnic groups (Substance Abuse and Mental Health Services Administration [SAMHSA], 1993). Chronic liver disease and cirrhosis are the fourth leading cause of death among AIs/ANs living in urban areas (Urban Indian Health Institute, 2004). The mortality rate from chronic liver disease and cirrhosis from 1990 to 1999 among AIs/ANs in urban areas was 27.5 per 100,000 and nationwide was 25.5 per 100,000 compared with the general population at 12.2 per 100,000 and 10.4 per 100,000, respectively. The Urban Indian Health Institute (2004) found that mortality rates ranged by area from 2.9 per 100,000 in the New York City area to 82.3 per 100,000 in the Tucson, Arizona area. In addition, at least 80% of homicides, suicides, and motor vehicle accidents in the AI/AN population are alcohol related (Hodge, 1997). Habitual smoking and regular alcohol consumption place Native people at risk for throat cancer, lung cancer, neoplasm of the pharynx, and accidental fire injuries and fatalities. The following are alcohol-related injuries reported by Hodge:

- Alcohol abuse has been implicated in 50% of adult crime on American Indian reservations.
- In 90% of homicides, the perpetrator, the victim, or both were intoxicated at the time of the act.
- Among Indians, 85% of suicides and suicide attempts are alcohol related (4 times the percentage for the nation).
- Among Indians, 75% of fatal accidents (some of which may actually be suicides) are alcohol related.

Comparing the 1985 U.S. Indian age-adjusted mortality rates with those reported for all races in the U.S. population, the Indian Health Service reported the following for American Indians (Hodge 1997):

- Alcoholism was 321% greater.
- Tuberculosis was 220% greater.
- Diabetes mellitus was 139% greater.
- Accidents were 124% greater.
- Homicide was 72% greater.
- Pneumonia and influenza were 34% greater.

According to Hodge (1997), chronic diseases are serious problems among AIs/ANs, and alcohol mortality is 10 times the rate for all races combined (Gill, Eagle Elk, & Deitrich, 1997). The high rate of mortality may relate to patterns of consumption in certain AI/AN communities. In some of these communities, there is a tendency for sporadic high-dose binge drinking. In addition, drinking by AIs/ANs appears to be typified by blackouts as well as a high degree of violence and physical fights when intoxicated (Manson, Shore, Baron, Ackerson, & Neligh, 1992).

The combination of stress, depression, substance abuse, and psychological frustration also contributes to increases in violent and abusive behaviors throughout the AI/AN community. Among the manifestations are child physical and sexual abuse, child neglect, domestic violence, assault, homicide, and suicide. It is not surprising that accidents and violence, often a consequence of alcohol and substance abuse, accounted for 19% of AI/AN deaths in 1988, almost 3 times the national figure (Gill et al., 1997). The national rate of suicide, homicide, and accidental deaths among AI/AN male youths is approximately 3 times that of the national average. In short, available data strongly suggest that AIs/ANs have the highest suicide rates (4 times that of all races nationwide).

In addition, AI/AN women have a much higher alcoholism rate than women in the general U.S. population (LaFromboise et al., 1994). Manson et al. (1992) found that the alcoholism rates for AI/AN women are the same as those for AI/AN men, which contrasts with previous reports that alcoholism rates for Native women are lower than rates for Native men. The alcohol and substance abuse death rate of young AI/AN women 15 to 24 years old exceeds that of AI/AN men by 40% (U.S. Department of Health and Humans Services, Indian Health Service, 1991). The rates of alcoholism, particularly among women, vary from tribe to tribe, and in some tribes only a small proportion of women have serious alcohol abuse problems (U.S. Department of Health and Human Services, Indian Health Service, 1991).

Studies indicate a high rate of fetal alcohol syndrome (FAS) and fetal alcohol effect among the children of AI/AN women (May, Hymbaugh, Aase, & Samet, 1983). FAS is 33 times higher among AIs/ANs than among non-Indians. The incidence of FAS among Southwest Indian tribes is highly variable but increasing. May et al. (1983) reported a range of 10.3 per 1,000 births (1 per 97) for the Plains tribes to 1.3 per 1,000 births (1 per 749) for Navajos. They also reported a Pueblo rate of 1 per 495, which, although lower than the Plains rate, is higher than those for the other Southwestern populations they studied.

Historical Background

The AI/AN populations have historically suffered tremendous cultural, spiritual, emotional, and economic losses. These losses, spanning many generations, have had a significant cumulative impact on the psychological well-being of individuals growing up in these cultural communities. In many cases, the impact has been devastating. Among the phenomena currently observed are major depression, behavioral problems, and thought disorders, all of which can be linked directly or indirectly to sociocultural deprivation and discrimination.

There is good reason to postulate that both specific and cumulative trauma among American Indian people are significant contributory factors to high rates of alcoholism, drug abuse, and depression and also to the relationships among these disorders (Robin, Chester, & Goldman, 1996). According to Robin et al. (1996), sociocultural and traumatic environmental factors specific to AI/AN communities that may be precursors to and associated with psychiatric disorders have rarely been studied. Many AIs/ANs have been separated from their families and communities for extended lengths of time because of government policies and missionary placement programs. Many lived their formative years away from their homes and communities of birth, having been adopted away and placed into foster care. The mental health consequences for American Indian children placed out of their homes and especially for those placed in non-Indian homes are not known (Nelson, Cross, Landsman, & Tyler, 1996). Nonvoluntary placement in boarding schools is a phenomenon common to AI/AN groups that many believe has contributed to substance use and abuse problems as has uninvolved, nonnurturing, punitive, and authoritarian parenting found to varying degrees among AIs/ANs (Brave Heart, 1999, 2000). However, only limited data have been collected to demonstrate the effects on involuntary placement (Piasecki et al., 1989).

Recent AI/AN urbanization has brought new, serious threats to the demographic survival of Natives in the United States. Also, AIs/ANs have a history of forced displacement, ethnic demoralization, and hardships both on and off the reservations that have contributed to a sense of alienation and mistrust. Other manifestations of the threats to their demographic survival are evident in the number of biethnic and multiethnic American Indians and the widely varying degrees of acculturation to the dominant culture among those living in urban areas (Herring, 1994). In addition, current socioeconomic, educational, and cultural challenges to the positive development of AIs/ANs can be attributed, in large measure, to the treatment they have experienced at the hands of the federal government. Their history has been characterized by military defeat, ethnic demoralization, and forced displacement. Centuries of injustice have resulted in feelings of suspicion and distrust of European American professionals and institutions.

Living in an urban environment undermines the strength of AI/AN communities and tribal affiliations and complicates family and clan support systems (LaFromboise et al., 1994). In cities, the majority of Indian communities are disadvantaged by poverty, substandard living conditions, frequent relocation, dispersal of the community, and pervasive unemployment. Further, those who place themselves in greater contact with the majority culture by increasing their interactions with outsiders, migrating to cities, working in professional jobs, or attending boarding schools and universities may face considerable acculturation stress, which makes them even more vulnerable to developing substance abuse and psychological problems (LaFromboise et al., 1994). In addition, there are those who increase their interactions through membership in gangs and other negative affiliations.

Many have suggested that the extensive use of alcohol and drugs by AIs/ANs may be a response to the stress of cultural disruption and exploitation that they have suffered for generations (LaFromboise et al., 1994). Studies offering a sociocultural explanation for AI/AN alcoholism indicate that excessive substance abuse also may be a response to the demands for integration into and identification with the dominant culture. This may be coupled with integration and identification with other ethnic groups as well, including African Americans, Asian Americans, and Latinos. The AI/AN urban community is often overshadowed by other groups because of their small numbers and dispersion throughout urban environments. As a result, they not only have to deal with the pressures of assimilating to mainstream culture but also of adapting to other predominantly ethnic communities that misidentify them and do not recognize them as tribal members. This misidentification contributes to the invisibility of urban Indians.

Finally, the stereotype of the "drunken Indian" has been pervasive within the United States through history, governmental policies, and the media. Many contend that negative stereotypes such as the drunken Indian contribute to pathological drinking patterns and adverse consequences after drinking. The demoralizing negative stereotypes that characterize AIs/ANs as not being able to behave normally (i.e., being uncivilized) or stay within boundaries when consuming alcohol contribute to the discrimination and oppression of the community, which then manifest themselves in intergenerational trauma and subsequent disorders.

Despite the many challenges, Native values and traditions continue to thrive. American Indian identities and cultural practices remain resilient while Indian people continue to develop coping strategies and become bicultural. Indian people, as a result, can be both highly acculturated and tribally or ethnically identified (Walters, 1999).

Current Research

Current research into some of the major problems confronting American Indians today is discussed below.

DUAL DIAGNOSIS

The prevalence, patterns, and problems of drinking alcoholic beverages vary enormously even in tribes closely linked geographically. In some American Indian communities where lifetime prevalence of substance abuse and mental health problems is high, more than half of the alcoholics are likely to develop at least one other major disorder, most often depression (Robin et al., 1996). The issue of cause and effect between alcoholism and other disorders is sometimes unclear, particularly in regard to alcoholism as it relates to drug abuse and depression. Research indicates that major depression is found most often in nonalcoholic AI/AN women, which is consistent with results of studies in non-Indian women (Baron, Manson, Ackerson, & Brenneman, 1990).

Depression has been observed at disproportionate rates (50%–90%) among drug-abusing mothers (Boyd, 1993). In addition, women who abuse substances have been characterized in the literature as having a number of issues related to poor well-being including guilt, anger, low self-esteem, and irritability (Boyd, 1993; Robin et al., 1996). Researchers have found that posttraumatic stress disorder (PTSD) has a high rate of comorbidity with substance abuse, ranging from 46% to 11% in some studies (McFall, MacKay, & Donovan, 1991).

Robin et al. (1996) suggested that both specific and cumulative traumas among AIs/ANs are significant contributors to the high rates of substance use, PTSD, and depression. Present generations of AIs/ANs face layers of repetitive and cumulative traumatic losses that are physical, cultural, and spiritual in nature. These layers of repetitive loss, in addition to the major traumas of the past, are often associated with destructive coping styles and may increase the likelihood that AIs/

ANs have co-occurring PTSD and substance use disorders (Simoni, Sehgal, & Walters, 2004).

CHILD ABUSE

Substance abuse is the most frequently associated factor contributing to child maltreatment across cultures (Berlin, 1987; DeBruyn, Lujan, & May, 1992). Miller, Downs, and Testa (1993) reported that children who have been physically or sexually abused are more likely to become addicted to alcohol or other drugs than other children. The U.S. Department of Health and Human Services, National Center on Child Abuse and Neglect (1999) reported that 79.8% of American Indian girls had experienced sexual abuse compared with 22.8% of American Indian boys.

ALCOHOL AND DRUG PATTERNS

Limited data are available on the alcohol and drug use patterns among urban AIs/ANs. Researchers can postulate from the data available nationally and from reservation-based samples that alcohol and drug use are high among urban AIs/ANs. Gill et al. (1997) looked at patterns of alcohol and drug use in a sample of 105 AIs/ANs living in Denver, Colorado. The percentage of abstinent or irregular drinkers (50.5%) found in this study is close to that found in previous studies on urban AIs/ANs. In 60.6% of the sample, either one or both parents were considered to be alcoholic, with only 11.1% having no primary or secondary alcoholic family members. Blackouts, binges, and physical fights were very common symptoms of alcohol dependence in this population, and these data were similar to data gathered by Manson et al. (1992). Of particular note is the very high prevalence of symptoms of physical dependence (82.4%) as well as the inability to stop drinking (80.0%) despite attempts to quit or set rules (68.6%).

In 2002, SAMHSA reported that for persons over 26 years old, the rate of heavy alcohol use is highest among AIs/ANs (7.4%) and increasing, whereas for all other groups, severe alcohol use rates are either stable or decreasing. In addition, SAMHSA reported that tobacco use disparities level off in college years (ages 18–25) when 50% of both Whites and AIs/ANs report use within the past month. However, after age 26, the rate of tobacco use among AIs/ANs (38%) is substantially higher than that for Whites (26%) and persons of mixed race and ethnicity (30%). From 1999 to 2000, the rate of illicit drug use among AIs/ANs jumped 21% (from 10.4%–12.6%), whereas for all other major ethnic groups, the rate declined. The increase among AIs/ANs was mostly due to excessive use of marijuana. (See U.S. Department of Health and Human Services, SAMHSA, Center for Substance Abuse Prevention, 2002.)

In a National Institute for Drug Abuse study, Baldwin, Maxwell, Fenaughty, Trotter, and Stevens (2000) reported very high rates of alcohol consumption in the past month among 147 AI/AN drug users (100%), with 42% reporting drinking every day and 50% reporting drinking until drunk half of the time or more. Additionally, focus group participants reported episodes of blacking out while drinking and also engaging in unprotected sex during blackout periods. Intravenous drug users reported the highest frequency of alcohol use in the past 30 days, and crack use was also associated with alcohol use. Respondents who reported alcohol use before or during sex were more likely to engage in unprotected sexual intercourse (Baldwin et al., 2000).

Successful Substance Abuse Services and Treatment for Urban American Indian and Alaska Native People

The most successful substance abuse treatment programs with the AI/AN population have been those that have incorporated traditional healing practices and included American Indian values and identity (LaFromboise, Trimble, & Mohatt, 1990; Spicer, 2001). Beauchamp (1997) posited that many American Indian substance abuse counselors believe that the incorporation of cultural and spiritual values into treatment programs is the only lasting solution to the substance abuse problems for AIs/ANs. In fact, AI/AN providers have long been incorporating traditional healing practices along with Western-based approaches in the treatment of substance abuse and have been able to secure funding to support these efforts.

In 1992, the Robert Wood Johnson Foundation announced the Healthy Nations Initiative: Reducing Substance Abuse Among Native Americans (Noe, Fleming, & Manson, 2003). The program was designed to provide grants to support the development of community-wide efforts to combat substance abuse. The incorporation of traditional cultural values was encouraged as a key component. Although some programs were more successful than others, there were several commonalities that characterized successful programs, including consistent and effective leadership, incorporation of a culture-focused approach, community ownership, thinking outside of the box, comprehensive efforts, and effective collaboration.

Buchwald, Beal, and Manson (2000) reported that 70% of urban AI/AN patients in primary care used traditional health practices. Although in some urban environments, AI/AN patients are able to use traditional health practices, the incorporation of traditional healing practices becomes increasingly difficult with the diversity of tribal affiliations in urban environments. This cultural diversity necessitates the provisioning of a variety of traditional cultural options for substance abuse treatment clients (Y. Edwards, 2003). Urban Indian treatment providers have addressed this challenge by bringing in Native traditional practitioners from different cultural backgrounds and traditions to work with both clients and staff.

A variety of cultural healing activities are used in urban settings, including prayer, singing, drumming, purification ceremonies (i.e., sweat lodge), smudging, herbs, and use of tobacco in ceremonies. In addition, talking circles are used for clients and staff. Traditional practices such as the talking circle, storytelling, and sweat lodges have been studied (Murillo, 2004). Talking circles have produced improvements in knowledge about cancer, and storytelling and talking circles have been used as tools for improving health. Finally, the sweat lodge ceremony has been examined in the jail-based treatment of alcohol abuse.

Barriers to Access to Substance Abuse Services and Treatment for Urban American Indian and Alaska Native People

A minority population colonized by Europeans and forced to assimilate into the majority culture, AIs/ANs today are subjected to health policies and practices based on Western cultural values and models (Champagne, 1994). Historically, AI/AN people have good reason to mistrust government agencies and organizations run by the mainstream (see the Introduction and chaps. 1 and 3, this volume). This includes a history of far-from-adequate health care for this population because of poverty, isolation, misunderstanding of jurisdictional responsibilities, and a variety of other governmental policies (such as repealing acts that would strengthen sovereignty among tribes; see Introduction, this volume). The situation is further aggravated by the fact that access to health care is greatly influenced by the race, language, and socioeconomic circumstances of an individual.

Although substance abuse services do exist, they are often underfunded. The lack of services and inadequate numbers of culturally competent providers are issues that must be confronted. There are a number of barriers to Indian people accessing substance abuse services in urban areas. Specifically, AI/AN people struggle with economic, geographical, institutional, and cultural barriers when seeking these services. Although abundant substance abuse treatment services are available in urban environments, AI/AN people do not use them (Nebelkopf & King, 2003). There are issues of accessibility, acceptability, affordability, and accommodation that determine the usage of available services in urban settings (Evaneshko, 1999). In a mental health needs assessment of Tucson's urban American Indian population, lack of knowledge of availability, lack of understanding of the processes or resource agencies, discouragement as a result of bureaucratic systems, and perceptions of agency unresponsiveness were frequently mentioned issues (Evaneshko, 1999). This mental health needs assessment also found that services were not used because of excessive waiting time, inconvenient hours, distant locations, lack of transportation, unaffordable services, and negative experiences. As a result, many wait until their substance abuse problems are in more advanced stages, thereby thwarting any opportunity for preventative services.

In addition, AI/AN clients might also be reluctant to access services in non-Indian settings and facilities as a result of traditional values and styles of living and healing processes. In some cases, AIs/ANs may underuse available services because of their perception that existing services are unresponsive to their needs. Many times, non-Indian professionals propose interventions with AI/AN clients that are incongruent with their clients' worldviews and culture.

Services for urban AI/AN people are also usually spread over a wide geographical area, making it difficult for individuals to negotiate access to services. For example, in some urban communities, the population tends to be dispersed over an entire county. Moreover, many AI/AN clients must rely on public transportation and complain that lack of adequate transportation is a major barrier to their seeking services at facilities serving AIs/ANs. They may have large families that cannot travel easily on public transportation or may be less mobile because of age or disabilities that may make it difficult to access public transportation. In addition, many AI/AN families are unable to afford the cost of transportation, which inhibits their ability to seek culturally sensitive services. In very large cities, the size of the transportation system may make it difficult to get around (i.e., the need to take multiple buses, subways, or trains), or the distances may mean it takes hours to get to one appointment. Sometimes the geographical barriers are so prohibitive that individuals may not seek treatment at all.

Finally, there are a number of barriers to treatment for AI/AN women with children. They are often reluctant to go into inpatient treatment programs because of child-care responsibilities (LaFromboise et al., 1994).

Limitations to Research

The urban Indian population is geographically dispersed and relatively small compared with the general population, which contributes to the lack of information available about their general health status (Urban Indian Health Institute, 2004). There are few sources of reliable statistics on the rates or causes of morbidity and mortality or the patterns of substance abuse treatment service use among urban AIs/ANs (Gill et al., 1997). Because accurate prevalence data are not available, the degree of alcohol and drug problems within any AI/AN community is typically based on indirect estimates of mortality from various causes that are known to be alcohol or drug related.

There are overwhelming social and environmental issues such as child abuse, marital breakdown, alcoholism, and drug abuse as well as a high degree of delinquency, school dropouts, and unplanned pregnancies (Gill et al., 1997). However, epidemiological data relating to these issues are lacking. The information required to make comparisons between the health and well-being of American Indians living inside cities versus those living on reservations is not available. Large-scale epidemiological studies have not been conducted in this population, partially because of the difficulty of random sampling in a transient minority population that is spread out over the urban environment. Data on AIs/ANs are often collapsed into an "other" category; as a consequence, American Indians are often misclassified as members of other ethnic groups. In other cases, they are simply excluded altogether. Researchers typically justify this decision on the basis of the relatively small size of the population relative to other ethnic groups. The majority of research studies addressing American Indians are in tribal communities and leave out the large urban population.

Conclusion

In working with AIs/ANs, the helping professional must take into account the family style, which may range from traditional to assimilated (Herring, 1994). This may include not only integration or adaptation to mainstream culture but to other ethnic communities. E. D. Edwards and Egbert-Edwards (1990) advocated for a comprehensive system-of-care community approach to the substance use problems of AIs/ANs. The approach recommends a coordinated prevention, education, and treatment model for AI/AN youth, their families, and their communities, which includes a variety of systems to address the multiple issues facing the community. Substance abuse treatment programs that integrate a system-of-care approach are most effective when leaders, including tribal council members, elders, and spiritual leaders, are involved and supportive. Support must be generated from all aspects of the community. Citizens of all ages must be engaged in the problem-solving process to create community ownership and investment in improving the quality of life in their communities. This may include forming a community coalition to ensure community involvement and acceptance.

Providers must also develop a strong collaboration philosophy. This includes collaborating with both Indian and non-Indian service providers. Programs should also consolidate prevention, intervention, and aftercare efforts to create seamless continuum-of-care services for clients and the community.

Service providers who are effective with AIs/ANs must be aware of the attitudes and customs particular to a client's ethnic and cultural heritage and be knowledgeable about alternatives in a client's background, both self-disclosed and from sources other than the client. The service provider's goal is to uncover, respect, and learn to understand differences in culture, community, and past and present experience.

Understanding and awareness of past and present experience include identifying different types of traumatic stressors that may contribute to increased substance use, including sexual trauma, domestic violence, child abuse, and historical trauma. Addressing co-occurring issues in addition to the potential role of multigenerational and current traumas in substance abuse treatment is important to healing the generations. Simoni et al. (2004) suggested it is important to directly deal with justifiable mistrust, historical trauma, and individual and familial responses to historical and present traumas.

The most successful intervention and treatment programs build on local values and traditions (U.S. Department of Justice, Office of Justice

Programs, 2000). This includes using the cultural knowledge, methods, and resources in one's urban community to make the program culturally appropriate and relevant. It is important to use culture as a resource to strengthen protective factors and to build on the tribe's cultural strengths. Emphasizing individual, familial, and tribal survival strategies can assist AIs/ANs in recovery and healing (Simoni et al., 2004). Most tribes have abundant examples of healthy lifestyles that advocate spiritual, mental, and physical well-being. In addition, AI/AN communities have the insight, wisdom, and strength to successfully address substance abuse given the resources available to them (Noe et al., 2003). The use of cultural values, philosophies, and practices can enhance the credibility of programs and the success of client treatment (Sanchez-Way & Johnson, 2000). For treatment to be culturally relevant, it must be based on holistic philosophy or principles that combine the biological, psychological, social, and spiritual aspects of a person's life. It must also acknowledge that multiple factors contribute to substance abuse and addictions. Over time, AIs/ANs have preserved and revitalized a number of traditional healing practices and applied these to the treatment of alcohol-related problems. Traditional values of AIs/ANs promote physical and emotional well-being among all Indian people (E. D. Edwards & Egbert-Edwards, 1990).

In seeking to understand the many emotional and psychological factors that affect AIs/ANs and contribute to substance abuse issues, one must use culturally sensitive research methods. Cultural sensitivity should extend to data collection techniques, choice of instrumentation, and interpretation of results. The assessment of substance use in AIs/ANs may differ significantly from that of other cultural and ethnic groups. The majority of research related to acculturation and mental health and substance abuse issues in minority populations is based on studies of immigrant populations. Therefore, generalizing these results to AIs/ANs may be problematic.

A community assessment of substance use and abuse along with other related factors is essential. Because some tribes are at a higher risk than others, more culturally specific treatment approaches need to be developed for these tribes, and this need becomes more challenging when dealing with multiple tribes in an urban environment. Data should be collected to show the scope and prevalence of alcohol and substance abuse problems as well as the root causes and the contributing risk factors. Improvements in data collection and reducing the incidence of racial misclassification are critical to understanding the health needs of urban AIs/ANs. Without accurate data, the health disparities impacting urban Indians are undetected and not analyzed (Urban Indian Health Institute, 2004). Finally, a community-wide program review and resource analysis should be conducted to understand how services are currently used, how they can be enhanced, and what programmatic resources are needed.

References

Baldwin, J. A., Maxwell, C. J. C., Fenaughty, A. M., Trotter, R. T., & Stevens, S. J. (2000). Alcohol as a risk factor for HIV transmission among American Indian and Alaska Native drug users. *American Indian and Alaska Native Mental Health Research, 9*(1), 1–15.

Baron, A., Manson, S. M., Ackerson, M., & Brenneman, D. (1990). Depressive symptomatology in older American Indians with chronic disease: Some psychometric considerations. In C. Attkisson & J. Zich (Eds.), *Depression in primary care: Screening and detection* (pp. 217–231). New York: Routledge.

Beauchamp, S. (1997). Healing alcoholism in indigenous people. *Social Work Perspectives, 8,* 35–40.

Berlin, I. (1987). Effects of changing Native American cultures on child development. *Journal of Community Psychology, 15,* 299–306.

Boyd, C. J. (1993). The antecedents of women's crack cocaine abuse: Family substance abuse, sexual abuse, depression and illicit drug use. *Journal of Substance Abuse and Treatment, 10,* 433–438.

Brave Heart, M. Y. H. (1999). Oyate Ptayela: Rebuilding the Lakota Nation through addressing historical trauma among Lakota parents. *Journal of Human Behavior and the Social Environment, 2,* 109–126.

Brave Heart, M. Y. H. (2000). Wakiksuyapi: Carrying the historical trauma of the Lakota. *Tulane Studies in Social Welfare, 21/22,* 245–266.

Buchwald, D. S., Beal, J., & Manson, S. M. (2000). Use of traditional healing among Native Americans in a primary care setting. *Medical Care, 38,* 1191–1199.

Champagne, D. (1994). *Native America: Portrait of the peoples.* Detroit, MI: Visible Ink Press.

DeBruyn, L., Lujan, C., & May, P. (1992). A comparative study of abused and neglected American Indian children in the Southwest. *Social Sciences and Medicine, 35,* 305–315.

Edwards, E. D., & Egbert-Edwards, M. (1990). American Indian adolescents: Combating problems of substance use and abuse through a community model. In A. R. Stiffman & L. E. Davis (Eds.), *Ethnic issues in adolescent mental health* (pp. 285–302). Newbury Park, CA: Sage.

Edwards, Y. (2003). Cultural connection and transformation: Substance abuse treatment at Friendship House. *Journal of Psychoactive Drugs, 35,* 53–58.

Evaneshko, V. (1999). Mental health needs assessment of Tucson's urban Native American population. *American Indian and Alaska Native Mental Health Research, 8*, 41–61.

Gill, K., Eagle Elk, M., & Deitrich, R. A. (1997). A description of alcohol/ drug use and family history of alcoholism among urban America Indians. *American Indian Alaska Native Mental Health Research, 8*, 41–52.

Herring, R. (1994). Native American Indian identity: A people of many peoples. In E. P. Salett & D. R. Koslow (Eds.), *Race, ethnicity, and self: Identity in multicultural perspective* (pp. 170–197). Washington, DC: National Multicultural Institute.

Hodge, F. S. (1997). *The health status of American Indians in California.* Woodland Hills: California Endowment & California HealthCare Foundation.

LaFromboise, T. D., Berman, J. S., & Sohi, B. K. (1994). American Indian women. In L. Comas-Diaz & B. Greene (Eds.), *Women of color: Integrating ethnic and gender identities in psychotherapy* (pp. 30–71). New York: Guilford Press.

LaFromboise, T. D., Trimble, J., & Mohatt, G. (1990). Counseling intervention and American Indian tradition: An integrative approach. *Counseling Psychologist, 18,* 628–654.

Manson, S. M., Shore, J. H., Baron, A. E., Ackerson, L., & Neligh, G. (1992). Alcohol abuse and dependence among American Indians. In J. E. Helzer & G. J. Cannino (Eds.), *Alcoholism in North America, Europe, and Asia* (pp. 113–130). New York: Oxford University Press.

May, P. A. (1996). Overview of alcohol abuse epidemiology for American Indian populations. In G. D. Sandefeur, R. R. Rundfuss, & B. Cohen (Eds.), *Changing numbers, changing needs: American Indian demography and public health* (pp. 235–261). Washington, DC: National Academy Press.

May, P. A., Hymbaugh, K. J., Aase, J. M., & Samet, J. M. (1983). Epidemiology of fetal alcohol syndrome among American Indians of the Southwest. *Social Biology, 30*, 374–387.

McFall, M., MacKay, P., & Donovan, D. (1991). Combat-related PTSD and psychosocial adjustment problems among substance abusing veterans. *Journal of Nervous and Mental Disease, 179*, 33–38.

Miller, B., Downs, W., & Testa, M. (1993). Interrelationships between victimization experiences and women's alcohol use. *Journal of Studies on Alcohol, 11,* 109–117.

Murillo, L. (2004). Perspectives on traditional health practices. In E. Nebelkopf & M. Phillips (Eds.), *Healing and mental health for Native Americans: Speaking in red* (pp. 109–115). Walnut Creek, CA: Altamira Press.

Nebelkopf, E., & King, J. (2003). A holistic system of care for Native Americans in an urban environment. *Journal of Psychoactive Drugs, 35,* 43–52.

Nelson, K., Cross, T., Landsman, M., & Tyler, M. (1996). Native American families and child neglect. *Children and Youth Services Review, 18,* 505–522.

Noe, T., Fleming, C., & Manson, S. (2003). Healthy nations: Reducing substance abuse in American Indian and Alaska Native communities. *Journal of Psychoactive Drugs, 35,* 15–25.

Piasecki, J., Manson, S., Biernoff, M., Hiat, A., Taylor, S., & Bechtold, D. (1989). Abuse and neglect of American Indian children: Findings from a survey of federal providers. *American Indian and Alaska Native Mental Health Research, 3*(2), 43–62.

Robin, R. W., Chester, B., & Goldman, D. (1996). Cumulative trauma and PTSD in American Indian communities. In A. J. Marsella, M. J. Friedman, E. T. Gerrity, & R. M. Scurfield (Eds.), *Ethnocultural aspects of posttraumatic stress disorder: Issues, research, and clinical applications* (pp. 239–254). Washington, DC: American Psychological Association.

Sanchez-Way, R., & Johnson, S. (2000). Cultural practices in American Indian prevention programs. *Juvenile Justice, 7*(2), 20–30.

Simoni, J. M., Sehgal, S., & Walters, K. L. (2004). Triangle of risk: Urban American Indian women's sexual trauma, injection drug use, and HIV sexual risk behaviors. *AIDs and Behavior, 8,* 33–45.

Spicer, P. (2001). Culture and the restoration of self among former American Indian drinkers. *Social Science and Medicine, 53,* 227–236.

Substance Abuse and Mental Health Services Administration. (1993). *National Household Survey on Drug Abuse, 1991–1993.* Rockville, MD: National Clearinghouse for Alcohol and Drug Information.

U.S. Department of Health and Human Services, Indian Health Service. (1991). *Indian women's health care: Consensus statement.* Rockville, MD: Author.

U.S. Department of Health and Human Services, National Center on Child Abuse and Neglect. (1999). *Annual report: National incidence and prevalence of child abuse and neglect, 1998.* Washington, DC: Author.

U.S. Department of Health and Human Services, Substance Abuse and Mental Health Services Administration, Center for Substance Abuse Prevention. (2002, November 22). American Indians/Alaska Natives and substance abuse. *Prevention Alert, 5*(16).

U.S. Department of Justice, Office of Justice Programs. (2000). *Promising practices and strategies to reduce alcohol and substance abuse among American Indians and Alaska Natives.* Washington, DC: Author.

Urban Indian Health Institute. (2004). *The health status of urban American Indians and Alaska Natives: An analysis of select vital records and census data sources.* Seattle, WA: Seattle Indian Health Board.

Walters, K. L. (1999). Urban American Indian identity, attitudes, and acculturation styles. *Journal of Human Behavior in the Social Environment, 2,* 163–167.

Walters, K. L., & Simoni, J. M. (1999). Trauma, substance use, and HIV risk among urban American Indian women. *Cultural Diversity and Ethnic Minority Psychology, 5,* 236–248.

Tawa M. Witko, Rae Marie Martinez, and Richard Milda

Understanding Domestic Violence Within the Urban Indian Community

5

A Nation is not defeated until the hearts of its women are on the ground. Then it is done, no matter how brave its warriors or how strong its weapons.

—Cheyenne Proverb

D omestic violence is a problem that faces many communities across the nation. The impact this violence has on the American Indian population has proven devastating. It is believed that the root to this violent behavior can be found in the history of the Indian people and the impact that history has had on the generations that followed. In this chapter, we explore some of the historical causes of domestic violence as well as offer solutions to end the cycle. We also discuss the power-and-control issues related to violence that may be unique to Indian people and the effects of domestic violence on children.

Violence Statistics

According to the U.S. Department of Justice (USDOJ), in their report *American Indians and Crime* (USDOJ, 1999), American Indians have a violent crime victimization rate that is 2.5 times higher than the national rate (124 violent crimes per 1,000 vs. 50 per 1,000, respectively). Further, the violent crime rate was highest for American Indians living in urban rather than rural areas (207 per 1,000 vs. 89 per 1,000, respectively). Although American Indians experienced higher rates of violent victimization than persons of other races at every income level, American Indians with an annual income of less than $10,000 reported the highest rate of violent victimization (182 per 1,000). Of particular note is that more than half the violent victimizations of American Indians involved offenders with whom the victim had a prior relationship, and about one in six violent acts against American Indians involved an offender who was an intimate or family member. Violent crime against Whites and Blacks is primarily interracial; although the majority of American Indian victims reported their offenders as White (60%) and Black (10%), almost a third (30%) were victimized by other American Indians (USDOJ, 1999). Such statistics illustrate that American Indians who are living in urban areas and who are struggling with severe poverty are among the individuals at highest risk for violent criminal victimization.

Similarly to other groups, intimate and family violence accounts for approximately 9% of victimization for American Indians. However, when one examines the racial composition of offenders in intimate and family violence incidences, an interesting trend emerges. Among victims of violence across all races, 11% of intimate victims and 5% of family victims report the offender to have been of a different race; among American Indians, these rates are 75% and 25%, respectively. Alcohol and drug use are also significantly correlated with intimate and family violence among all racial groups. Nearly 75% of American Indian victims of family violence reported that their offender had been drinking at the time of the offense (USDOJ, 1999). Violence and alcohol and substance abuse often go hand in hand. The data suggest that the concurrence of domestic violence and alcohol abuse varies widely, from 25% to 80% (Sacred Circle 1, 2002). Often violence is considered a symptom of addiction; however, the two are separate entities that must be treated separately in order for true change to take place (Heer, 2002).

Violence appears to be a learned response that involves the changing of the belief system that encourages and accepts violence as a norm. In addition, it has been documented that children who come from violent homes are at greater risk for physical abuse and neglect as well as serious mental health problems (Geffner, Jaffee, & Sudermann, 2000).

Historical Background

Many historical factors have influenced the increased level of violence in Indian communities. For the centuries before Columbus arrived, the

Indian way of life was that of natural order, and women were respected and honored. The introduction of alcohol and Christianity into the Indian community brought with it a clear message that female subservience was literally the will of God (Gunn-Allen, 2000). With the Christian belief system of the time that stated women were to be subservient to men, many Indian and non-Indian men treated women as property, which also led men to believe that abuse of women and children was not only acceptable but required (Mousseau, 2000). Although changes have been made in the general population in relation to how women are treated and the opportunities that are afforded them, this has not been true in Native communities. Within Native communities, there has been systematic and growing abuse against Native women both on reservations and in urban environments set against the backdrop of racism, terrorism, and genocide. It is this history that has altered Native lifestyle today.

IMPACT OF COLONIZATION

When Columbus came to the Americas, he brought with him more than diseases; he brought a new way of looking at the world and a new way of viewing women. Prior to Columbus, women were valued, respected, and honored. Women were not abused, talked down to, or violated. Women had equal status with men. Often, if women did not agree with a particular course of action by men, the women would intervene, and their word on the situation was final. No more discussions would take place on the subject. With colonization came the breakup of tribal ways, exposure to sexual assault and violence, and the beginning of internalized oppression (Sacred Circle 2, 2002). Women were no longer safe, not only because they were Native but also because they were women (Sacred Circle 3, 2002).

IMPACT OF BOARDING SCHOOLS

With the introduction of boarding schools, Indian children were separated from their families and taken to schools where they were taught that being Indian was bad and where they were punished severely for speaking their language or practicing their traditions. With this came a loss of cultural history, because children were not able to learn their stories and practices. As part of this loss of Indian parenting, children were taught that physical punishment was the way to correct behavior, and abuse in all of its forms became the norm (Morrissette, 1994). One of the impacts that boarding schools had on future generations of Indian people was to teach violence as a norm.

IMPACT OF RELOCATION

Relocation to urban areas was also a factor adding to the problems of violence within American Indian communities. American Indians were moved to urban areas away from family and community. They were often not prepared for these changes and faced many difficulties. As a result, when difficulties arose, they were not able to fall back on traditional ways of solving conflict, ways that involved cooperation and respect. Instead, violence often prevailed as Indian men struggled with their new role in a community that did not accept them. The separation from tribal lands and communities as well as the isolation and loss of identity all led to more internalized oppression that encouraged violence in the community (Mousseau, 2000).

Men Who Batter

Native programs that work with men who batter are in uncertain territory. Most offender programs base their work on one of four theories (Paymar, 2000): psychological (something wrong with the individual, such as self-esteem or depression), relationship conflict (something wrong with the relationship, both parties contribute), anger causes violence (cycle of violence), and male beliefs about women (power and control, male superiority). However, Native programs seek to incorporate how their culture changed to treat women in ways that do not follow their traditions. Although many Native programs have used all four methods at some point, the most commonly used is the power-and-control model, which is discussed below.

Power-and-Control Model

The cultural genocide of Indian people led to the formation of unnatural life-destroying power, which has led to an increase in violence within the Indian community. Indian people's way of life was changed from one that recognized the equality of women to one that allowed violence against women. This change led to *internalized oppression*: It was no longer necessary for outside forces to destroy Indian people, because Indian people were destroying themselves. The community began to internalize the hate and loathing that the Europeans felt for them, and community members began to hate their own Indianness. This self-loathing is often difficult to identify because it comes from the thoughts and actions of those within the group (Sacred Circle 4, 2002). Programs such as those of Cangleska, Inc. (see discussion below), have conceptualized the power-and-control model as a pyramid to represent the belief system of hierarchy and competition, one that is unnatural for Indian people but now pervades the community and is prevalent in mainstream society. The power-and-control pyramid takes the power-and-control wheel and updates it to serve Indian people.

On the outside of the pyramid, one side is physical violence. This type of violence involves punching, kicking, choking, pushing, slapping, and pulling hair. To the other side is sexual violence. This type of violence includes physically attacking the sexual parts of a woman's body, marital rape, and treating a woman as if she is a sex object. These two areas of assault make up less than 25% of actual domestic violence cases (Sacred Circle 5, 2002). Often these two types of violence are the final stages, the stages in which the abuse is finally reported. It is what is on the inside of the pyramid that allows for the physical and sexual violence to occur and is often what remains with a woman even after she has left the relationship.

The power-and-control model found within Indian communities includes some of the main tactics seen in this type of model, for example, male privilege; isolation; intimidation; emotional abuse; minimizing, lying, blaming; using the children; economic abuse; and coercion and threats. What makes this model different from other power-and-control models is the inclusion of cultural abuse and ritual abuse. We briefly address the first eight tactics and then explain in detail the last two often-used tactics.

As with most models related to power and control, the impact of male privilege must be considered. Prior to Columbus's landing in America, women were active participants in the tribe. In many tribes, they selected the chiefs, decided if war was prudent, and served as healers. After colonization and the physical and cultural genocide of Indian nations, this concept changed. Indian men began seeing Indian women the way Europeans saw their women, as property. Indian men began to endorse the concepts that women were to be servants and were incapable of making decisions on their own. Women's roles changed, and one consequence of this was the perceived right of men to batter.

Once an Indian man viewed his woman as merely property, he could do as he wished with her. One tool he used was isolation. With isolation he was able to control what she did, who she talked to, and what she read. He limited her outside involvement with friends and family and often used jealousy to justify his actions. For Indian women living in the city, this became more complicated as they struggled to make friends and to lead their lives, often without any family support. It was not unheard of for a man to tell his Indian partner that she could not go back home to the reservation to visit relatives, further isolating her from anything outside the home. For example, one urban Indian woman was not allowed to visit her family on the reservation for 2 years because her partner stated that if she went back, he knew she would cheat on him. In addition, he told her that he no longer wanted her to go to school because he did not like the people there. As a result, she had no contact with her family and had a difficult time making friends in the city.[1]

Intimidation is often used in conjunction with male privilege and isolation as a way to control a woman's actions. This intimidation involves making a woman afraid of her husband with simply a look, action, or gesture. She knows by this look that she has violated one of his "rules." He might destroy her property, break things, and display weapons around her—anything to make her realize that if she does not do what he says he will hurt her. For an urban woman, this can also include threatening her family if they come to see her or call her. For example, one urban Indian woman stated that her partner would not accept calls from her family on the reservation and would give her a mean look every time the phone rang to ensure that she would not answer the phone.

Emotional abuse can include demeaning a woman and making her feel worthless. A man may call his wife names, such as "squaw," or humiliate her in front of others. He may make her feel guilty about the abuse, implying that it is her fault; he may even make her feel as if she is crazy. The batterer uses these power-and-control tactics to break the woman down and lower her self-esteem.

The practice of minimizing, lying, and blaming is consistent with the tactics described above. The batterer makes light of the abuse or shifts the responsibility to the woman. He is not willing to take responsibility for his actions. Indian men may imply that their behavior is the result of colonization or boarding schools. They may state that it is not their fault because it is really alcohol that made them violent. Although many of these behaviors can be attributed to the impact of colonization and boarding schools, and understanding the origins of violence is the first step in changing patterns of abuse, it is important not to use this as an excuse to be violent.

---

[1] The individual women described here worked with the chapter authors within the Los Angeles and San Bernardino Counties of Southern California. Their identities are not listed to ensure their confidentiality and protection.

Using the children is also an important tactic for men who are battering their partners. The man may threaten to take the children away. He may use visitation to harass his wife. He may also tell her that he is going to take the children to the reservation and that he will make sure she loses custody. She may feel that if she leaves him, the courts will take the children away because she has no job or place to live. One Indian woman living in a major metropolitan city was told by her partner that if she left, he would take the children and he would get custody because she was poor. This woman stayed with the batterer until she received help in filing for custody of her children. In some states, there is also the added threat that exposing a child to domestic violence is considered willful cruelty or unjustifiable punishment and therefore must be reported as abuse (Jablon, 2002), which may prevent many Indian women from leaving their partners even though they are abusive.

Economic abuse is also a commonly used tactic. An Indian man may tell his wife that she cannot get a job or go to school. He may not allow her access to any of the family income or may even take the money that she does earn. More than half of women who are able to work are at risk of losing their jobs as a result of violence, and nearly 75% have been harassed on the job by their partner (Davies, Lyon, & Monti-Cantania, 1998). The batterer makes it difficult economically for a woman to leave him. Many women feel that if they leave, they will not be able to care for their children or survive without the economic support of their partner.

Coercion and threats are a part of most of the above-mentioned tactics, and a batterer may actually carry out his threats against his wife or her family. A man may state that if his wife leaves him, he will hurt himself or report her to welfare or social services. He may also have her commit illegal acts on his behalf and later use this information against her if she leaves him. For example, one Indian woman stated that her partner forced her to steal for him and then told her that if she left him, he would report her to the police and she would go to jail. Often, if a woman does press charges against her batterer, he uses coercion and threats to makes her drop the charges. This behavior typically continues even after she leaves.

The two tactics that make this power-and-control model different from other models are cultural abuse and ritual abuse. Understanding of these two areas was developed by Sacred Circle, a program of Cangleska, Inc., that is aimed at ending violence against Native women.

Cultural abuse involves conflict around the aspects of being Indian in a relationship. For two Indian people, this may mean that they compete over Indianness. A man may use the culture to prove male superiority or female submission. He may even engage in blood quantum debates, indicating that he is more Indian than his partner and dismissing her needs. If they are from two different tribes, he may stress that his tribe's way of doing things is better than hers. He may even use her tribal affiliation against her by stating that her tribe sold out, whereas his did not. He may also force her to live on his reservation and not allow her to visit her own. If the couple is of mixed race, a non-Indian man may imply that being Indian is bad. If an Indian woman's partner is of another ethnic minority heritage, he may state that her heritage is inferior to his. He may force her to adopt his lifestyle and ignore her traditions. If a woman's partner is of European descent, he may indicate that she needs to assimilate, that the Indian way is wrong, or that it is sacrilegious for her to practice her traditions or customs, forcing her to adopt his lifestyle and ignore her cultural heritage.

Ritual abuse involves a man's using religion against his partner. He may pray against her or define spirituality as masculine. He may not want her to practice her ways. This is especially important in urban environments, because Indian women in the cities struggle to establish a sense of identity away from the reservation. He may use this against her by stating that if she practices her religious beliefs she will go to hell. He may even use this to indicate that she is not "allowed" to divorce him.

All 10 of these tactics are used interchangeably to force women to remain in battering relationships. Many women do not know that there is help available to them and that they can leave. Urban Indian women may feel the added pressure of not having anywhere else to go. They may have left their reservation and feel ashamed to go back because of the abuse or because they were with someone who was non-Indian. In addition, the effects of the abuse may have led to other psychological problems, such as depression, anxiety, sleep disturbances, and eating disorders. The abuse may also lower a woman's self-esteem, allowing her to have unrealistic expectations about her partner's ability to change and intense feelings of danger if she were to leave (Deaton & Hertica, 2001). All of these factors contribute to why a woman may stay in or leave an abusive relationship.

Impact of Violence on Children

It is important that interventions are developed that address the long-lasting effects on the well-being of children who witness violence, in particular, domestic violence. One of the effects that has been documented is posttraumatic stress disorder, which some contend is similar to what war veterans have experienced. In addition, Geffner et al. (2000), in *Children Exposed to Domestic Violence: Current Issues in Research, Intervention, Prevention, and Policy Development*, discussed the effects on children of being exposed to violence in the home. They found these children to be at high risk for both externalizing and internalizing behavior problems. Some of the externalizing problems they observed included temper tantrums, impulsivity, aggression, conflicts with siblings and friends, and bullying. Internalizing problems may be evidenced through somatic complaints, sleep disturbances, anxiety, social withdrawal, and depression. In addition, it has been noted that children from violent homes are at higher risk for injuries as well as school problems such as truancy. They also experience an increased frequency of childhood delinquency (see *Addressing Domestic Violence and Sexual Assault in Indian Communities* by Two Feathers Native American Family Services, 1999). Finally, Wasserman (2005), in *Understanding the Effects of Childhood Trauma on Brain Development in Native Children*, explored the connection between childhood trauma and brain development, including how the brain changes when exposed to trauma. Her groundbreaking document highlights the negative impact that witnessing violence as well as being exposed to other childhood trauma has on children. What all these data suggest is that Indian children require special care to ensure that the situation in which they are being raised does not negatively impact their mental health functioning.

Breaking the Cycle

How does this cycle of violence end? How can the community go back to a more natural life way that honors men and women? There are a few programs that have been designed to do this. One program designed to address domestic violence within the Indian community was developed by Cangleska, Inc. The components of the Cangleska, Inc., program are unique to tribal communities and are discussed below as a model program for ending violence in Indian communities, both rural and urban. Although there are few urban programs that address the issue of violence within Indian communities in a comprehensive format, one in particular bears discussion. Native Pathways to Healing, a program of United American Indian Involvement, Inc., has been designed to work with the large urban Indian population in Los Angeles, California. This program was developed to use the many principles outlined by Cangleska, Inc., and then reformatted to best serve the unique needs of an urban Indian population.

CANGLESKA, INC.

Cangleska, Inc., was originally known as Project Medicine Wheel (PMW), a project of the South Dakota Coalition Against Domestic Violence and Sexual Assault. Specifically, PMW was a comprehensive domestic violence prevention and intervention program designed to provide advocacy to Oglala women living on and off the Pine Ridge Reservation in South Dakota. When an initial 3-year grant ended, the Oglala Sioux Tribe assumed responsibility for the program, and PMW became a tribal agency. The mission and work of Cangleska, Inc., remain the same as the objectives of PMW: to provide a comprehensive domestic violence and sexual assault prevention and intervention program serving the citizenry of the Oglala Sioux Tribe.

Cangleska, Inc., developed seven program components in responding to domestic violence and sexual assault on the Pine Ridge Indian reservation and throughout Indian country. These components were designed to minimize barriers of geographic isolation and poverty; to provide victims with easier access to law enforcement services, victim services, and tribal court protections; and to monitor offenders and provide rehabilitation activities. The components of Cangleska, Inc., include shelters, outreach advocacy, Stronghold (a legal assistance program), coordinated response systems, a probation department, an offenders program, and a sacred circle.

There are currently two shelters operated by Cangleska, Inc. One, which opened in Kyle, South Dakota, in 1997, is located on the Pine Ridge Indian Reservation, and one, which opened in Rapid City, South Dakota, in 2000, is located in the nearest urban center to the Pine Ridge Reservation. The shelters provide safety for approximately 600 women and their children each year by providing food and housing as well as mental health treatment.

The outreach advocacy program is designed to assist women who are battered but do not desire shelter or feel a need to go to a shelter. Advocates are on call with tribal law enforcement and serve over 1,500 women and their children each year. These advocates help women find the needed resources required to stay out of abusive relationships. Part of this advocacy involves referral to Stronghold, another program of Cangleska, Inc., designed to provide civil legal services to women who have been battered.

The coordinated response system is a mechanism for policy, protocol, and procedure development to enhance the criminal justice system's domestic violence response and infrastructure development. One of the goals of the program is to monitor the system's response to domestic violence. Cangleska, Inc., has assumed responsibility for development and implementation of a technology information sharing project, Smoke Signals, to electronically link the tribal criminal justice system and Cangleska, Inc., departments. Previously, the tribal criminal justice system's record keeping had been completely manual.

The probation department and offenders' program are designed to work with the batterer. The probation department is an independent domestic violence specific probation department; it is the first probation monitoring service available to the Oglala Sioux tribal courts. The offenders' program, on the other hand, offers court-ordered and volunteer participants who are domestic violence offenders the opportunity to examine their violent behavior and make changes. The offenders' program involves attending 26 weekly group meetings to address the origins of violent behavior and to look for alternative solutions. What makes this program unique is that the cultural heritage is intricately involved in each session. In addition, offenders are offered the opportunity to visit one on one with the facilitator to further understand and change their violent behavior patterns.

The final program offered by Cangleska, Inc., is Sacred Circle, which is designed to become a national resource center to end violence against Native women. Sacred Circle provides training, consultation, and technical assistance to the Indian community both on and off the reservation on domestic violence response. In addition, Sacred Circle provides training on all aspects of domestic violence.

Although the Cangleska, Inc., programs are designed to meet the specific needs of the Lakota people, many other programs and tribes have adopted the principal program components and adjusted the cultural pieces to meet the needs of their specific communities. In cases in which this involves urban Indian centers, the concepts of understanding culture and history and the need to work with all members of the community are the important features that should be translated.

NATIVE PATHWAYS TO HEALING

Drawing on the inventive work of Cangleska, Inc., Native Pathways to Healing attempts to apply Native philosophy and principles to an urban environment. Under this program, Indian women who are currently in or have been in battering relationships are able to receive individual and group counseling. In addition to counseling, Indian women have access to extensive case management assistance, including help with emergency housing, clothing, and food; help from advocates for clients who must attend court to get restraining orders, to file for custody, or to testify; and help obtaining the necessary tools needed to acquire permanent employment. A resource center for women is also being developed to provide access to information on domestic violence and sexual assault through pamphlets, videos, and the Internet.

One unique feature of the Native Pathways to Healing programs is their extensive case management activities that involve helping women with anything they may need to successfully leave the battering relationship. For example, one Indian woman's ex-husband took her children from her while they were at school, stating he would not allow her to have contact with them. She was removed from her home and had lost her job. He told her on several occasions that he would leave the state and she would not know where he was. He also battered her on several occasions. A case manager worked with this woman in many ways, first helping her get a restraining order against her husband. The case manager then contacted the department of children and family services to have an assessment done on both families. Because this woman was American Indian, the case manager ensured that the American Indian unit or someone familiar with the Indian Child Welfare Act was assigned to the case. The case manager then worked with the woman helping her complete the paperwork required for welfare or tribal temporary assistance for needy families; she then referred her for a job skills assessment and accompanied her to court.

This type of response is especially important for urban Indian women because they are often isolated from their families and tribal reservations. In addition, the court systems and social environment differ from the reservations, and, for many Indian women, are scary and foreign. Urban Indian women often feel as if there is no one available for them. Having case managers or advocates who are there for them can help them see that there are people who care about their needs and are willing to help.

Conclusion

For true change to take place in the elimination of family violence within Indian communities, both rural and urban, Indian people must be able to go back to a more natural way of life. An old Indian philosophy states that the decisions and actions we make now should be made with the best intentions for the seventh generation, the generation that will follow our grandchildren's grandchildren. We must not do anything that will harm this generation or there will be no more generations to follow.

The natural life-supporting power, represented as a circle, puts equality back in the middle and nonviolence on the outside. The circle symbolizes the power of the medicine wheel, a power that is related to honor and respect, not control and terrorism. Inside the circle are spiritual reflection; economic partnership; negotiation and fairness; nonthreatening behaviors; respect, trust, and support; honesty and accountability; responsible parenting; shared responsibility; sexual respect; partnership; and cultural respect. In this model, the qualities are those of generosity, love, being spiritually centered, having courage, being respectful, mutual sharing, humility, compassion, being hardworking, and having fortitude. This belief system contains the qualities that were the cornerstone of the Indian way of life before Indians were terrorized into believing another group's philosophy was accurate and true.

Indian people must not excuse the use of violence in the past but must use history to understand where the violence comes from. By understanding this connection, both men and women may change their attitudes about violence, and then healing can begin. For without a clear understanding of the circumstances involved, it is difficult to establish appropriate services to effectively end violence against Native women and support the renewal of traditional culture (Sacred Circle 6, 2002). This is challenging work, but it is work that must be done if Indian people are to end violence within their communities.

References

Davies, J., Lyon, E., & Monti-Cantania, D. (1998). *Safety planning with battered women: Complex lives/difficult choices.* Newbury Park, CA: Sage.

Deaton, W., & Hertica, M. (2001). *Growing free: A manual for survivors of domestic violence.* Binghamton, NY: Haworth Maltreatment and Trauma Press.

Geffner, R., Jaffe, P., & Sudermann, M. (2000). *Children exposed to domestic violence: Current issues in research, intervention, prevention, and policy development.* Binghamton, NY: Haworth Maltreatment and Trauma Press.

Gunn-Allen, P. (2000). Violence and the American Indian woman. In M. C. Burns (Ed.), *The speaking profits us: Violence in the lives of women of color* (pp. 18–21). Seattle, WA: Center for the Prevention of Sexual and Domestic Violence.

Heer, C. (2002). *Domestic violence and substance abuse: How can we integrate?* Rapid City, SD: Ending Violence Against Native Women Training Institute.

Jablon, S. (2002). *Study materials for the California Jurisprudence and Professional Ethics Examination.* Los Angeles: PsychPrep.

Morrissette, P. J. (1994). The holocaust of First Nation people: Residual effects on parenting and treatment implications. *Contemporary Family Therapy, 16,* 381–392.

Mousseau, M. (2000). *A herstorical view of violence against women.* Rapid City, SD: Sacred Circle, Natural Resource Center to End Violence Against Native Women.

Paymar, M. (2000). *Violent no more: Helping men end domestic abuse.* Alameda, CA: Hunter House.

Sacred Circle 1. (2002). *Facts about alcohol abuse and domestic violence.* Rapid City, SD: Ending Violence Against Native Women Training Institute.

Sacred Circle 2. (2000). *Domestic violence information packet.* Rapid City, SD: Ending Violence Against Native Women Training Institute.

Sacred Circle 3. (2002). *Tactics of oppression and colonization: Power and control over Native women.* Rapid City, SD: Ending Violence Against Native Women Training Institute.

Sacred Circle 4. (2002). *Internalized oppression in action.* Rapid City, SD: Ending Violence Against Native Women Training Institute.

Sacred Circle 5. (2002). *The reality: Statistical facts.* Rapid City, SD: Ending Violence Against Native Women Training Institute.

Sacred Circle 6. (2002). *Violence against Native women: Battering statistics and implications.* Rapid City, SD: Ending Violence Against Native Women Training Institute.

Two Feathers Native American Family Services. (1999). *Addressing domestic violence and sexual assault in Indian communities.* McKinleyville, CA: Author.

U.S. Department of Justice. (1999). *American Indians and crime.* Washington, DC: U.S. Government Printing Office.

Wasserman, E. (2005). *Understanding the effects of childhood trauma on brain development in Native children.* West Hollywood, CA: Tribal Law and Policy Institute.

Nadine Cole

Trauma and the American Indian

6

American Indian people have been exposed to traumatic events since the colonization of the New World beginning over 500 years ago. In recent decades, the concept of historical trauma, also called *intergenerational trauma*, has emerged. *Historical trauma* involves exposure of an earlier generation to a traumatic event that continues to affect the subsequent generations. The exact mechanisms of such transmission of trauma have not been fully explored but are believed to involve effects on relationship skills, personal behavior, and attitudes and beliefs that affect subsequent generations. This concept of historical trauma has affected American Indian peoples of today. This destruction of the Native peoples of America involved policies of extermination by the colonial powers and emerging government, the introduction of diseases that were unknown in the Americas, and fear from the new immigrants and settlers that resulted in the goal to eradicate the Native population of the Americas (Stannard, 1992).

These policies, both official and unofficial, provided for the destruction of much of the original culture of American Indian peoples. Culture is important in that it provides a sense of meaning and purpose along with ways of looking at, understanding, and capturing the world. It provides for a structure within which to understand and cope with the world. This destruction of culture and people on such a wide scale eroded family and tribal structure, sense of meaning and purpose, worldview, and spiritual ties to the community and environment. Survivors had to contend with these issues as well as with continuing violence perpetrated against them as these policies continued. The lack of understanding and acknowledgement of this genocide in current society continues to perpetrate the effects on Native peoples. In many parts of our society, the policy on genocide in relation to Native peoples is looked on as necessary for colonization, and current prejudicial and racist attitudes are tolerated and encouraged.

The trauma that urban American Indian peoples have experienced has been exacerbated by relocation from rural to urban centers, the largest number occurring after the establishment of a government policy of relocation in the 1950s. These relocations forced people away from their families and tribes, disconnecting them from their support systems. This tore many families apart, destroying the sense of connection and belonging. Those relocated were not around other American Indians, and when problems and issues arose, the necessary connections to elders, Native healers, and other family members were not available. Healing rituals were abandoned, and transmission of cultural mores and values were lost without such support.

To understand the effects of historical or intergenerational trauma, it is important to look at two main bodies of research. The first area to consider is intergenerational trauma and its effects on subsequent generations. Two such groups include the Nazi Holocaust survivors, most notably the Jewish population, and Japanese American internment survivors. A second important area of consideration is the concept of complex posttraumatic stress disorder (PTSD). This area includes the effects of multiple current traumas on functioning.

Holocaust Survivors

There is a wide body of research in the area of the Nazi Holocaust and its effects on subsequent generations of Jewish survivors. Auerhahan and Laub (1998) pointed out some of the conflicts in the Holocaust survivor literature. The survivor community is torn between wanting recognition of the strength of the survivors and showing that there were no lasting effects on the Jewish people versus wanting recognition of the negative effects. This issue was highlighted by Yehuda et al. (1998). They noted the difficulty in documenting the horror while also showing the dignity of the Jewish people and their capacity to survive. Some of the fear of recognizing the negative effects is in pathologizing the survivors and their families, which is tantamount to admitting that Nazi oppressors "won." Indeed, there is evidence that although there were negative effects, there was also tremendous resiliency. Solomon (1998) looked at survivors and their families who relocated to Israel after the Holocaust. This work showed that there were effects from the Holocaust; however, there was no evidence of greater pathology in survivors or their families. Indeed, there was evidence that survivors viewed the world as more meaningful and less benevolent than nonsurvivors. Children of survivors evidenced greater anxiety, depression, guilt, anhedonia, despair, somatization, and an obsessive preoccupation with the Holocaust. However, none of this led to greater diagnoses of pathology. These same children showed greater optimism about the world and more moderate political views. It appears that overall there are specific psychological issues that are raised in both survivors and survivor families; however, this does not lead to greater pathology.

This conclusion was confirmed by Felsen (1998), who reviewed studies done in North America. These were empirical, controlled studies of the nonclinical population of survivors and survivor families. Overall, the children of survivors are functioning within normal range. There are specific psychological issues that they are dealing with, which include less differentiation from parents, less independence, increased anxiety, guilt, depression, and more difficulty in regulating aggression. In addition, the importance of examining cultural differences within the survivor population was emphasized. It was noted that Eastern European Jewish immigrants value greater familial closeness and place greater importance on family. This influences individuation and independence for children.

The research among second-generation survivors within the clinical population shows some significant psychological problems. These problems include difficulty with relationships and attachment to others (Barocas & Barocas, 1980; Bar-On et al., 1998; Davidson, 1980; Levav, Kohn, & Schwartz, 1998; Tytell, 1999), extreme reactivity to stress (Baider et al., 2000; Jucovy, 1983), and an overall hostile worldview (Jucovy, 1983; Roden & Roden, 1982). Impairment in parenting skills has been noted with first-generation survivors (Davidson, 1980; Levav et al., 1998). Survivor families also show specific patterns of communication about the Holocaust. There tends to either be an excessive, obsessive retelling of the traumatic events or avoidance and silence about these events (Baranowsky, Young, Johnson, Williams-Keeler, & McCarrey, 1998; Davidson, 1980).

Japanese American Internees

Another population that shows intergenerational effects of trauma is that of the Japanese American internees during World War II. The bulk of those interned were issei (first-generation) and nisei (second-generation) Japanese. Nagata (1998) examined the effects of the internment on the sansei (third generation), those born after the internment. She noted a "shroud of secrecy" that surrounded the discussion about the internment with nisei parents. The communication was brief, and internees discussed only small fragments of their experience. Despite this lack of meaningful and detailed discussion, the sansei children showed effects of the internment on their sense of security, accelerated loss of Japanese culture, and sense of shame and its impact on self-esteem. A later study looking at nisei internees noted that they reported having more frequent (although brief—only about 15 minutes) conversations about the internship with their family members than had the previous study of sansei children (Nagata & Cheng, 2003).

Complex Posttraumatic Stress Disorder

The idea of complex PTSD was first proposed by Lenore Terr in her work with survivors of childhood abuse. She suggested a differentiation between Type I trauma, which involves a single event, and Type II trauma, which involves multiple, repeated, and prolonged events (Terr, 1991). Several clinicians have agreed with such a differentiation, most notably J. Herman, who has been a proponent of the idea of complex PTSD (Herman, 1992). Complex PTSD is believed to cause changes in affect regulation, consciousness, self-perception, perception of the perpetrator, relationships, and systems of meaning.

Exposure to multiple, repeated, and prolonged traumatic events has only begun to be a focus of research in the American Indian. More recent research has focused on establishing the prevalence of trauma exposure and diagnosing PTSD. In such research, one must also consider the differences across the American Indian population, including differences between children and adults, as well as the characteristics of special populations such as combat veterans.

Robin, Chester, Rasmussen, Jaranson, and Goldman (1997) examined 247 adult members of a Southwestern tribe. They found that 81.4% had been exposed to at least one traumatic event. The lifetime prevalence for the diagnosis of PTSD was 21.9%. This was compared with the prevalence rate among the nonclinical, non-Indian population, which ranged from 1% to 9%. Factors that were predictive of developing PTSD differed according to gender. Physical assault was most predictive of developing PTSD for women, whereas a history of combat and exposure to more than 10 traumatic events was predictive for men.

Jones, Daughinais, Sack, and Somervell (1997) used the Diagnostic Interview Schedule for Children with 109 Northern Plains adolescents in 8th to 11th grades as part of the Flower of Two Soils study. Amongst these adolescents, 61% experienced at least one traumatic event. They found a 3% rate of diagnosable PTSD, though high rates of partial PTSD (having two out of three symptoms clusters) were noted.

Manson et al. (1996) noted several studies that were attempting to quantify both exposure to traumatic events and prevalence of PTSD in American Indian populations. One such study was the above-noted Flower of Two Soils study. Another study was with adolescents in a tribal school in the Southeastern United States, as part of the Health Survey of Indian Boarding School Students. In this study, 85 out of 163 survey participants were selected for clinical interviews on the basis of their scores on the Suicidal Ideation Questionnaire. These were students in the first and third quartiles (very high and moderate levels of suicidal ideation). Interviews were completed on all those in the third quartile (43) and on 18 in the first quartile. More than 60% had experienced at least one traumatic event. Of these, 1 subject was diagnosed with PTSD, less than 3% of those reporting a traumatic event. In other words, there was a high percentage of exposure to traumatic events, but the rate of PTSD diagnosis was very low.

Another study involving American Indian adolescents noted by Manson et al. (1996) was the Foundation of Indian Teens project. In this study, 297 Southwestern Indian adolescents were given a self-report survey followed by a clinical interview if their score showed eight or more traumatic events. The results indicated that 51% reported at least one traumatic event. In addition, about half of these reported more than eight events. In terms of diagnosable PTSD, 26.9% met full criteria.

These studies seem to indicate that many American Indian youth have been exposed to multiple traumatic events. They suggest the possibility of complex trauma, though more studies are needed to examine the prolonged and repeated aspects of these traumas. Additional research is needed for other age groups and tribes as well as urban and reservation populations.

A final study attempting to show the prevalence of PTSD is the Matsunaga Vietnam Veterans Project (National Center for PTSD and National Center for American Indian and Alaska Native Mental Health Research, 1997). This study came about because the National Vietnam Veterans Readjustment Study failed to sample American Indian and Asian Pacific Islander Vietnam veterans. The portion of this study sampling American Indian veterans (the American Indian Vietnam Veterans Project) was divided into Northern Plains and Southwestern Indian populations. This study showed that 57.2% of the Northern Plains and 45.3% of the Southwestern Indian veterans had a lifetime prevalence of PTSD. The overall best predictor of developing PTSD was combat exposure.

Although these studies help delineate the current traumas and their prevalence within the American Indian communities, the impact of historical trauma is also present. Perhaps one of the largest difficulties in examining historical trauma is the fact that we are about 120 years past the last major massacres and battles. We have no living eyewitnesses to these events, though certainly the events have been kept alive in stories and family and tribal histories. Current effects can only be proposed and assumed rather than validated by scientific means. This is the limit of scientific method. This does not mean that these events are any less real or valid.

Limitations of Research

The biggest limitation of the research is the small number of studies done in the area of historical or intergenerational trauma. As a result, a clear understanding of how traumatic memories are transmitted across generations as well as the effects of these memories is lacking. The populations studied have been limited to those in which the traumas have been within the past 60 years.

RESEARCH ON THE HOLOCAUST

Research on the Holocaust is by far the largest portion of the research that has been done on immediate survivors as well as second- and third-generation survivors. There are several important factors to consider when looking at this research, factors that may clarify the sometimes conflicting research results. One factor is the amount and type of exposure for the survivors. The experience of the Holocaust differed widely across people. There were some Jewish people who went into hiding, some were in the ghettos blocked from any escape and exposed to poverty and hunger, and some experienced the death camps. These experiences were widely different, and the amount and type of trauma that survivors experienced differed accordingly. The problem with much of the research literature is that it does not control for amount of exposure. There is also no easily quantifiable way to account for the effects of rumors and word-of-mouth information that were circulating and horrifying those hearing it.

A second factor to consider when looking at the intergenerational Holocaust data involves the population studied. Intergenerational Holocaust data are taken from both clinical and nonclinical samples. Much of the research data was taken from clinical populations in which one might expect significant problems both for the individual and his or her family. A more accurate account of the effect of the trauma would be from the general, nonclinical population.

In addition, as a third factor, it is likely that there were differences across the communities studied. A Jewish survivor's experience was different depending on which country he or she settled in. Survivors in Europe had different experiences from those in America and those in Israel. Some environments were supportive and acknowledged the horror of the Holocaust, which provided for deeper processing of the trauma and allowed for healing to take place. An interesting study would be to examine Holocaust survivors and their families who continued to live in Germany. This would involve looking at the effects of trauma when one continues to live with the identified perpetrators of the trauma, much like the American Indian's experience in the Americas. This is an area that has yet to be addressed in the literature on trauma and the American Indian.

RESEARCH WITH AMERICAN INDIAN PEOPLE

Research with American Indian people requires knowledgeable researchers who recognize the huge differences across tribes and living situations. There is a need for additional studies concerning the prevalence of exposure to trauma and PTSD among nonclinical populations. Perhaps the most difficult aspect of such research will be looking at the urban population, which is a mix of tribes and socioeconomic situations. To date there has been no study examining prevalence rates of trauma and PTSD in an urban Indian population. There are certainly no studies examining historical trauma and its effects, and the feasibility of such studies is limited by the numbers of generations that have passed.

Trauma Model

Some initial ideas for treating trauma, and especially historical trauma, have been presented by B. Duran, Duran, and Brave Heart (1998). They specifically proposed a model that uses both Western and Native American healers. This requires a fundamental understanding of the Native American worldview. They also suggested using healing rituals for the community. Braveheart-Jordan and DeBruyn (1995) discussed one such model that was developed and used with the Lakota people. This model incorporated the historical trauma experienced with traditional ceremony and group work to bring about resolution of grief and mourning. This model continues to be applied to other tribes, and work is being done through the Takini network regarding healing for the nations.

EFFECTS ON THE TRIBE

The tribe is one of the unique factors of American Indian peoples. Within the tribe, there are smaller groupings, usually described as clans. It should be noted that every tribe has different customs, languages, and values. As an example, some tribes are matrilineal, whereas others are patrilineal. Because of these differences, it is impossible to discuss all tribes as one group and get the full sense of each. The tribal differences are vast and more extreme than differences found across European cultures. These differences include language, parenting practices, lineage considerations, gender roles, and familial obligations.

Perhaps the place to start is with the effect of colonization on the tribes. The tribes in North America were self-governing, with control and power over the territory and the people entrusted to them. They had developed trade with neighboring tribes to the extent that goods were traded over hundreds of miles. One of the effects of colonization was to emasculate the tribal governments. Tribal governments were subject to the federal government of the United States. Their jurisdiction was limited and no longer included governance of punishments and establishment of trade. In current times, some tribes have regained greater control and power, though none have the level of self-governance that once was. Despite such terms as *sovereign nations*, there is still the reality that tribes exist within a larger country and government.

A second effect on the tribes was caused by the vast numbers of people who were annihilated during the colonization. Stannard (1992) described the figure of 95% of the population annihilated as being conservative. This resulted in general knowledge as well as important customs and cultural information being lost. There is no adequate way to assess the amount and extent of what was lost. In addition, the amount of destruction to each tribe differed widely. Some tribes that were colonized first were heavily affected, whereas some were more resistive and less accessible to the colonizers and thereby left more intact. Some examples might include the smaller tribes originally found along the New England coasts, which experienced great destruction of lands and loss of tribal members. In contrast, the Navajo, who were living in areas that were not highly desirable, were able to resist some of the destruction that others experienced.

Communication within the tribe is the place to begin the healing of the historical trauma. There is the need to tell about what has happened, for in the telling comes the opportunity to make sense of it, to fit it to the worldview, and to see the spiritual meaning of it. There is the need to avoid both silence about the events as well as excessive retelling. These patterns, as seen with Holocaust survivors (Baranowsky et al., 1998; Davidson, 1980), seem to be at polar opposites. One risks the reoccurrence of the event, and the other serves to traumatize those around. A balance somewhere in the middle is the best option.

Urban American Indians must deal with the disconnection they feel from the tribe. The amount of contact with the tribe may differ widely. There are certainly some urban American Indian people who have regular contact with their tribe, whereas others may have little or no contact. There are urban American Indians who have lived away from the tribe for several generations, even prior to the relocations of the 1950s. This means that the amount of influence and support from the tribe will differ. This support is important in dealing with the historical trauma, working on rebuilding the worldview, and finding meaning in life events. The urban American Indian must turn to other American Indians in the community for this support and recognition. There is a need to develop a sense of community and caring so that there is support during crises. This support is important in helping to rebuild worldview and a sense of identity. Urban Indians need to turn to others as they begin the journey of healing.

EFFECTS ON THE FAMILY

The American Indian family has also had to adapt to the dominant culture to survive. Many of the tribal effects can also be seen in the family. Again, there are differences across families. Colonization by a dominant society that was patriarchal and patrilineal and in most cases misogynist created a great amount of damage for American Indian families, especially those from matrilineal tribes. The structures of influence and power in the tribes were not understood and were ignored by the dominant culture. The role of women was not valued, and women were denigrated. There was a reductionism and devaluation in Indian families that was not there prior to colonization.

An area that must be examined when looking at the family is the attachment of members to each other. As was found in the Holocaust research (Barocas & Barocas, 1980; Bar-On et al., 1998; Davidson, 1980; Levav et al., 1998; Tytell, 1999), there is difficulty with relationships and attachment to others. Trauma, with its loss of meaning, also affects the meaning and value of relationships. This has been seen in the families of combat veterans. Fathers exposed to combat show several patterns of behavior, including intrusiveness into their children's lives, distancing themselves from their children, inability to meet their children's needs, and modeling self-defeating behavior (Curran, 1997). All of these interfere with appropriate, healthy relationships to children. This impairment in parenting skills is also seen in Holocaust survivor families (Davidson, 1980; Levav et al., 1998). Such breakdowns in family relationships can be seen in the high level of child abuse and domestic violence in American Indian families. There is a need to reestablish appropriate, committed family relationships that allow family members to thrive and blossom.

EFFECTS ON THE INDIVIDUAL

One effect of trauma on the American Indian individual is the development of PTSD, based on personal exposure to traumatic events. Prevalence rates in the American Indian community vary from 3% (Jones et al., 1997) to 21.9% (Robin et al., 1997). Some of these variations are due to the lack of application of standardized measures of PTSD and the population studied. Overall, the prevalence rates of both exposure to traumatic events and the diagnosis of PTSD are greater for the American Indian than for the general population. In addition to these higher rates of exposure to traumatic events, the American Indian person must also contend with the results of historical trauma. One of the long-lasting results of historical trauma, as seen in Holocaust survivors, is extreme reactivity to stress (Baider et al., 2000; Jucovy, 1983). This reactivity results in poorer coping responses to relatively minor incidents, and combined with both depression and substance abuse as comorbid diagnoses, amplifies the difficulty in coping. Developing coping skills and resiliency are important for healing.

The most frequent comorbid diagnoses with PTSD, outside of other anxiety disorders, include depression and substance abuse. A full evaluation must account for these diagnoses. In the area of substance abuse, the use or abuse of substances can be seen as self-protective. This may be a way to avoid and numb the emotions and recollections of trauma.

As such, substance abuse interferes with treatment and healing. An important component in treatment is the recollection of the traumatic event. This recollection needs to be as complete and whole as possible, including emotions, memories, and sensations. There must be a sense of what was lost. In the American Indian community, the recollection must include an understanding of the historical trauma, its effect on one's tribe and family, and the continuing effect today. More exploration and research about understanding the historical trauma is needed, because the history is not well known or apparent. In addition to the historical trauma, the individual's specific traumatic events must be explored.

ESSENTIAL ELEMENTS

There is the sense of deep shame that is part of the understanding of trauma, especially for the American Indian community. Shame is a deeply held belief that one is bad, horrible, impaired, tainted, and more. This deep sense of shame for the American Indian client is the unfortunate result of hundreds of years of oppression and annihilation. It is deeply held and can be seen in self-denigration, negative self-image, and low self-esteem. Such deeply rooted shame is also seen in disorders and problems such as substance abuse and dependence, child abuse, depression, and suicide. Treating such shame in the American Indian population is an extreme challenge because of the additional difficulty of overcoming the dominant culture's traditional view of the American Indian. There is either a romanticized view of the culture or an extremely negative view, neither of which is accurate or realistic. The effects of shame can lead to self-defeating and self-sabotaging behavior.

The treatment for shame requires a change in the deeply held beliefs about oneself. There is the need to examine these beliefs and to have the capacity to believe that one is good. One way to develop this is by seeing others in one's own group as role models such that one can begin to see that who one is, is not all bad. This gives a glimmer of hope to begin the process of seeing the self in a positive light. It is important to develop role models and mentors within the urban American Indian community.

Another essential consideration in treatment is the thrill and risk-seeking behavior that frequently accompanies trauma and PTSD. There can be an "addiction" to the physiological response to stress or danger. This response includes an adrenaline release that increases heart rate and muscle tension and gives a sense of power and control. This is a very powerful response. Many traumatized persons enjoy this response and seek out situations that produce it. The desire to experience the adrenaline release may be largely unconscious, though some individuals readily recognize this response. They place themselves in dangerous and risky situations. For some this involves living in a family situation that is chaotic with many problems. Arguing, physical fighting, and living on the edge can all produce this response. This situation must be dealt with in treatment because without intervention, it can lead to further traumatization. There must be an interruption in this cycle for the individual and family to heal.

Perhaps the most important aspect of treatment involves the spiritual nature of American Indian people and of trauma. Overall, American Indian people do not hold the Western view of the person as having separate parts of themselves. Frequently these parts are discussed as body, soul, and mind in the dominant culture. The American Indian view is that all of these parts are one. They are connected and related to each other. There can be something that happens in the physical world that damages the soul, as an example. This is especially true in the area of trauma; for Indians, a physical trauma affects soul, mind, and body. E. Duran, Duran, Brave Heart, and Yellow Horse-Davis (1998) described this as "soul wound." Therefore, the idea that spiritual concerns can be separated and removed to be dealt with in other arenas, such as a church, is counter to traditional culture. Spiritual concerns are an everyday life occurrence. Contact with the spiritual is seen every day, and many American Indians are mindful of this. There is a sense of the sacred (as opposed to the secular) in everything. This spiritual dimension must be addressed in treatment with American Indian clients.

There has been a recent awakening and concern for addressing spiritual issues in treatment of traumatized clients. There has also been a recognition that trauma affects the spiritual life of the individual. Decker (1995) noted that traumatic events appear to disrupt one's sense of invulnerability and cause one to seek purpose and meaning. He described spirituality as "our search for purpose and meaning involving both transcendence (the experience of existence beyond the physical/psychological) and immanence (the discovery of the transcendent in the physical/psychological)" (Decker, 1995, p. 1).

Janoff-Bulman (1992, 1995) approached the treatment of trauma from the perspective of the assumptions made about the world. These assumptions can be seen as part of the search for purpose and meaning, thereby making them part of the spirituality of the person. Generally, the assumptive world is based on beliefs that the world is benevolent, events are meaningful, and one's person is positive and worthy. Traumatic events defy these beliefs. The world is no longer benevolent but hostile and dangerous. Events can be chaotic and randomly destructive. One impact on the individual is the belief that one is to blame for the traumatic event. This blame takes on two aspects. One aspect is behavioral self-blame in which there is the belief that one could or should have done something different to prevent the traumatic event. This self-blame may be adaptive in that it allows the person to lessen his or her vulnerability, and thereby, begin to rebuild his or her assumptive world. A second type of self-blame is characterological. This self-blame is evidenced by the belief that one is inherently bad, and therefore, deserved the traumatic event. This can be very destructive, adding to issues of shame and depression. Healing is focused on rebuilding the assumptive world of the individual. This rebuilding is not to resurrect the old worldviews but to account for the traumatic events. The traumatic events must be assimilated into an overall worldview. Individuals who achieve this frequently talk about the meaning of the trauma and how it has changed them.

Program Recommendations and Conclusions

Perhaps the best model for rebuilding and healing is that proposed by Braveheart-Jordan and DeBruyn (1995). This is a model developed out of traditional healing and sociological and psychological understanding of trauma and the Lakota people. This work continues with the Takini network and its work with various peoples.

One factor in this model is the understanding of the history of the effects of colonialism on the tribes. It is important to discover and establish the history of each person's tribe and what traumatic events have happened through the years. This is not information that can be gotten from history books, because most books either do not cover these events or only cover them inaccurately (e.g., I remember as a child reading about the massacre at Wounded Knee and having it presented as a battle). This knowledge begins to set the background for one's personal history and understanding of the forces and losses. An important part of this for the urban American Indian is also establishing the reasons why the family left the tribal areas and moved to the urban setting. How did this move come about? What were the factors influencing prior generations to make the move? It is also helpful to know whether the family retained its sense of being Indian or tried to deny this. Did the family continue to be involved with American Indian events? Did they proclaim their heritage to others? The answers to these questions help to define how each individual fits into the social world.

The rebuilding of the assumptive world is necessary for the urban American Indian and is part of the individual's spirituality. This rebuilding must include the aforementioned historical trauma and involve the community. How do a people explain, find meaning and purpose, and rebuild the essence of good? It is necessary for the community to come together to talk about these issues, helping each other to find a resolution and belief that will provide them positive support and connection to the larger world. The role of ritual and traditional ceremony can be significant here. Ritual provides nonverbal recognition and resolution of such issues, allowing the physical, verbal, and spiritual to come together. Wholeness develops, with a deep sense of connection with the physical world as well as a sense of sacredness. The complete person joins with the tribe, earth, environment, and all others, and the transcendent, immanent, and universal are most apparent. Ritual is necessary for healing and must include traditional healers. Some concepts that are understood best are harmony and the completeness of the circle.

Most urban American Indians have more than one spiritual foundation. They frequently hold both traditional tribal beliefs as well as (most likely) Christian beliefs. Both of these worlds must be explored and resolution found concerning the meaning of each world and their lives. There must be a way of reconciling these worlds and of developing a sense of how they fit and what is necessary for healing to take place.

A final important piece for the healing model is that of grieving the loss. It is important to grieve and fully recognize the loss of culture, people, and history. This grieving can only be done fully in the context of the understanding of the effects of colonialism, as noted earlier in this chapter. To grieve fully, one must know what exactly is lost.

Rebuilding meaning and purpose in life enhances healing. It thus becomes central to providing the sense of pride and self-esteem that comes from awareness of where one fits in one's family and ever-widening circles of the community; the tribe; and ultimately, the world. The recovery from trauma is necessary to provide strength and wholeness for the future generations, even unto the seventh generation.

References

Auerhahan, N., & Laub, D. (1998). Intergenerational memory of the Holocaust. In Y. Danieli (Ed.), *International handbook of multigenerational legacies of trauma* (pp. 21–41). New York: Plenum Press.

Baider, L., Peretz, T., Hadani, P., Perry, S., Avramov, R., & DeNour, A. (2000). Transmission of response to trauma? Second-generation Holocaust survivors' reaction to cancer. *American Journal of Psychiatry, 157,* 904–910.

Baranowsky, A., Young, M., Johnson, D., Williams-Keeler, L., & Mc-Carrey, M. (1998). PTSD transmission: A review of secondary traumatization in Holocaust survivor families. *Canadian Psychology, 39,* 247–256.

Barocas, H., & Barocas, C. (1980). Separation–individuation conflicts in children of Holocaust survivors. *Journal of Contemporary Psychotherapy, 11,* 6–14.

Bar-On, D., Eland, J., Kleber, R., Krell, R., Moore, Y., Sagin, A., et al. (1998). Multigenerational perspectives on coping with the Holocaust experience: An attachment perspective for understanding the developmental sequelae of trauma across generations. *International Journal of Behavioral Development, 22,* 315–338.

Braveheart-Jordan, M., & DeBruyn, L. (1995). So she may walk in balance: Integrating the impact of historical trauma in the treatment of Native American Indian women. In J. Adleman & G. Enguidanos (Eds.), *Racism in the lives of women* (pp. 345–368). New York: Harrington Park Press.

Curran, E. (1997). Fathers with war-related PTSD. *National Center for Post-Traumatic Stress Disorder Clinical Quarterly, 7,* 30–33.

Davidson, S. (1980). The clinical effects of massive psychic trauma in families of Holocaust survivors. *Journal of Marital and Family Therapy, 6,* 11–21.

Decker, L. (1995). Including spirituality. *National Center for Post-Traumatic Stress Disorder Clinical Quarterly, 5,* 1–3.

Duran, B., Duran, E., & Brave Heart, M. (1998). Native Americans and the trauma of history. In R. Thornton (Ed.), *Studying Native America* (pp. 60–76). Madison: University of Wisconsin Press.

Duran, E., Duran, B., Brave Heart, M., & Yellow Horse-Davis, S. (1998). Healing the American Indian soul wound. In Y. Danieli (Ed.), *International handbook of multigenerational legacies of trauma* (pp. 341–354). New York: Plenum Press.

Felsen, I. (1998). Transgenerational transmission of effects of the Holocaust. In Y. Danieli (Ed.), *International handbook of multigenerational legacies of trauma* (pp. 43–68). New York: Plenum Press.

Herman, J. (1992). *Trauma and recovery.* New York: Basic Books & HarperCollins.

Janoff-Bulman, R. (1992). *Shattered assumptions: Towards a new psychology of trauma.* New York: Free Press.

Janoff-Bulman, R. (1995). Victims of violence. In G. Everly & J. Lating (Eds.), *Psychotraumatology* (pp. 73–86). New York: Plenum Press.

Jones, M., Daughinais, P., Sack, W., & Somervell, P. (1997). Trauma-related symptomatology among American Indian adolescents. *Journal of Traumatic Stress, 10,* 163–173.

Jucovy, M. (1983). The effects of the Holocaust on the second genera-tion: Psychoanalytic studies. *American Journal of Social Psychiatry, 3,* 15–20.

Levav, I., Kohn, R., & Schwartz, S. (1998). The psychiatric after-effects of the Holocaust on the second generation. *Psychological Medicine, 28,* 755–760.

Manson, S., Beals, J., O'Nell, T., Piasecki, J., Bechtold, D., Keane, E., & Jones, M. (1996). Wounded spirits, ailing hearts: PTSD and related disorders among American Indians. In A. Marsella, M. Friedman, E. Gerrity, & R. Scurfield (Eds.), *Ethnocultural aspects of posttraumatic stress disorder* (pp. 255–283). Washington, DC: American Psycholog-ical Association.

National Center for PTSD and National Center for American Indian and Alaska Native Mental Health Research. (1997). *Matsunaga Vietnam Veterans Project: Final report.* White River Junction, VT: National Center for PTSD.

Nagata, D. (1998). Intergenerational effects of the Japanese American internment. In Y. Danieli (Ed.), *International handbook of multigener-ational legacies of trauma* (pp. 125–139). New York: Plenum Press.

Nagata, D., & Cheng, W. (2003). Intergenerational communication of race-related trauma by Japanese American former internees. *American Journal of Orthopsychiatry, 73,* 266–278.

Robin, R., Chester, B., Rasmussen, J., Jaranson, J., & Goldman, D. (1997). Prevalence and characteristics of trauma and posttraumatic stress disorder in a Southwestern American Indian community. *American Journal of Psychiatry, 154,* 1582–1588.

Roden, R., & Roden, M. (1982). Children of Holocaust survivors. *Adoles-cent Psychiatry, 10,* 66–72.

Solomon, Z. (1998). Transgenerational effects of the Holocaust. In Y. Danieli (Ed.), *International handbook of multigenerational legacies of trauma* (pp. 69–83). New York: Plenum Press.

Stannard, D. (1992). *American holocaust.* New York: Oxford Univer-sity Press.

Terr, L. (1991). Childhood traumas: An outline and overview. *American Journal of Psychiatry, 148,* 10–20.

Tytell, T. (1999). Trauma and its aftermath: A differentiated picture of aftereffects of trauma in daughters of Holocaust survivors. *Disserta-tion Abstracts International, 59,* 4490B.

Yehuda, R., Schmeidler, J., Elkin, A., Wilson, S., Siever, L., Binder-Brynes, K., et al. (1998). Phenomenology and psychobiology of the intergenerational response to trauma. In Y. Danieli (Ed.), *Inter-national handbook of multigenerational legacies of trauma* (pp. 639–655). New York: Plenum Press.

III

New Directions for Working With Urban American Indians

This part of the book provides information about new clinical models developed specifically for urban Indian populations. The four chapters focus on the use of stories to heal old wounds and the use of community healing models to develop culturally appropriate treatment interventions and strategies.

Chapter 7, "Storytelling as a Healing Tool for American Indians," by Dolores Subia BigFoot and Megan Dunlap focuses on the use of stories as a healing tool for American Indians. The authors explore some of the historical background of stories, including the different types of stories and why they were used. They discuss the concept of how we need to view ourselves as storytellers and what that means to the next generation. The authors conclude with other ways in which stories may be used to heal the wounds of the past and connect this generation with its historical roots.

Chapter 8, "A Framework for Working With American Indian Parents," by Tawa M. Witko focuses on some of the historical factors that influence parenting, such as the effects of boarding schools and urban migration. The author explores the components of the traditional family system and some of the issues currently being faced by urban Indian parents as well as current treatment modalities. The author concludes with recommendations regarding program development and treatment of the urban Indian family as a whole.

Chapter 9, "Growing Up Indian: Treatment With Urban Indian Adolescents," by Rose L. Clark and Tawa M. Witko, focuses on the issues affecting teenagers and ways in which clinicians can reach them. The authors begin with some historical background, including the effects of urban migration, living off the reservation, the boarding schools, and what it means to be a city Indian. The chapter includes current treatment issues, such as identity development, being mixed blood, and the high rates of alcohol and drug use and suicide among this population. The authors conclude with ways in which therapists and community leaders have successfully used the old ways to connect adolescents with their heritage and ease the transition into adulthood.

Chapter 10, "An Innovative Healing Model: Empowering Urban Native Americans," by Carrie Lee Johnson focuses on a new approach to understanding urban Indians. The chapter explores the impact of colonization, residential schools, and historical factors such as forced relocation. The chapter also addresses some of the mental health and substance abuse problems as predecessors to family dysfunction and child abuse. The author then examines the use of the traditional medicine wheel as a way to assist with the healing process and concludes with a new model, developed by the author, aimed at empowering urban American Indians.

Dolores Subia BigFoot and Megan Dunlap

Storytelling as a Healing Tool for American Indians

7

"Long ago, when turtles laid eggs . . ." begins a story of Coyote. Coyote, Iktome, and Rabbit are all tricksters who exist in the words spoken by storytellers and who have been created thousands of times over in the imaginations of Native people. Tricksters serve the purpose of letting people know when behavior is profitable or unprofitable. The trickster that exists in the stories sometimes plays out the actions with the help of the teller.

The oral history of tribes preserved stories that included tricksters and their unbecoming behavior as well as explanations of why things are the way they are and how things came to be. Sometimes they simply offered a sense of something tangible when confusion reigned. The stories held the keys to the traditions, rituals, and social organization of the people. A story could always be found that would show someone the consequences of his or her behavior. Stories were used to explain how things happen and what can be expected about the present and the future. Storytelling time was a time for filling in the past and helping to make sense of things when challenges seemed overwhelming; it was also a time for learning, listening, interacting, and sharing with one another. Like the parables of the New Testament, the stories taught a moral lesson. Storytelling was the form of transmitting how things were and why things came to be. Storytelling gathered people together to share recreation time and also served their listening and oratory skills. Stories provided the answers to when, where, how, and how come. It is through stories that people could be accountable for actions and for teaching each other what is expected behavior and how to attend to one another.

Creation stories are the history and tradition of the tribes; they tell how the world began and explain how the world, people, animals, and plants are related. Through creation stories, people can better understand the natural order of life and from what direction they came and in what direction they are going. Stories give reason to the overall scheme of things. It is important to understand the creation of things because understanding provides the framework within which wise decisions can be made. Stories about the animals that helped bring the First People into the world are told as creation stories. In many creation stories, the animals help the Creator bring about the beginning of a place safe for mankind. Creation stories were retold and retold many times in the growing-up years and through childhood, adolescence, and old age. These stories not only explained the beginning of the tribe; they also had different significance depending on the circumstances.

There were winter stories and summer stories, stories for days that the rains fell, and stories for early morning. In several tribes, creation storytelling time was reserved only for the winter months or for ceremonies. For some tribes, these special stories could only be told at certain times, in certain seasons, and in certain places. The telling of the tale was recreational and embodied lessons to be learned. Winter tales, reserved for the season of cold and snow, showed respect for the elements that confined the tribe to their shelters. Limiting the stories to particular times demonstrated respect for the conditions the tribe lived under and thereby increased appreciation of the external world and how closely connected the elements were to the survival of the tribe.

Some stories lasted long into the winter nights and were shared by several storytellers. Many storytellers were trained from an early age to listen and repeat the exact words within the story. The story had to be told accurately because it embodied the correct history of a tribe. Over time, individuals occasionally embellished and adapted certain stories or built one story on another. Using this method, many storytellers could contribute to the story line. The creation stories demanded exactness; the *how come* and *why* stories permitted flexibility in expression.

Different objects were used to aid the imagination of the listener. Voice, silence, drum, and song all contributed to the playing out of the story line by the teller of the tales. Feathers, rocks, grass, fur, sticks, and other items helped the listener pay attention and served as a reminder of the story after the story was no longer being told. The storyteller's use of hand gestures, facial contortions, body movements, and other creative features added to the drama and excitement of the story. Sometimes only the voice changed as the teller recreated the long tribal legends lasting into the night, night after night.

Elders, teachers, guides, leaders, helpers, and relatives always had the opportunity to use the oral tradition of teaching to share their ideas, thoughts, feelings, beliefs, and expectations. Their stories contained messages about loyalty, love, respect, responsibility, honesty, humility, trust, and sharing, all qualities that helped American Indian and Alaska Native people to live the lives they did and to be the people they were. The stories existed to explain all of creation: the spirits of the mountains, the spirits of the rocks, the spirit of the streams, the spirit of the plants, and the spirit of the trees; the ways of people and their beliefs; the interactions between all creatures, both those here on earth and those that left long ago. All objects had life, and each contained a different medicine that could be used in both spiritual and physical healing. Objects were instilled with movement, emotions, speech, or other kinds of power to assist people in their journey from other worlds, through this world, and into the next. The relationship between the Indian people and the animals is one of mutual dependence. The animal world contained all manner of explanations. Explanations could change as greater understanding came about, yet there was still the element of belief that some things are unexplainable and are to be accepted without question. Stories allowed for the repetition of words so that eventually some things became so completely accepted, they were not questioned again. But children are curious and seek knowledge. That is part of their way of growing, as is explained by the stories of the Medicine Wheel (BigFoot, 2003). Parents, grandparents, and other relatives used stories to help children understand their place in the world and how they could show their gratitude for their existence. Respect for all living creatures was repeated with each telling of a story. Demonstrating respect and being able to give offering were two constants with storytelling.

The formal use of storytelling is common in urban settings rather than in rural or reservation areas, as can been seen by the proliferation of Internet sites and storytelling events such as Web sites that contain information on Native storytelling; see, for example, Canku Ota—An Online Newsletter Celebrating Native America (http://www.turtle track.org), as well as sites maintained by the City of Takoma Park, Maryland (http://www.takomapark.info); the Presbyterian Church (http://www.pcusa.org); and the Worcester Art Museum, Worcester, Massachusetts (http://www.worcesterart.org). The documentation of the use the storytelling as a healing art is limited within the American Indian population and even less common with youths, whether reservation or urban. However, urban youths have a much greater likelihood of being exposed to formal storytelling than nonurban youths because urban youths have more access to the Internet and the resources of larger school systems, which are the settings of many storytelling events.

Clinicians serving urban American Indian youths may lack formal training in the use of traditional storytelling, but the concepts and examples provided in this chapter are applicable to urban youths. Two constants still remain: respect and offering gratitude. The clinician can provide the model for respect, and the listener (youth) can provide the model for offering gratitude, a listening ear. At some point in the therapeutic relationship, the listener should become the storyteller, and then the offering becomes the story.

Storytelling as a Useful Tool for All Children

Storytelling has a long tradition and has served many purposes in the lives of American Indian children.

HOW TO LIVE

The oral transmission of rituals, ceremonies, feats, and kinship was accomplished by stories and legends told to children. Stories were living histories that could always be shared with children. Revealed through the stories were the tribal expectations, individual consequences, and possible punishments of unbecoming behavior. The stories were examples to children about how to behave. They clearly illustrated behaviors that would be tolerated and behaviors that were unacceptable.

One would hear the same tale many times from infancy to adulthood as the child moved from one stage of development to the next. The story never changed, but the message in the story would be appreciated with a different attitude because different parts of the story would be emphasized. Different aspects of the story would be stressed depending on the age of the child and how much impact the teller wished to have on the child.

During the telling of stories, children developed their listening ability and increased their attentive behavior. Listeners were not passive. From beginning to end, the storyteller actively engaged them. The teller would sometimes stop the story to get a response from the listeners or to explain something within the story that might have application for that time and setting. The teller built a relationship with the listeners. That relationship could extend to objects the teller used or places the teller took the listeners with his or her oral journeys.

DEFINING SELF

Understanding who we are and why we are here through stories can be comforting and inspirational, or it may appear to be confining and unpleasant. Children can learn about the trials and triumphs of their ancestors, about the supportive environment in which they were raised, and about the wonder of the future through storytelling. Stories can give children a sense of belonging to their family, community, and tribe, and this can instill a sense of purpose, identity, and hope. Stories could be an extremely positive force in the life of children. Stories are powerful tools that can exert a potential positive or negative force. Negative tales are stories that could limit children's views of themselves and the world. Children raised hearing stories about the shortcomings of their ancestors, the deficits in their own abilities, and the hopelessness of the future might have a worldview that includes the bleak tone of these stories.

Parents have always told stories about activities their children engaged in. The importance of these stories should not be underestimated because they have the potential to shape the way in which a child views him- or herself and his or her family, the community, the tribe, and the world. With a bit of story structure, parents can develop their own stories about their children that can be told and retold. The telling of stories from one generation to the next helps children form a link between those living today and those who lived before, illustrates the traits and characteristics that can be seen in each generation, and it carries forward humor and gratitude about those whose lives are touching them with words. Many elements contribute to children's emotional and cognitive development as well as their sense of self, and it is important to recognize that the spoken word can increase knowledge and understanding of how one fits into the world. Native children may become lost when they are not able to imagine their place in the world among their family members and within their tribal community.

STORIES AS DEFINITIONS OF REALITY

The use of stories to provide a context for creating and understanding reality is universal and captured well as a concept within the tribal culture of American Indian and Native Alaskans. However, this approach in not unique to Native people, with many non-Native individuals exploring this arena. This is evident in the proliferation of Web sites that link to the National Storytelling Network (http://www.storynet. org/). Courses in and about storytelling are taught in colleges and universities, with many established institutes or centers for storytelling. Folklore and storytelling are combined with formal teaching, traditional healing, psychotherapy, professional development, guidelines in education, multicultural applications, and much, much more. The range of involvement spans professional associations devoted to storytelling to individuals who just like to tell a good story and see themselves as the teller of tales. Conferences and festivals abound, as evidenced by schedules posted on the Internet. Stories can remind us all of where we came from, who we are, and what we can hope to become. Stories shared by a large group of people can help individuals feel connected to others and embrace other individuals, but certain stories can also serve to set up a system in which particular individuals or groups are alienated or excluded. Stories can be manipulated to express ill will. People with good and not-so-good intentions have attempted throughout the years to use popular stories to motivate and manipulate masses. War movies with their visual telling of stories during World War II are a wonderful example of this.

Stories influencing the perception of reality have been examined not only on individual, family, or community bases but at the level of society as well. For example, the stories printed in popular women's magazines through the ages have been correlated to the view of the "proper" way in which women are expected to live and behave (Friedan, 1963). Not surprisingly, it appeared that the dominant culture's view of what place women served in society was related to the stories distributed and available to women. After being exposed to society's stories for a period of time, many women reported that they (sometimes unsuccessfully) altered their own view of their place in society to fit that of the stories being told.

Teaching Values With Family History Stories

Storytelling is a method that is well suited to the learning style of children. Many psychologists (e.g., social learning theorists and behaviorists) believe that children learn by example. Stories can provide children with characters going through circumstances similar to their own. Children can observe, through stories, the problem-solving process, possible actions to take, and the consequences of each action. Through repeated telling of a story, children can develop an understanding of these processes and behaviors without physically engaging in them.

CHILDREN'S STORIES

Bringing children into a circle is a traditional teaching based on the concept of honoring children and extending family relationships, and it reaffirms the concept of children being at the center. Being the center of a story is a way of reenforcing to children that they are the center of the circle. Children love to hear stories about themselves, and knowing they are at the center of a story is one way of making children feel that they are important.

There are different ways to share a child's story. A simple way is to tell a child about what he has done in the past, which most parents do naturally and automatically. Many times stories are short and funny, with something that stands out because of some action.

Parents who are having difficulty with a child can be instructed to establish a story time. For example, when a parent would like to spend more time one-on-one with a child or do a special activity with a child, this can be the time for telling a story. The stories should have a positive feature. Participants can use any story they have been told about a family member that is enjoyable to tell. Parents can be encouraged to think of some story from their experiences growing up or how they married; they can use any event from their lives or their parents' lives. The subject of the story can be anything: how they lived, where they went to school, what they ate, or how they kept warm in the winter. Identifying thoughts, feelings, and actions helps with the story line. The basic structure of the story is as follows: Identify an event; establish the players or characters; and develop a beginning, middle, and ending. The beginning should explain the setting and the characters in the story. The middle should tell the event and how the characters felt, thought, acted, or looked. The ending should conclude the story, telling what happened to the characters and why. The storyteller should emphasize the story with voice levels, facial expressions, hand movements, and enthusiasm.

An example of a simple family story is as follows:

> There was once a little boy who was born to his mother and father. His father was very proud of him and was teaching him about his heritage of being Cheyenne, Arapaho, and Navajo. When the family had a reunion, his dad wanted him to share who he was with everyone. So with great encouragement by the father to the son, the little boy stood very proud and straight and with clarity stated, "I am SUNSHINE and HO-HO what daddy?"

Children love hearing stories about who they are, what they said, how they acted, and the reactions of others. This can be expanded, especially when children need to know more about themselves and their relationships to others. This helps build their sense of belonging and identifying. Their relationships can be with their parents, grandparents, siblings, extended family members, animals, or others. A simple story pattern may start with an introduction similar to that provided above and proceed as follows:

> Once upon a time a child was born to a mom and dad [if there is something you know about the day, then that can be added] when the snow was blowing and the sun was far to the south [a name and siblings can be added at any point]. The name of the boy was _____, and he decided he wanted to drive his father's pickup truck, which was parked in the driveway, even though he was not long enough or tall enough and did not have a driver's license and had not asked permission. [Describe the action that happened.] He crawled in the door of the pickup truck; he sat in the seat. He had seen his father drive the truck many times, and it was always a special time when he went with his dad in the pickup truck because his dad would smile at him and put him in the front right next to him. [Describe the outcome.] He knew his dad would pull the long stick, so that is what he did, and the truck rolled backward, hit the trash can, and stopped at the end of the driveway when his dad realized what was happening. [Describe the reaction.] Dad was very surprised to know his pickup truck was at the end of the driveway and his son was in the driver's seat. Dad ran to the pickup truck and said "Did you start driving already? You are not old enough!!!!!" [Describe how it ended.] And now dad knew that his son loved being in the truck with him, and dad always turned and smiled at his son but did not let him drive again. This was the story about when _____ learned that being old enough to drive was not when he was short and could not reach the foot pedals.

This is an easily applied method of teaching parents to tell stories to their children.

JOURNAL RECORDING

Individuals can chronicle their life stories in a daily or other regularly timed recording of their activities, thoughts, reactions, or encounters, either in diary form or in letters. Regular letter writing can form a journal. George Bent's letters to George Hyde are the basis of much information about Cheyenne and Arapaho culture and history in the late 1800s. *Life of George Bent* (Hyde, 1968) is a narrative of letters written to Hyde by Bent beginning in 1905 and lasting until 1918, when Bent died. George Bent was the half-Cheyenne son of William Bent and Owl Woman. These letters discuss life at Bents Fort, Bent's life with the Cheyennes, and the military events that occurred on the southern plains during this time.

Young children respond to hearing stories, and it can be helpful to have children tell their stories without written words or recognizable pictures. Young children can create a daily log of their thoughts, feelings, and reactions just by using colors on pages of a loose-leaf notebook or pages stapled together, if necessary. This was successfully done with a 4-year-old boy who experienced severe trauma over a period of time. The child responded well in play therapy, but the parents were concerned about how withdrawn he was during the week. The child actually came up with creating a diary. A seven-page notebook was sent home after each weekly session with instructions that on each day, the child would record his impressions, thoughts, anxieties, reactions, and fears on a single sheet of paper using only different colors. The colored journal continued each week, with the child being able to verbalize what was on each sheet and recall reactions from several weeks back by reviewing each page of the journal. He was able to see his progression from the beginning of the journal keeping to the end of the therapy. As his anxiety decreased and he became less withdrawn, he moved toward allowing his parents to write down his daily events so that the journal moved from colors to a written record given to the parents. This allowed the child to build a stronger attachment to the parents while the parents learned to listen to their child and continued the commitment to maintain a daily activity introduced by their child. The journal keeping became the storytelling of the child's life and the integration of his daily living with a permanent record.

Historically, record keeping within Native culture was done with markings on sticks, paintings on rocks, or other creative methods. Record keeping today is much easier with the use of pen and paper, and one can be quite prolific with a computer and printer. Researching one's genealogy has increased the motivation for some to write in a journal regularly, because people are discovering family stories by reading ancestors' personal journal records. A record-keeping activity does not need to be confined to words alone but can be creative storytelling with paintings, sculpture, or other art objects. One individual used his Dream Catcher to display his achievements, goals, and aspirations in a symbolic way. (A Dream Catcher is a hoop that is woven with thread similar to a spider web; attached to the weaving would be objects of importance such as feathers, pictures, and rocks.) Recording one's daily activities and aspirations can help to sort out thoughts and mend sorrows. Being able to review different times in one's life with short stories and illustrations can bring laughter, memories, appreciation, and determination. Journal keeping can become the source of stories for future generations.

Current Treatment Modalities and Research

Storytelling is an art as old as the spoken word, with the telling of the tale holding wonder for the teller and the listener. The wonder extends to a greater power within the telling of a story that goes beyond the words alone. What has been discovered is that with hand gestures, reflected emotions, and imagination, the telling of a story can create new meanings and understanding for the listener as well as the teller. Healing can be within the words, gestures, emotions, meanings, and imagination. Within a therapy context, storytelling can be used with individuals for a variety of purposes: teaching a point, examining past events, increasing coping strategies, using less direct approaches to address sensitive subjects, dealing with grief, or rewriting stories. Teresa LaFromboise (personal communication, August 1985) considered this when she proposed using tribal legends and tales, similar to what Malgady, Costantino, and Rogler (1986) developed with Cuento Therapy using folktales as a culturally sensitive psychotherapy tool for Puerto Rican children. This approach was further developed with hero and heroine modeling therapy for adolescents (Costantino, Rogler, & Malgady, 1990). The results indicated that children in Cuento therapy demonstrated increased social adjustment and reduced anxiety.

The therapeutic value of storytelling is evident by the use of projective storytelling cards created by Northwest Psychological Publishers, Inc. (Caruso, 1990), with children who are in therapy for inappropriate sexual behavior or who have a history of abuse (Bonner, 2000). Barbara L. Bonner (1999) and Dolores Subia BigFoot have been conducting training with Project Making Medicine, a national project to train Native mental health professionals in the treatment of child physical and sexual abuse using projective storytelling. Abuse-focused therapy and treatment of children with sexual behavior problems incorporate the use of projective storytelling to allow youth to create a story line based on what they view as having occurred between individuals portrayed on the cards. Children are allowed to describe events prior to, during, and after the picture. Each picture is independent of the others; therefore, they are interchangeable and do not need to be sequential. The use of the pictures in therapy provides an opportunity for a child to explore within a safe environment fears, hopes, changes, new understandings, and new behaviors or skills learned during therapy. Children are prompted to explain in their own words their perception of what they see and what they understand to be true about their world.

Additional efforts to use traditional Native stories have been undertaken by tribal child sexual abuse programs. The Hopi Child Sexual Abuse Project (Leviton, Schacht, & Quamahongnewa, 1994) developed children's stories as part of their intervention to help children and the community recover from sexual abuse. The intent was to provide an acknowledgement of conflicts within families with a method of healing within a cultural context. The Navajo New Mexico Coalition of Sexual Assault Programs (1993) developed a child abuse prevention manual that presents a contemporary story of an assault against a young girl. The story emphasizes the strength and healing she receives from her family, culture, and environment with the use of Navajo legends, animals, song, music, humor, and language.

Animals have always been considered helpers and healers within Native teachings. The story of the turtle was based on a turtle technique to help children develop self-control. Today the turtle technique (Bonner, 1999) is used extensively with Native children. In the Southwest, it has been revised to incorporate animals native to the desert, such as the rabbit, and the names have been changed to names more common to the local culture (Larry Salway, personal communication, May 7, 2000). The turtle story is adapted from Marlene Schneider and Arthur Robin (n.d.). The turtle story presented here (Bonner, Walker, & Berliner, 1999) is part of the manual developed for treatment of children with sexual behavior problems in which a number of Native children have participated.

THE TURTLE STORY

Once upon a time there was a handsome young turtle. He was ___ years old, and he had just started school. His name was Ralph. Ralph was very upset about going to school. He didn't want to learn school things. He wanted to run outside or stay at home to watch television. It was too hard to learn the ABCs. He would rather play and laugh with friends. He got into lots of fights with other children, but he really didn't know how they started. He felt he had to fight. He didn't like listening to his teacher. He wanted to make wonderful loud fire engine noises he used to make with his mouth. It was *hard* to be good in school. It seemed like he was mad or unhappy most of the time and always in trouble.

Every day on his way to school he would say that he would try his best. But, despite his plans, every day he would get mad at somebody and fight, or he would get angry because he made a mistake, and then he would rip up his papers. He began to feel like a "bad" turtle. He went around for a long time feeling very, very bad.

There was another turtle in his class named Lesley. She lived close to Ralph and sometimes they would walk home from school together. She was a pretty young turtle, but she didn't like school either. In fact, she didn't like much of anything. She felt sad or worried most of the time. She would worry that her mother might get sick or that her father might lose his job. She worried that her teachers would get mad at her. When she wasn't worried, sometimes she was sad. She lost her cat and she was sad. She didn't like the way she looked. In fact, she didn't like much of anything.

She didn't do very well in school either. She was so worried and sad that she never really got interested in doing her schoolwork or even in playing with friends. She was always thinking about other things.

One day Ralph and Lesley were walking home from school together. They were both feeling very unhappy when they met the biggest, oldest tortoise in their town. The wise old turtle was 200 years old and as big as a house. Both Ralph and Lesley had heard stories about how the wise old turtle helped other turtles feel better about themselves.

So, Ralph told the old tortoise that he was feeling bad. He told the old turtle about the fights, the papers, and getting into trouble. Lesley told the old turtle about feeling sad and worried all the time.

The old tortoise smiled at them in a kindly way and seemed eager to help them. "My goodness," the tortoise said in a big, bellowing voice. The old turtle's voice became soft and quiet. "I'll tell you a secret. You are carrying the answer to your problem around with you," he said. Ralph and Lesley didn't know what the old turtle was talking about. Still whispering, the old turtle said, "Your shell! Your shell! That's why you have a shell. You can go inside your shell when you feel sad or you seem to be heading for trouble. When you are in your shell, you can have a moment to rest and figure out what to do about it."

Lesley and Ralph still looked a bit puzzled. So the old turtle said, "Here's what you can do when you feel like you are troubled. Ralph, say to yourself, 'I feel angry,' and Lesley, say to yourself, 'I feel worried (or sad).'"

"Then say to yourself, 'Shell to relax.' In your shell, you are safe. You can relax all the muscles of your body. You can let them get limp, like cooked spaghetti. Take a deep breath, and for a few seconds, blow your troubles out of your mouth, right out of your shell. Just rest for a moment.

"Then say, 'I can think of a way to help myself.' Think of something you can do that is good for you, something that will help you feel better, something you can do that will help you avoid trouble.

"Then come out of your shell and do it. Do the best thing you can to help yourself."

Ralph and Lesley liked the idea, but they didn't understand it very well, so they asked the turtle to describe it again. The old turtle repeated what to do. This time, they practiced the steps as the old turtle told the story. The old turtle said, "When you feel troubled, remember the four parts of the 'secret':

"Say what you are feeling and that you don't like it.

"Go into your shell and relax.

"Think of something you could do to help yourself.

"Then do it."

After they left the old turtle, Lesley started to worry. She started to wonder if her mother and father would be in a good mood. But then she remembered what the old turtle told her. She said, "I feel worried and I don't like it," and went into her shell to relax. After she rested for a moment, she thought that worrying about her mother and father wouldn't do her any good. She decided to sing a new song she had heard on the radio. She liked the song and it helped her feel better. She felt proud that night with her new skill.

The next day, Lesley started to feel sad at school because she didn't like the way she looked. She remembered the four parts of the secret. She said she felt sad about the way she looked and didn't like feeling sad. Then she relaxed in her shell and figured out that she could look better if she washed the dirt off her shell during recess. She also figured out that she could be happier if she got her work done. She did it, and it helped again. Her secret helped her with a lot of her worries and sad feelings.

That evening, Ralph also thought about the special secret. He practiced saying its four parts: "Say what you feel, relax in your shell, think about helping yourself, and do something to help yourself." He said them over and over again. He told his parents about his secret, and they seemed to like the idea. The next day came, and he again made a mistake on his nice clean paper. He started to feel that angry feeling again and was about to lose his temper, when suddenly he remembered what the old tortoise had said.

"I feel mad, but I don't need trouble," Ralph said to himself. Instead of ripping up his paper, he pulled in his arms, legs, and head and rested until he knew what to do. He was delighted to find it so nice and comfortable in his shell. The mistake didn't bother him there. He figured out that the best thing to do was to go on with his work as best he could. When he came out, he felt better. As he continued working, he was surprised to find his teacher smiling at him. He told her he was angry about the mistake, but he decided to continue working. She said she was very proud of him.

Both Ralph and Lesley continued using the secret for the rest of the year. When they got very angry, very sad, or felt themselves heading for trouble, they figured out what they could do to help themselves. They felt happier, and they both were proud of themselves. Everybody admired them and wondered what their magic secret was.

Turtle Rhyme

When I think of doing something wrong
I stop and think of this song
I pretend like I'm a turtle
And go in my shell
'Cause that is a place
Where I relax well
I think about
What I am doing wrong
And blow it off
And just go on
I think of things
That I could do
And when I do that
Then I am through

This technique helps children to be less impulsive and develop self-discipline by providing structure and helping them recognize that they can maintain self-control in a step-by-step process.

USE OF IMAGERY

The use of imagery is an essential element in encouraging American Indians to tell stories about their lives in a way that is nonthreatening. Imagery can transform impression, thoughts, and feelings into a story format by shifting who uses the words. Use of imagery can help youths to focus, restructure, concentrate, and transform. Helping Native adolescents use imagery has been successful for pain management and for raising their level of participation in their medical treatment. It was proving very difficult for hospital medical personnel who worked with several Native youths who required regular and painful medical procedures to do their jobs. It was critical to have patients as calm and relaxed as possible for procedures that were, in fact, highly uncomfortable and intrusive. To lessen their anxiety, Native youths were encouraged to verbalize places or events they found soothing and comforting. Imagery has longed been used in relaxation exercises, so the natural extension of using familiar places seemed appropriate with these youths. With guided instruction, one Native youth was able to reproduce images and began to tell a story of the images, which included color, sensations, smell, wetness, wind, and hardness. The story images completely removed him from the hospital bed to a remote rock in the middle of a pond where he told of birds and sounds and rocks and recalled the stories of his father. One could see the physical changes that occurred when the tension decreased. He told his feelings in a story and in the process created for himself a safe and familiar place. His story became a journey that he could travel when he needed to disassociate from the painful procedure.

PICTORIAL STORYTELLING

Many urban areas are confronted with young adults with fetal alcohol syndrome or secondary disabilities as a result of neurological disorders from in utero drug exposure who are rearing children of their own. A successful effort initiated with young mothers with fetal alcohol syndrome and fetal drug exposure has been to help them use pictures to learn how to care for their infants. A storybook format with pictures of appropriate parenting or caregiving behaviors with somewhat exaggerated details is used to instruct the young mothers (Carol Yakish, personal communication, February 18, 1997). For example, the first picture prominently shows a clean disposable diaper, and the last picture shows a diapered baby. A young mother views a series of behaviors taken in sequence to accomplish the particular tasks. All of the pictures are in a three-ring, 8.5-inch × 11-inch binder, which allows for the placement of captions with the pictures. Captions provide statements such as, "Brenda is holding her daughter, Irene, with her right hand to hold Irene's head up and with her left arm under Irene to support her back. See how Brenda's arm circles Irene almost all the way around." Finger rings or other markings are used to help designate right from left. If there is a problem with bottle-feeding, the mother is first taught and shown how to wash bottles, measure formula, heat a bottle, hold the infant, and place the infant after feeding. Pictures are taken sequentially so that when a mother has questions or has difficulty remembering the next step, she can review the book. She can also see the outcome of her actions by the condition of the infant—full, asleep, contented, or unhappy. The mother is taught to ask for help when she realizes that she has tried each strategy and it is not working. Assisting the mothers with the story of their caregiving creates great satisfaction, and the picture book becomes a record of their child's development. It also offers a record of the mother's mastery of caregiving skills. Each mother is presented with a picture book of a different situation in which she is pictured taking care of her child in an appropriate manner. For example, when a mother may not realize that she is making choices between her infant and her partner, a wrong decision can place the child at risk. Using pictures allows her to see her decision making with the outcome of her choices. The pictures tell a story of her choices and depict the way she may think or feel; the pictures provide reasons to decide between her child's safety and her partner.

Service providers teach each skill by having the mother practice the skill, take a picture, and then add the picture to the book. The picture book is a reminder of physical activities she needs to do on a daily basis to care for her child and a reminder of what she has accomplished. The book and the praise from the social service providers serve as constant reinforcement of appropriate caregiving behaviors.

SUBSTANCE ABUSE

There are many different approaches for intervening with Native people seeking help in substance abuse treatment programs (Nixon, Phillips, & Tivis, 2000; Trautman, Phillips, Hallford, Borrell, & Nixon, 2000). One technique is to present these individuals with a pictorial account of their behavior and the consequences of their behavior (Candice Stewart Sabin, personal communication, August 2001). The pictorial account allows these individuals to have a tangible and visual connection to how their decisions affect their lives and what behaviors evolve out of those decisions. For some individuals, having a tangible representation of their choices makes the choices appear more real. The pictorial account does not rely on a verbal or cognitive presentation of sequences; it is a story of the person's thoughts, behaviors, and emotions and their impact on the person. The pictorial account presents a sequence of choices to assist individuals with their method of decision making. A critical portion of this pictorial account is to depict the actions of the person when the person is in recovery and engaging in sober behaviors. Rather than focus on past decisions, individuals are encouraged to consider immediate decisions and create pictures anticipating the outcome of those immediate decisions. They are able to create a story based on their choices, with each decision being a new part of their life story. The pictorial account helps them connect their thoughts, behaviors, and emotions to allow them to see the links. This method has the advantage of being less directed but tangible. John Sipes Jr., a Cheyenne historian and Chief, described this method as similar to a Winter Count, typical of Plains tribes' activities when winter gatherings took place (personal communication, February 22, 2000).

Another technique used with individuals with a history of substance abuse is the sweat lodge, which has been implemented into several programs, including one Southern Plains tribe treatment center. Within the sweat lodge, people have the opportunity to tell their stories.

As part of the story and the experience, the heat, rocks, wood, fire, offerings, songs, drums, cleansing, and ceremony all become centered within the person. Participants can envision themselves as being worthwhile because they are centered. Each person is encouraged to recall success in maintaining sobriety and to establish connection with the helpers (heat, rocks, wood, etc.). Participants also have the opportunity to describe their sense of self and how they will recapture it when out of the sweat. They are encouraged to recreate their life story and to call all of the helpers, including the treatment personnel and other clients, for assistance in maintaining sobriety. Conducting traditional ceremonies is typically restricted to an individual with the authority either by inheritance or by some designation. Clinicians may find it difficult to encourage a sweat ceremony in the majority of urban sites. However, a clinician can develop a corresponding safe setting to help youths describe their sense of self with the use of helpers (rock, wood, song, water, etc.) and to experience how those helpers can be reminders of maintaining a healthier, more respectful lifestyle.

Other Concepts of Storytelling

Some clients have initiated their own method of storytelling. A young urban male Native American who was a fancy dancer used his dance outfit to create his story. He or a relative made each piece of his dance outfit, and he would tell who the relative was, the nature of the relationship, what the item was for, where it came from, why it was a part of his dance regalia, what the colors represented, when it would be replaced, where the design came from, and what it meant to him as a person and as a dancer. He discovered that when he needed a place of retreat but could not physically remove himself, he could rearrange his breast plate with its numerous bones, beads, and straps. This allowed him to relax and concentrate. With this process, he could regroup and reorganize not only the breast plate but also his mind and world. He used the degree of complexity of the pattern as an indication of the degree of difficulty he was experiencing. The breastplate patterns began to represent his ability to work through his difficult times, and they became a part of the story he told as he described his dance outfit.

This process can be used with weaving or other pattern-making materials to help youths understand and develop decision-making skills. Each step can be explained in a story format.

VIDEO STORYTELLING

Carved From the Heart (Frankenstein & Brady, 1996) is a documentary about a Native father who loses his son to a drug overdose. The father, as a result of his grief, decides to create a totem pole, and eventually the entire town of Craig, Alaska, is invited to participate in the carving. It brings together people who are Native and non-Native, and more importantly, it acknowledges common problems of personal loss, inter-generational grief, substance abuse, suicide, and violence. It seeks to promote healing within the community and intertwines the process of carving the Healing Heart Totem pole with participants' stories of involvement and healing. This powerful film opens up questions of death and dying, suicide, family relationships and parenting, substance abuse, family violence, and the impact of the Vietnam War on veterans and their families, and it shows the importance of ceremony and culture in facing tragedy and how communities can provide support to their members. The film also acknowledges the intergenerational grief that grows out of rapid changes in lifestyle and interruptions to the passage of tradition and knowledge within Alaska Native and American Indian communities. Many similar story films with discussion guides are available and can be a source to open a discussion with youths and their families.

Future Treatment and Research Needs

The Reach Out and Read programs (see http://www.reachoutandread. org/) seek to make early literacy a standard part of pediatric primary care. Pediatricians encourage parents to read aloud to their young children and give books to their patients to take home at all pediatric checkups from 6 months to 5 years of age. Parents learn that reading aloud is the most important thing they can do to help their children love books and to start school ready to learn. Mark Wolraich and Dolores Subia BigFoot have initiated a similar program with two tribes in Oklahoma. With the help of tribal volunteers, we are attempting to record oral children's stories into storybook form with Native language translations. Tribal elders, parents, children, and young adults are tell-ing the stories, and the response has been overwhelming. What has been apparent is the increase in pride in sharing tribal stories. Most of the participants view this as beneficial in preserving the stories, thereby preserving the culture and language. In addition, the stories explore what is expected behavior, and many agree that this helps in the teaching of boundaries and consequences. The unexpected benefit has been that families are gathering together to tell their stories. We had assumed that most recording sessions would be one on one. Instead, there has been an unexpected outcome. When the volunteer arranges for an individual to tell a story, the scheduling prompts family members to gather to listen. When more people listen, more questions are asked, and more detailed explanations are given about events or legends. Of course, one story often triggers additional stories and additional explanations. During this process, children can become visually more attentive and more spontaneous, resulting in parents practicing more patience and young and old alike communicating about expectations and tribal lifestyles. This effort is in the early stages. Few stories are written, and most stories are being recorded to be translated later. We anticipate that more specific outcomes will be presented in the future when the storybooks are printed and available to the parents to read in their Native language.

Conclusion

By telling and hearing stories, Native Americans can begin the healing process for their youths, but it is up to the clinicians to see the importance of this useful tool in the treatment of their American Indian clients, especially within urban Indian communities where many do not know or have immediate access to their tribal elders. They do, however, have access to the Internet and the community of urban elders. Storytelling is a natural part of telling how one fits in the world. Clinicians can use the natural inclination to tell tales to help Native youths better understand how they fit in the world and in their community. They can help Native youths reconstruct stories to picture themselves better able to handle the gifts and challenges of life.

This chapter presents clear examples for practitioners to apply in practice and provides encouragement to be creative in developing storytelling techniques in working with Native clients. Native and non-Native practitioners need not be master storytellers to engage their clients; however, they must not limit themselves to just a cognitive approach when listening, watching, doing, and telling are also important healing skills.

A traditional way to close is with a story, and this story is still alive. This story was told by an older Native man living in an urban community in an eastern state. He told of his father who took him past the buildings, past the city, past the woods, and beyond the lake and guided him to a rock. The rock held the story of a young boy on a hunt. The first picture was of a youth traveling in his canoe; in the second picture, the youth saw a deer; in the third picture, the youth shot the deer; in the fourth picture, he hauled the deer into his canoe; and in the last picture, he returned in his canoe. This Native man said that each generation of males in his family, father to son, had been brought to that place beyond the city's sounds but still within the city limits, toward the lake, and guided to that rock. He knew that each pair of parent and offspring had experienced the wonders of that trip, and he had also brought his son. The young hunter in the story is important; but more important is the connection between each father and son pair. They have a story that connects them, and they are grounded in their history. They use the story as a way of telling one another the meaning of life and that there is a way to produce more laughter than sorrow and more hope than despair. Stories hold so much for Native youths. Stories continue to heal even when the teller is no longer telling the story and the story remains alone on a rock to be seen by a father and his son.

References

BigFoot, D. S. (2003). *Medicine wheel* [PowerPoint presentation]. Unpublished document.

Bonner, B. L. (1999, June). *Definitions, incidence, and indicators of child abuse and neglect, treatment of children with sexual behavior problems, and abuse-focused therapy* [PowerPoint presentation]. Unpublished document.

Bonner, B. L. (2000, March). *Cognitive behavioral techniques for children with sexual behavior problems: Two approaches to group therapy for children with sexual behavior problems*. Paper presented at the meeting of the American Professional Society on the Abuse of Children, Somerset, NJ.

Bonner, B. L., Walker, C. E., & Berliner, L. (1999). *Children with sexual behavior problems: Assessment and treatment* (Final Report, Grant No. 90-CA-1469). Washington DC: U.S. Department of Health and Human Services, Administration of Children, Youth, and Families. Available at http://ccan.ouhsc.edu/csbp%20cognitive-behaviorial%20child.pdf

Caruso, K. R. (1990). *Projective story telling cards*. Redding, CA: Northwest Psychological Publishers, Inc.

Costantino, G., Malgady, R. G., & Rogler, L. H. (1986). Cuento therapy: A culturally sensitive modality for Puerto Rican children. *Journal of Consulting and Clinical Psychology, 54,* 639–645.

Frankenstein, E., & Brady, L. (Producers). (1996). *Carved from the heart* [Video]. (Available from Newday Films, 190 Route 17M, P.O. Box 1084, Harriman, NY 10926; http://www.newday.com)

Friedan, B. (1963). *The feminine mystique* (2nd ed.). New York: Dell.

Hyde, G. E. (1968). *Life of George Bent.* Norman, OK: University of Oklahoma Press.

Leviton, B., Schacht, A., & Quamahongnewa, B. (1994). *Talking cousins* (2nd ed.). Second Mesa, AZ: Hopi Child Sexual Abuse Project.

Malgady, R. G., Rogler, L. H., & Costantino, G. (1990). Hero/heroine modeling for Puerto Rican adolescents: A preventive mental health intervention. *Journal of Consulting and Clinical Psychology, 58,* 469–474.

Navajo New Mexico Coalition of Sexual Assault Programs. (1993). *Child abuse prevention manual: Information and activities.* Albuquerque, NM: Author.

Nixon, S. J., Phillips, M., & Tivis, R. (2000). Characteristics of American Indian clients seeking inpatient treatment for substance abuse. *Journal of Studies on Alcohol, 61,* 541–547.

Schneider, M., & Robin, A. (n.d.). *Turtle technique.* Unpublished manuscript, Point Woods Laboratory School, Stony Brook, NY.

Trautman, R. P., Phillips, M. E., Hallford, G., Borrell, G. K., & Nixon, S. J. (2000). An overview of women seeking substance abuse treatment in Oklahoma. *Journal of the Oklahoma State Medical Association, 93,* 437–443.

Tawa M. Witko

A Framework for Working With American Indian Parents

8

any Indian people, as a result of factors such as internalized oppression and multigenerational trauma, have lost the cultural parenting that once dominated Native society. Prior to the cultural genocide that followed the "discovery" of North America, Indian children were valued and cherished; women were considered sacred and honored; and men cared for and provided for their families and tribes. This all changed after colonization, and Indian people have been struggling to resolidify what was once strong. In this chapter, I examine ways mental health practitioners can help parents regain the cultural parenting that was lost as a result of cultural trauma, incorporate traditional American Indian parenting with mainstream parenting techniques, and explore how family therapy and community responsibility can heal the wounds of the past.

Traditional Family Systems

Strong family ties are important in American Indian culture and must be maintained across the different family systems within the diverse community of tribes and nations.

FAMILY TYPES

The traditional American Indian family system incorporated spirituality, culture, and a connection to the tribe or nation (Stauss, 1995).
Most Indian people would state that "the most important source of
connection and intrinsic worth is the family" (Garrett & Garrett, 1994,
p. 137). Families make up the essence of Indian nations and therefore
must be kept strong. Research has indicated that there are at least three
types of American Indian families, all of which retain American Indian
core values as a constant (Herring, 1989). In this chapter, I introduce
another group that has not been addressed in most literature, which
is the urban Indian family. Understanding how families fall into these
categories helps in the development of culturally appropriate treatment
plans because not all Indian families require a traditional approach to
treatment in the beginning.

The Traditional Family

This family adheres to the culturally defined styles of the tribe or nation.
They are less likely to come to a counselor for help. They generally
turn to a traditional healer for services. These families tend not to
relate well to mainstream service professionals and generally ignore
mainstream methodologies.

The Nontraditional Bicultural Family

These families have adopted many non-Indian styles of living. They
are more likely to see a counselor for help. They have accepted contemporary or mainstream forms of treatment and tend to relate better to
mainstream service professionals.

The Pan-Traditional Family

These families struggle to redefine and reconfirm traditional styles that
have been lost. This group does not use contemporary or mainstream
treatment. They reject these mainstream forms of treatment and the
service professionals who administer them. Their goal is to recapture
the traditional cultural heritage, and they look to that system for solutions to any problems within the family.

The Urban Family

These families struggle with adhering to the cultural norms of their
tribes or nations while trying to function in mainstream city life. They

are often at a loss as to where to seek treatment and, depending on how long they have been in the city, either look for an urban Indian center for help or seek help from other ethnic minority treatment centers. These families appear to be in constant struggle to define their Indianness as they try to hold on to what they feel has been lost. These families may exhibit some of the characteristics of the previous three groups, with the added pressure of trying to define themselves in a world that has ignored them.

FAMILY ROLES

The roles within the American Indian family often differ from the roles within families in mainstream society, and without taking this into consideration, therapists might actually do more harm to the family than good. Elders are honored and respected for the wisdom they have obtained and play a vital role in the community. In many Indian communities, the primary role of the grandparents is to rear the children, and the primary role of the parents is to provide economic support. In urban environments, the pressure underlying these roles can be amplified as a result of economic necessity (the need for both mother and father to be working), and the result is a lack of suitable role models for the children. The child is seen as a gift, someone very special who all members of the family should take part in raising. In addition, the American Indian family functions on a multigenerational support system that relies on everyone to provide continuity for all. This continuity allows the cultural transmission between generations to take place (Garrett & Garrett, 1994). Although this continuity is difficult for Indian families living in urban areas, they still try to maintain a lifestyle that honors children, family, community, and the earth (Champagne, Goldberg-Ambrose, Machamer, Philips, & Evans, 1996).

In urban communities where actual kin may be far away, *fictive kin* emerge. Fictive kin are individuals from other tribes or nations who become another mom and dad or grandmother and grandfather to the children and family (Kawamoto & Cheshire, 1997). These fictive kin help provide support for the family in many ways (economic, social, and emotional). This is especially important for families who have only one parent. In addition, the traditional roles of boys and girls, although similar to those roles in European society, tend to focus more on the balance of masculine and feminine aspects of self versus what boys do and girls do (Kawamoto & Cheshire, 1997).

DISCIPLINE

Although there is great heterogeneity among tribes in the United States, there are some common beliefs about discipline as well. In many traditional American Indian tribes, parents did not use harsh discipline when teaching their children. Although there are tribes who used such concepts as "whip men," most believed that harsh discipline should be avoided. Even in those tribes in which children were spanked, it was done as a last resort and in a nonabusive way. Generally speaking, it was believed that noninterference was the best way to correct behavior. This noninterference was done through shunning, ignoring, or removing children from their surroundings (BigFoot, 1989). This is very similar to what is now called "time out." Children in American Indian communities were valued and respected and were often disciplined gently (McDade, 1995). It was believed that correct behavior could be achieved if the child was first ignored, and if that did not work, the child was removed from the situation (BigFoot, 1989). In addition, it was believed by many tribes that children learned best through the observation of others. They were encouraged not to ask a lot of questions but to pay attention to what their parents and elders were doing, and in so doing, children learned respect and appropriate behavior.

Past Cultural Trauma

As stated in the introduction to this volume, the past cultural trauma experienced by Indian nations has had tremendous impact on the way Indians live today. The effects of boarding schools and urban migration in particular have had specific impacts on how children are raised.

Some of the residual effects of the boarding schools on parenting have been that "the American Indian parent was left unsure of generational boundaries, behavioral expectations, and limits" (Morissette, 1994, p. 386). These same people who were taught to be ashamed of their culture are now struggling with a sense of inferiority, which affects how they parent their children (Morissette, 1994). The children of these parents are reacting the same way their parents did before them as they repeat the "generational experience of discrimination, unemployment, poverty, anger, depression, and alcoholism" (Berlin, 1987, p. 301). American Indians have experienced such shame and guilt associated with the boarding schools that their feelings have prevented them from sharing these events with their children. It is important to realize that this experience, not the incompetence of the parents, has been a block to effective parenting. For these parents to be effective, the past trauma needs to be linked with the current parental difficulties (Morissette, 1994). If parents can begin to deal with their experience and share this with their children, everyone can be helped and the healing can begin.

Urban migration left parents without the kinship bonds and culture that they once had. Parents were forced to raise their families in unaccustomed ways. They no longer had their aunties and grandparents around to help them rear their children in a traditional way and were forced to turn to others. As was mentioned previously, this resulted in the formation of fictive kin, which enabled Indian parents to have some support, but this support was not tribe specific. Overall, although more opportunities may have become available to Indian families through schools and employment, other tribe-specific opportunities (ceremonies, rites of passage, etc.) were lost. However, there is great resiliency among urban Indian families. In many cases, families get together to bring out a medicine man or healer, although the connections Indian people make with their relatives are no longer tied along blood lines. Urban Indian families are finding the support they need from the community in many different ways.

Current Treatment Issues

There are two issues of particular concern for the mental and physical health of American Indians. These are the effects of acculturation and assimilation on Indian's self-image and urban health problems, particularly lack of access to health facilities and alcohol and drug use.

ACCULTURATION ISSUES

According to Arthur S. Reber's (1985) *Dictionary of Psychology*, acculturation means "the gradual acquisition of the behavior patterns of the surrounding culture, in particular the subculture within which you are raised *or* the adoption of cultural elements from another culture" (p. 5). *Assimilation*, by Reber's definition, means "to take in, absorb, or incorporate as one's own" (p. 56). These two concepts are important to understand because of the implications they have for American Indian people. The attempts by the boarding schools and missionaries to assimilate the American Indian people into mainstream culture led to a dismantling of the Indian way of life. This dismantling has had a detrimental effect on parenting and the well-being of American Indian people (MacPhee, Fritz, & Miller-Heyl, 1996). Parents struggle with their own sense of ethnic identity, and their children are left to wonder about their own sense of self as well. This identity conflict is particularly disruptive during adolescence and becomes a serious problem as adolescents try to define themselves in a world that does not truly accept their cultural beliefs (Flynn, Clark, Aragon, Stanzell, & Evans, in press). As stated in the introduction to this volume, understanding acculturation and assimilation is a major key to working with Indian parents.

URBAN INDIAN HEALTH CONCERNS

On the reservation, Indians have access to facilities sponsored by Indian Health Services; however, urban Indians do not have this access. There are few centers that serve the physical and mental health needs of urban Indian populations, and it appears that many non-Indian providers seem to be reluctant to serve this particular population, possibly out of fear that they may not be paid for their services (Champagne et al., 1996). The needs of urban American Indian women are also not being met. They are in need of prenatal, maternal, and child-care services as well as adequate parenting programs that are sensitive to the specific needs of the Indian population (Champagne et al., 1996). In addition, families suffer as a result of lack of educational services, employment opportunities, and family and social support systems. Many families feel uprooted, having left their family and friends on the reservation, and tend not to be comfortable living in the city (Flynn et al., in press). These issues affect the family in a negative way, and as a consequence, family members are at greater risk for mental health problems, including but not limited to alcoholism, substance abuse, suicide, and various stress-related disorders (Flynn et al., in press). There simply are not enough resources available to the urban Indian population, particularly culturally appropriate programs and services.

A modest amount of research is available on the drug and alcohol patterns of American Indian youths, and this research indicates that this population tends to use alcohol, tobacco, and drugs more frequently and at earlier ages than other ethnic minority groups (Champagne et al., 1996; for a more in-depth discussion on this topic, see Clark, chap. 4, this volume). Although there are a few centers and programs within the American Indian community that have been developed to deal with such issues, many have been shut down, which leaves a void in the care of these youths. In addition to the issues surrounding drugs, alcohol, and tobacco, American Indian youths are also in tremendous need of culturally appropriate day care and educational facilities (Champagne et al., 1996). Moreover, the stress and mental health problems related to parenting can lead to more violence in the community, which may manifest itself in child physical and sexual abuse, child neglect, domestic violence, assault, homicide, and suicide (Flynn et al., in press). Overall, the needs of the urban Indian have been weakly addressed in social and mental health facilities, an oversight that must be resolved if the urban Indian community is to thrive.

Current Treatment Modalities

Although there are no specific books that blend American Indian culture and heritage with parenting, a few programs have attempted to do so, and I look briefly at three programs that have been effective. In addition to culturally competent parenting programs, effective work with Indian families involves the use of family therapy, couples therapy, and community responsibility.

POSITIVE INDIAN PARENTING

Positive Indian Parenting was a collaborative effort on the part of the National Indian Child Welfare Association, mental health providers, and traditional healers (National Indian Child Welfare Association, 1996). It is considered the model for American Indian parent training. It involves an eight-session program that incorporates lectures, group discussions, and homework assignments. The eight sessions are Traditional Parenting, Lessons of the Storyteller, Lessons of the Cradleboard, Harmony in Child Rearing, Traditional Behavior Management, Lessons of Mother Nature, Praise in Traditional Parenting, and Choices in Child Rearing.

The first three sessions of this program involve traditional Indian techniques. In the first session, parents learn about the heritage of Indian culture as it pertains to parenting as well as to recognize how they learned to parent, to understand how some of the old ways of parenting have been lost, and to begin to make choices about the kind of parents they want to be. In the second session, parents learn to understand the importance storytelling had in traditional child rearing, to appreciate how stories can be used to develop good judgment in children, and to recognize the importance of good communication with their children. In the third session, parents learn to recognize traditional nurturing techniques, to understand how important nurturing is, to understand how traditional nurturing helped children develop, and to understand that development is tied to the child's readiness. In each of the sessions, a historical overview is given, and a group discussion follows. Parents are then split into groups in which they are able to participate in exercises based on the theme of the session. Each of the sessions ends with a brief social time.

The fourth and fifth sessions deal with harmony in child rearing and traditional behavior management. The fourth session helps parents recognize some of the different historical beliefs and concepts about harmony and balance within a family and how these beliefs and concepts were used to prevent parenting problems before they started. The fifth session helps parents to recognize some of the historical ways for managing children's behavior, to understand that discipline is a way of teaching self-control, and to recognize that providing limits and consequences will help the child learn respect and kindness for others.

The final three sessions look at how to prepare children for life, how praise should be used, and the type of parenting style one chooses. The sixth session helps parents to understand how examples from nature were used in traditional Indian culture to teach children life skills and to recognize how important the parent's role is in teaching children life skills. The seventh session helps parents learn to recognize ways in which praise can be used in parenting techniques, to understand how praise was used traditionally, and to apply praise in their parenting style. The eighth session deals with the choices Indian parents face. This session helps parents learn about some of the issues and challenges that Indian children must face and how positive Indian parenting can help children manage and overcome these challenges.

This program is effective in its effort to combine traditional Indian parenting with modern parenting techniques. This program is used in most Indian agencies and by parent-training professionals in the Indian community.

PARENT TRAINING FOR AMERICAN INDIAN FAMILIES

Dolores BigFoot (1989) developed the Parent Training for American Indian Families program specifically for American Indian parents. This program incorporates many of the principles outlined previously and is a good example of how culture can be incorporated into parent training.

The Parent Training for American Indian Families program consists of six sessions that address three traditional child-rearing practices in contemporary terms. The three concepts include honoring children, the traditional talking circle, and storytelling. Each session involves the use of a video, role-playing, and homework assignments. Parents are instructed on the traditional use of each concept and how they can still be applicable today. After each session ends, there is a brief social gathering at which participants can talk and ask the instructor any questions they might have.

The first three sessions involve honoring children with words and actions. Traditionally, "Indian parents knew they could encourage behavior by acknowledging those traits that would be helpful as the child grew into adulthood" (BigFoot, 1989, p. 53). The focus was on letting the child know that he or she was respected and that his or her positive behavior was appreciated. The first session of this program addresses the concept of praising good behavior. Time is spent on addressing what praising good behavior means. The benefits of praising behavior are explored, and then the parents are able to role-play praising statements with the other parents and facilitators. Homework is assigned that has the parents practice what they learned in class with their own children. The second session continues the concept of honoring children with words and actions but addresses the use of praising alternate behaviors. Parents are once again given a definition for what praising alternate behavior means, and time is spent understanding the concept. The third session begins with honoring children with discipline and introduces the concepts of ignoring and removal. The definitions of *ignoring* and *removal* are given, and role-playing exercises are done to allow the parents to practice ignoring annoying behavior and removing children for more serious problems.

The fourth session introduces the concept of the talking circle for family unity and the use of the family council. Traditionally, the family council served as a way to honor parents, relatives, and children. Each person had a voice, and each person was respected. It was seen as a means by which "one could safely approach others for talking, listening, learning, sharing, crying, and healing" (BigFoot, 1989, p. 89). In this session, parents are given the definition of the *family council* as "a gathering to bring families together to learn, discuss, and problem-solve in a democratic way that helps each member of the family" (BigFoot, 1989, p. 93). Reasons are given for why the family council should be used, and a format is introduced that helps parents establish and maintain an ongoing council. Role-playing allows the parents to practice the concept of the family council before they initiate it at home. The homework for the week involves approaching family members and beginning the process of establishing a family council.

The last two sessions introduce the concept of storytelling. Storytelling, as it related to parents, traditionally provided a time when "parents and children could be together, a time for parents to fill in the past with history for children, and a time for learning, listening, interacting, and sharing one with the other" (BigFoot, 1989, pp. 104–105). Storytelling is an integral part of the American Indian experience. The fifth session of this program deals with developing a family history story. The format for developing a family history story is introduced, and parents are asked to develop a story based on their family using an event that they are familiar with. The homework for this week involves developing at least one story that will be shared with their child or at the family council meeting. The final session continues the use of storytelling. This time the story is child-centered. The purpose of this is to encourage the interaction between parents and children, to increase listening skills and attention span in the children, and to remember special events that happened within the family. A positive story about a child is also a way to increase the self-esteem of the child. Parents again engage in role-playing, and they are given their final homework assignment, which involves developing at least two stories about their child. At the conclusion of this session, a potluck meal takes place, and certificates are handed out to the parents.

This program is useful because it incorporates traditional Indian parenting with mainstream parent-training techniques. This program is very effective with Indian families.

HONORING THE CHILD

Honoring the Child: An Urban Indian Parenting Program is designed to incorporate some of the mainstream parenting programs along with traditional American Indian parenting (Witko, 1999). The eight-session program involves understanding principles of mainstream parenting programs such as parenting styles, effective discipline, and active listening skills. In addition, the importance of storytelling and talking circles is explored; appropriate role models are examined; and parents are taught how to address issues of racism, discrimination, drugs and alcohol, and violence with their children. The program involves defining the main concepts, exploring the historical impact of the issues, and examining ways to resolve the issues from a traditional parenting approach. Each session first explores traditional and current approaches, and then discussions ensue on the combination of both. Parents are asked to role-play various situations, and homework that allows them to practice and implement what they have learned is assigned at the end of each session. In addition, a summary that highlights the key points outlined in the session is given to each parent.

Honoring the Child spends the first three sessions focusing on mainstream parenting strategies such as active listening, positive discipline, understanding parenting styles, and purposes for child misbehavior. This is done through interactive exercises and homework that is aimed at challenging parents' current perceptions about child rearing and the effectiveness of their current parenting tools.

The next three sessions focus on more traditional Indian parenting strategies such as talking circles, storytelling, and the development of a positive Indian identity. Because many urban parents do not have access to their families, reservations, or tribal society, they lack the cultural knowledge to pass on to their children. Many of these parents do not know their language, songs, or ceremonies, and these exercises challenge parents to explore these areas of themselves through interactive exercises such as development of family stories, initiating talking circles, and exploring issues of racism as it pertains to ethnic identity.

The final two sessions explore the impact of violence, drugs, and alcohol within the community as well as help parents to develop daily strategies for increasing a sense of positive Indianness in their children and themselves. Parents go over videos and review brochures related to these very serious issues. Parents are then asked to sit with their children and go over what they have learned. During the final session, they are given resource materials that show them ways to involve their Native culture in everyday activities and are encouraged to begin participating in local Native events and activities.

Reactions to this program have been positive. Many parents have stated that this was the first time they had a chance to explore their own Indianness, and most say they will continue to explore this with their children. This program has been effective with urban parents because it incorporates traditional Indian parenting techniques while still addressing the impact of living in an urban environment.

Table 8.1 provides a summary of these three parenting programs for American Indian families. However, parenting classes are only the first step in renewing the urban Indian family system. Family therapy, couples therapy, and community responsibility also play and important role.

FAMILY THERAPY

Family therapy with Indian families needs to incorporate mainstream family therapy techniques while embracing the collective history of the people. It is important to determine where a family fits in relation to acculturation, the boarding schools, and reservation life. These factors play a role in how one works with the family.

As explored in the introduction to this volume, it is important for a therapist to determine the levels of acculturation and assimilation of each urban Indian family at the beginning of the therapist's work. One can ascertain where a family "fits" by expanding on the general questions one asks when beginning the therapy process. These questions could include the following: Did your family always live in the cities or was there a time when they lived on a reservation? Does your family practice any of the traditions of your tribe? Does your family attend cultural activities? Does your family maintain ties with family members on the reservation? These kinds of questions can help the

TABLE 8.1

Summary of Parenting Programs for American Indian Families

Session	Positive Indian Parenting	Parent Training for American Indian Families	Honoring the Child
		Program	
1	Explores the heritage of American Indian culture, how Indian parents learned their roles, and how these roles were lost over time	Explores the importance of praising good behavior	Explores understanding self through identifying parenting styles and why children misbehave
2	Explores the importance of storytelling, the use of storytelling to teach good judgment, and the importance of good communication with American Indian children	Explores the importance of praising alternate behaviors	Explores understanding the use of praise as a way to change behavior and active listening
3	Explores nurturing and its importance in child development; explores developmental readiness	Explores the use of discipline to change behaviors; introduces the concepts of ignoring and removal	Explores the use of encouragement to change behavior and the use of I messages
4	Explores different historical beliefs about harmony and balance and how they played a role in parenting	Explores traditional themes such as talking circles and family councils	Explores the use of storytelling as a way to communicate with children and teach positive behaviors
5	Explores historical ways of managing children's behavior through discipline and limit setting	Explores the importance of storytelling; helps families begin to develop their family stories	Explores the use of discipline to change behaviors; introduces concepts of time-out, talking circles, and family councils
6	Explores how nature teaches us lessons about life	Explores the importance of storytelling with stories that are child-centered	Explores developing a positive Indian identity; discusses and confronts issues of stereotypes, racism, and discrimination
7	Explores the importance of praise and its use in good parenting		Explores issues of violence and alcohol and drug use within urban settings; explores concepts of social learning and modeling as ways to change behavior
8	Explores issues and challenges Indian children face and how to overcome them		Explores ways in which parents can incorporate their newly learned skills and their culture into daily activities

FIGURE 8.1

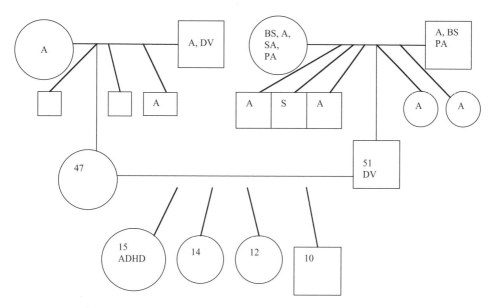

Genogram for a mixed-race couple with a Native father and a non-Native mother. The squares represent men and boys, the circles women and girls, ages if known are listed as numbers, and any significant diagnoses are listed on the inside of each shape. A blank shape indicates the data are unknown or not significant. Lines represent family relationships. A = alcoholism; BS = boarding school; DV = domestic violence; PA = physical abuse; SA = sexual abuse; and S = suicide; ADHD = attention deficit/hyperactivity disorder.

clinician ascertain what family type he or she is dealing with and work within that framework. This line of questioning can also help the clinician address any problems the couple may be having related to their cultural heritage and its role in parenting.

Family therapy techniques such as creating genograms have proven to be very useful in helping parents understand the impact of history on their current behavior. In addition, genograms help parents address behavior patterns that have a detrimental impact on their ability to parent effectively. Figure 8.1 shows a couple with four children. The parents presented their oldest daughter for treatment because of her aggressive behavior. The father was Native American from a reservation in South Dakota, and the mother was non-Native. The father was exposed to violence through alcoholism, boarding school violence, and domestic violence by his parents. The father had been violent with the mother and had become easily frustrated with his daughter who had been acting out. Through the use of the genogram, both parents were able to understand the origin of some of the patterns of violence and could then work toward making changes in how they parented their children. For the father, the visual display of his parents and their experiences in boarding schools allowed him to come closer to his cultural heritage and begin to see some of the same patterns in himself.

Inclusion of case managers and advocates can also be an important tool in working with Indian families. Case managers and advocates are able to help families access services that enable them to participate in treatment. Case managers work with families on issues related to transportation, food, and shelter as well as help them receive services outside the typical therapeutic process.

Practitioners working with Indian families will be required to go outside the realm of general psychological practice and meet families where they are. It is important to acknowledge the cultural heritage of the families one works with; to get a thorough history, in particular boarding school and urban migration history; and to make sure that the therapeutic process is in no way harming the family.

Assessing the family's acculturation and assimilation level, making the therapeutic process more easily accessible, and helping parents access services available to them are all important. The family's status in regard to these areas will determine the type of treatment that will be most beneficial to them.

COUPLES THERAPY

Couples therapy can be effective in helping parents understand their cultural expectations and thereby assist in rectifying parental difficulties in child rearing. This is an area that should be explored when working with Indian families and their children.

When working with Native families, one must take into consideration whether the couple is interracial—many urban Indian men and women are marrying non-Indians, and these interracial couples are raising families. This has tremendous impact on the type of treatment that will be effective.

The little research available in this area indicates that often when Indian people marry non-Indians they marry either White or Black partners, quite possibly because of their shared colonial history (Spickard, 1989). In addition, it has been estimated that by 1990, close to 70% of all American Indians were married to someone of a different race (Rinaldo, 1996). This is an interesting dynamic that must be addressed in treatment and program development.

In interracial marriages in which Native people marry non-Indians, a couple of interesting dynamics can emerge. One dynamic surfaces when Indians marry partners who are also ethnic minorities, and the Native culture is seen as the secondary culture in the family. This may indicate that the family is not acknowledging the impact Native culture has on their relationships and parenting struggles. Another dynamic emerges when the Indian marries a partner who is of European descent. When this happens, the Native culture is generally not acknowledged, and the children often are raised without the understanding of their cultural heritage. In the genogram in Figure 8.1, the couple did not realize the impact that the husband's culture had on their parenting difficulties. As a result of the past cultural trauma experienced by the husband's parents, he was not parented in the traditional ways of his culture and therefore did not himself have the appropriate parenting techniques. Through many sessions, this couple addressed issues surrounding their backgrounds and worked on ways to resolve their conflicts so that they were able to parent their children more effectively.

To understand this better, it may be helpful to use the concept of marital contracts. Each member of a couple may have different expectations from a partner on the basis of his or her cultural background. These expectations can lead to conflicts if the partners are not aware of the differences and are not able to communicate effectively with each other. Conflicts between partners can also lead to parenting difficulties. In addition, there may be problems that arise because the Native parent's concepts of parenting may be quite different from the non-Indian parent's concepts about parenting.

COMMUNITY RESPONSIBILITY

Community responsibility has to do with engaging others in the care-taking of the child. Traditional Indian families used the community as a resource for child rearing through the reliance on blood relatives and nonblood relatives (those adopted as members of the family through traditional ceremonies) who often supported parents in many different ways. However, urban Indian families struggle with this as it becomes increasingly difficult to identify other Indian people for support. This, of course, parallels overall societal trends in which the support of extended families is disappearing and parents are forced to rely on nonfamily for support, often at high financial costs. This trend, however, is further complicated when Native culture is added to the mix. Therapists must be aware of the Indian programs in their area and feel comfortable referring to or consulting with them as needed. Indian families need to have other families to turn to so that they can achieve positive mental health functioning.

Conclusion

With the large percentage of American Indians living in urban areas, every therapist or counselor needs to understand the intricacies of working with American Indian children and their families. Many Indian people may not indicate they are Native, but the stressors associated with being Indian still affect them, and a thorough history is necessary for effective treatment. It is also important for Native Americans not to deny the effects of their culture on the relationships they have with their significant other as well as their children. This is especially important with interracial couples in which the Native culture may not be the dominant culture in the home. In such a family, the Indian spouse may not realize that some of the conflict in the home may be related to some of the multigenerational trauma of his or her ancestors (acculturation, boarding schools, and urban migration).

References

Berlin, I. N. (1987). Effects of changing Native American cultures on child development. *Journal of Community Psychology, 15*, 299–306.

BigFoot, D. S. (1989). *Parent training for American Indian families.* Unpublished doctoral dissertation, University of Oklahoma, Norman.

Champagne, D., Goldberg-Ambrose, J. D., Machamer, A., Philips, B., & Evans, T. (1996). *Service delivery for Native American children in Los Angeles County, 1996.* Los Angeles: Drew Foundation.

Flynn, K., Clark, R., Aragon, M., Stanzell, S., & Evans, T. (in press). *The mental health status of at risk American Indian and Alaska Native youth in Los Angeles County, 1998.* Los Angeles: United American Indian Involvement.

Garrett, J. T., & Garrett, M. W. (1994). The path of good medicine: Understanding and counseling Native American Indians. *Journal of Multicultural Counseling and Development, 22,* 134–144.

Herring, R. D. (1989). The American Indian family: Dissolution by coercion. *Journal of Multicultural Counseling and Development, 17,* 4–13.

Kawamoto, W., & Cheshire, T. (1997). American Indian families. In M. K. DeGenova (Ed.), *Families in cultural context: Strengths and challenges in diversity* (pp. 15–34). New York: McGraw-Hill.

MacPhee, D., Fritz, J., & Miller-Heyl, J. (1996). Ethnic variations in personal social networks and parenting. *Child Development, 67,* 3278–3295.

McDade, K. (1995). How we parent: Race and ethnic differences. In C. K. Jacobsen (Ed.), *American families: Issues in race and ethnicity* (pp. 283–300). New York: Garland Publishing.

Morrissette, P. J. (1994). The holocaust of First Nation People: Residual effects on parenting and treatment implications. *Contemporary Family Therapy, 16,* 381–392.

National Indian Child Welfare Association. (1996). *Positive Indian parenting: Honoring our children by honoring our traditions.* Portland, OR: Author.

Reber, A. (1985). *Dictionary of psychology.* New York: Penguin Books.

Rinaldo, P. M. (1996). *Marrying the Natives: Love and interracial marriage.* New York: DorPete Press.

Spickard, P. (1989). *Mixed blood: Intermarriage and ethnic identity in twentieth century America.* Madison: University of Wisconsin Press.

Stauss, J. H. (1995). Reframing and refocusing American Indian family strengths. In C. K. Jacobsen (Ed.), *American families: Issues in race and ethnicity* (pp. 105–118). New York: Garland.

Witko, T. (1999). *Honoring the child: An urban Indian parenting program.* Unpublished doctoral dissertation, California School of Professional Psychology, Los Angeles.

Rose L. Clark and Tawa M. Witko

Growing Up Indian: Treatment With Urban Indian Adolescents

9

A merican Indian youths experience a variety of conditions related to mental health functioning. These include alcohol and drug abuse, depression, anxiety, suicide, and dual axis diagnosis (Flynn, Clark, Aragon, Stanzell, & Evans-Campbell, 1998). This is compounded when one adds the pressures of growing up in an urban environment in which the struggle to define oneself as an Indian person is difficult, especially if one is of mixed heritage. In large part, it appears that many of these issues stem from greater social, economic, and sociocultural problems within the community, including the intergenerational trauma that impacts all Native people.

Multigenerational Trauma

For Indian nations, the arrival of Columbus brought with it the destruction of the Indian way of life. The functioning of the family was slowly dismantled as parents were forced to attend schools that taught them to be ashamed of their Indianness as well as showed them that violence was the appropriate way to change behavior. Indian parents were not taught the traditional ways to be a parent, and in turn, their children were not taught that being Indian was something to be proud of (Morrissette, 1994). For Indian children being raised in urban areas, this is especially damaging because there are fewer Indian models to connect with, and the children lack the coming-of-age process that was once the norm.

In traditional American Indian tribes, young male and female youths entered adulthood at a very specific time and place, with initiation rituals clearly delineating the transition. These rituals helped the child transition into adulthood and become an active member in the tribe. These rituals also connected children and adolescents with their cultural heritage and helped them define their reality as Indian people, thus allowing them to feel a sense of pride in their ancestry as well as to develop a positive sense of self as an individual.

In today's urban reality, however, such rituals have for the most part fallen by the wayside. The lack of a meaningful rite of passage contributes significantly to various acting-out behaviors, including adolescent substance abuse and involvement in gangs (Nighthorse-Campbell, 2000; Sanchez-Way & Johnson, 2000). Teenagers are left to observe that Indian adults are also struggling with their own ethnic identity issues and that they are embittered by internalized oppression. As a consequence, teenagers often experience tremendous confusion and find it difficult if not impossible to achieve positive self-acceptance of their identities as American Indian people (Witko, 2002). There is little sense of pride or tribal tradition, reflecting the cumulative impact of forced acculturation in the hostile urban environment.

In addition, urban Indian youths are faced with the many struggles that emerge from living in an urban environment. Violence abounds, drugs and gangs dominate many urban neighborhoods, and many Indian youths feel they must go along with others in the neighborhood to survive. It is not uncommon for the ethnic identification of an urban Indian youth to be unclear because he or she may speak slang or Ebonics. Urban youths may even dress as many gang members do and deny their Indian ancestry, especially if they are of mixed blood. All of these factors hinder appropriate treatment as these youths struggle to find a place in the world that accepts their Indian heritage while maintaining a connection to the city.

Impact of Trauma on Indian Youths

For Indian youths, the impact of the cultural trauma of their parents affects them in many ways, especially with their sense of identity.

Adolescents in general struggle with a sense of who they are. It is a time not necessarily of storm and stress but of a readjusting and reawakening of the spirit within. Who they are to become begins to express itself during this time. This is particularly hard for Indian youths because they lack the cultural foundation to keep them strong in the face of the struggles that present themselves (Sanchez-Way & Johnson, 2000). The statistics related to alcohol and substance abuse, child abuse, and education in this population are alarming (Bechtold, 1994; Champagne, Goldberg-Ambrose, Machamer, Phillips, & Evans, 1996; DeBruyn, Chino, Serna, & Fullerton-Gleason, 2001; Geffner, Jaffee, & Sudermann, 2000). In addition, the consequences of being of mixed heritage appear to be especially relevant during this time in children's lives as they struggle to define themselves in a community in which they feel that they are the only ones of their background.

YOUTH ALCOHOL- AND SUBSTANCE-ABUSE-RELATED PROBLEMS

Disturbing statistics have been surfacing over the years from research studies regarding substance abuse problems among American Indian youths (Beauvais, Oetting, & Edwards, 1989; Edwards & Egbert-Edwards, 1990). Recent evidence shows that problem drinking is prevalent among adolescents and even younger Indian children. Beauvais, Oetting, and Edwards (1985), in research with over 1,400 American Indian youths, have shown that 82% of Indian adolescents report having used alcohol at least once compared with 66% of non-Indian youths sampled at the same time. In addition, 50% of the Indian adolescents reported that they had used alcohol in the recent past compared with 27% of the non-Indian population. Much of the alcohol use by these adolescents appeared to be heavy, with incidents of blackouts and extremely drunk behavior being reported. These authors also reported on a 1982 study with young American Indian children between the ages of 9 and 12. Over 33% of these Indian children, representing seven different reservations, indicated they had used alcohol. Although reports of usage were light, this early experimentation with alcohol is a definite concern.

Indeed, Beauvais et al. (1989) reported that by the 12th grade, lifetime prevalence of alcohol use is almost universal among American Indians: 96% for males and 92% for females. Compared with non-Indian youths, American Indian youths have higher rates of alcohol and substance abuse; tend to use alcohol earlier, more often, and in higher quantities; and have more negative consequences when drinking (Beauvais et al., 1985). In addition, the rate of deaths resulting from alcoholism for Indian youths ages 17 through 24 is greater than the national rate. The National Household Survey on Drug Abuse, conducted by the Substance Abuse Mental Health Services Administration, U.S. Department of Health and Human Services, compiled data on the prevalence of substance use among racial and ethnic groups in the United States from 1991 to 1993. The survey found that American Indians ages 12 and older had the highest percentage of illicit drug use in the prior year compared with other ethnic minorities (Substance Abuse and Mental Health Services Administration, 1993).

The U.S. Bureau of Indian Affairs Youth Risk Factor Survey, which was conducted in 1997, surveyed 5,606 American Indian 9th to 12th graders (U.S. Bureau of Indian Affairs, 1997). Of those surveyed, 54% reported drinking alcohol during the past month, 43% reported episodic heavy drinking during the past month, 52% reported using marijuana during the past month, 22% reported ever having used cocaine, 29% reported ever having sniffed or inhaled intoxicating substances; and 6% reported ever having injected illegal drugs. Out of 6,970 middle school (6th–8th grade) students, 59% reported ever having drunk alcohol, 51% reported having used marijuana, 11% having used cocaine, 29% reported having sniffed or inhaled intoxicating substances, and 3% reported having injected illegal drugs.

According to a 1985 congressional hearing on Indian juvenile alcoholism and drug abuse, 53% of urban American Indian adolescents engaged in moderate to heavy alcohol or drug use compared with 23% of their urban, non-Indian counterparts (LaFromboise, 1988). Los Angeles urban American Indian youths also suffer from alcoholism and substance abuse. A study conducted by the United American Indian Involvement of Los Angeles among Indian youths ages 8 through 18 years old found that 13.3% of the youths acknowledged drinking behavior and 8.3% admitted using drugs (Flynn et al., 1998). According to the Los Angeles County Department of Mental Health, during fiscal year 1999, of 186 children who received services, 50% had a substance-related diagnosis (Los Angeles County Department of Mental Health, 1999).

The Indian Health Service has reported that Indian youths often begin using alcohol, marijuana, and inhalants between the ages of 11 and 13 (Indian Health Service, 1997). Several surveys of Indian adults show alcohol use beginning between the ages of 11 and 15. Up to 25% of all respondents indicated a serious drinking problem by the 12th grade. The majority of all youths of most tribes report experimentation with alcohol, and heavy drinking has been called the main reason that one in two Indian students never finish high school. A 1987 Indian Health Service survey indicated that in 1985, 78% of Indian 7th to 12th graders had used alcohol compared with 57% of non-Indians in the same grades. Heavy alcohol use was reported by 2.2% of Indian students compared with 0.2% of non-Indians in 1975. Although drinking alcohol was the most frequently cited source of trouble, 56% of youths said they approved of it. From these studies, three factors have been identified by researchers as being particularly important in increasing behaviors that result in significant risk factors for Indian youths: (a) a sense of cultural dislocation or lack of integration into either traditional Indian or American life; (b) a lack of clear-cut sanctions within the Indian community against the abuse of cigarettes, smokeless tobacco, alcohol, and other drugs; and (c) a lack of strong peer group support for positive choices in lifestyles.

Epidemiological data clearly show that American Indian youths are at tremendous risk. Among the striking statistics are the following:

- The proportion of American Indian and Alaska Native individuals who die before age 25 years is 3.2 times greater than for the nation as a whole.
- The accidental death rate for Indian children ages 5 through 14 years old is twice that of the national norm.
- Homicide is the second leading cause of death among American Indians and Alaska Natives 1 through 14 years of age and the third leading cause for those 15 through 24 years of age.
- In some American Indian communities, fully 10% of children are in court-ordered foster care.
- Although American Indian and Alaska Native juveniles account for only 1.2% of all U.S. juveniles, they account for more than 60% of the youths in federal custody.

CHILD ABUSE

Numerous child welfare scholars have explored the etiology of child maltreatment across cultures, including child neglect, child physical abuse, and child sexual abuse, and have found a variety of contributing factors. Substance abuse is the most frequently associated factor contributing to child maltreatment across cultures (Berlin, 1987; DeBruyn, Lujan, & May, 1992; Gelles, 1987; Hauswald, 1987; Lujan, DeBruyn, & May, 1989; Piasecki et al., 1989). In addition, the impact of witnessing violence in the home is strongly correlated with child abuse. It also has been documented that children who come from violent homes are at greater risk for physical abuse and neglect (Geffner et al., 2000).

It has been noted that some of the long-lasting effects of children's witnessing domestic violence include posttraumatic stress disorder, anxiety, sleep disturbances, depression, and social withdrawal as well increased childhood delinquency (Geffner et al., 2000). Children who witness this type of abuse and trauma are at great risk of repeating the cycle of violence or viewing violence as an effective coping strategy.

EDUCATION

The relatively small number of American Indian students in urban settings renders them relatively invisible to school systems. American Indian students have the highest dropout rate of any racial or ethnic group (36%) as well as the lowest high school completion and college attendance rates of any minority group. Only 20% of adult male American Indians have graduated from high school. Further, even when Indian students attend college, many of them do not graduate. One study estimated that 75% of Indian college students drop out before attaining a 4-year degree (Champagne et al., 1996). These problems are particularly pronounced in Los Angeles, where Indian children are dropping out of school at over twice the rate of Indian children in other urban areas.

In addition, it is often difficult for Indian youths in urban schools to develop a sense of pride in their heritage. Although advances have been made in providing knowledge of Indian history, other areas are seriously problematic, such as the use of Indian mascots for sports teams, which can hinder positive self-image in Indian youths and reinforce negative stereotypes of Indian people (Chamberlain, 1999; Staurowsky, 1999; Witko, 2005). Although many tribes and organizations, including the Society of Indian Psychologists and the U.S. Commission on Civil Rights, have proposed resolutions advocating the retiring of Indian mascots, many schools are reluctant to change. So although Indian youths may learn about certain aspects of their heritage in schools, they must still contend with the stereotypes of their people and what those stereotypes reflect of themselves. This remains a struggle for Indian youths and an area that should be examined more fully in the literature.

BICULTURALISM

As Bechtold (1994) pointed out, coping with biculturalism poses a particular problem for American Indian youths, who are growing up as members of an extraordinarily disadvantaged minority. They find themselves growing up in urban environments dominated by other cultural groups, often minority, and are pressured to assimilate either to the norms of deviant groups (i.e., gangs) or to the mainstream (i.e., an ultimately rejecting society). These social forces make it extraordinarily challenging for youths to maintain an authentic sense of tribal identity.

Children of mixed blood often struggle with their sense of identity. This is particularly true of Indian children living in urban environments. One of the problems Indian youths face is that they do not live in areas where there are other Indian children. Indian people are dispersed within a large urban environment; it is not unusual for an Indian family to live on a block where there are no other Indian people in a 10- or 12-block radius. In fact, many Indian children grow up believing they are the only Indians left.

As adolescence approaches, these children are left with the idea that they must pick what part of themselves to claim. For Indian youths raised in environments where other Indian people are scarce, the idea of claiming one's heritage as an Indian person seems moot. For example, one 14-year-old Navajo boy raised in a large urban environment denied he was Indian to all who asked, even though he was half Navajo. His mother, who was Navajo, died when he was 2, and his father, who was of Latino descent, married another Latino and proceeded to have three more children. This young Navajo boy grew up in a house in which he was the only Indian and was often made fun of for his clear Indian features. He was not allowed contact with his maternal relatives, and therefore, knew nothing of his heritage. This changed when situations arose that forced the children out of the parental home. The American Indian unit of the Department of Children and Family Services was notified, and this child received treatment from a local urban Indian center. At that point in his life, he had had no contact with other Indian people and was ashamed of his Indian mother. Therapy with this child was difficult; he refused to go to the Indian center, stating he was not Indian. The Indian therapist who worked with this child spent more than the typical 3 to 4 sessions establishing rapport; she went to the child's home and focused therapy on issues not related to being Indian. After several months of therapy, the child began asking questions about his heritage, wondering what his maternal relatives were like, and he became curious about some of the traditions of his tribe. As he processed these issues, he began to discover the Indian within himself. This example illustrates the difficulties many urban Indians face in defining their sense of self as an Indian person. This young man struggled with knowing he was different from his siblings but not wanting to know why he was different. If the therapist had approached this child from a strictly traditional frame of reference, she might not have been successful. Yet with understanding and perseverance and the willingness to work with his issues, she was able to help him adjust to the changes in his life, and he began to establish a positive sense of self related to his Indianness.[1]

---

[1] This and other case-related anecdotes in this chapter describe some of Tawa M. Witko's former clients.

Current Treatment Modalities

The struggle to develop a sense of self in an urban environment is difficult. Indian youths struggle with many obstacles, as has been previously stated. There are few programs in urban environments that are able to address the needs of Indian people, let alone Indian adolescents. Because Indian adolescents in urban areas often attempt to blend into their environment, they are often misclassified and therefore not treated in a culturally appropriate manner (Witko, 2002). The programs that do exist are helping Indian youths achieve a positive self-image in a variety of ways, including attending youth camps and participating in group exercises, individual and family therapy, and traditional medicine.

YOUTH CAMPS

Many urban Indian programs have developed youth camps where Indian children and adolescents can begin to explore their Indianness. These camps take place in local mountain regions, and the children and adolescents are taught about indigenous wildlife and plants, horses, teepees, fishing, and ceremonies. Children are surrounded by other Indian youths who often have some of the same issues they do, and they begin to find comfort and realize that they are not alone. Children leave these camps beginning to understand the meaning of being Indian, not as the stereotype Hollywood portrays, but as it is relevant to their own lives. For example, one 12-year-old girl, after attending one of these camps, indicated that being Indian was a "cool" thing and that she now wanted to learn how to dance so that she could participate in the local powwows. This young woman's perspective had changed, and she became eager to learn about herself, her tribe, and her traditions, which had been something she had shown no interest in previously.

GROUP EXERCISES

Groups have a long-lasting effect on the way Indian youths see themselves. It is within these groups that youths begin to learn some of the aspects of Indian culture that normally the tribe would have explained. For Indian youths in the cities, these groups and centers become the tribe they never knew. They are able to learn about their heritage, ask questions, visit local museums, participate in weekend activities with other Indian youths, and develop a sense of self as an Indian. Many of these groups branch out into local tribal groups in which youths of a particular tribe can get together and learn about their specific history and traditions. For many of these youths, this becomes a time when they do not feel they have to pretend to be something they are not and when they can be proud of who they are.

INDIVIDUAL THERAPY

Incorporating culture within therapy has proven to be quite effective with urban Indian youths (DeBruyn et al., 2001; Sanchez-Way & Johnson, 2000; Witko, 2002). For many preadolescents, the use of play therapy has been a useful tool in effective treatment, whereas for older adolescents, individual therapy that focuses on activities has proven the most useful.

The principles of play therapy apply to Indian adolescents, but the added feature is that culture is also intricately involved. For preadolescents (11–13 years old), the use of play in many forms allows the child to express his or her feelings in a safe environment. This is important for Indian youths, because many who are referred for treatment have suffered from poor mental health primarily as a result of circumstances beyond their control. These children have often been removed from their homes because of abuse and violence, and many have the beginning stages of severe mental health and or personality disorders. For example, a simple exercise involving ceramics and pottery played a significant role in the work with a group of Pueblo children. The children had only lived on the reservation for a short time when they relocated to the cities. The children ranged in age from 8 to 16 years old. They knew nothing of their culture and did not seem willing to learn. After several months of therapy, the children gradually began asking about their culture after first observing a poster on the wall of many different types of moccasins. They became curious about what type of shoes their tribe wore, they wanted to burn sage at the beginning and end of sessions, and they began to actively participate in therapy. Because the children were showing an interest in their culture, the treatment team decided that sessions should be centered on their specific tribe, using their interest as a way to develop a stronger sense of self and possibly decrease some of their acting-out behaviors. One exercise involved shaping pottery out of clay, which was something their particular tribe was known for. Once the pottery was shaped, it was then painted. The children became extremely involved with this exercise and through the process started accepting their Indian heritage; they were also more motivated in treatment. Through these types of exercises, the children began exploring their ethnic identity, and some of their problematic behaviors did decrease.

When working with older adolescents, the therapist must redefine play therapy. Indian adolescents are dealing with many issues, not only within themselves but also within their environment. Gangs, violence, and drugs and alcohol are ever-present forces they must contend with, and attending therapy sessions is often not their choice. What has proven effective is play therapy that involves doing something that makes the environment safer and less threatening. Many Indian youths in the cities are into basketball and current music, such as rap. For one 15-year-old boy, the therapist listened to music with him and talked about the lyrics, often applying them to the boy's situation or feelings he might be experiencing. As a therapist, Tawa Witko has taken adolescents to parks to play ball or have done whatever was necessary to help them feel comfortable with her so that they could begin sharing. Once that has occurred, they are able to approach some of the specific issues associated with being Indian in the cities, such as isolation, discrimination, and lack of appropriate role models.

For some Indian children and adolescents, simple contact with other Indian people, particularly professional adults, makes a difference. Many Indian youths have very negative views of Indian people, a part of the internalized oppression passed down from their parents. The Indian professionals these children meet seem different from the familiar negative stereotypes. Perhaps their contact with these Indian professionals in a therapeutic environment allows them to see the possibilities available to them and challenges their concepts of what being Indian really means. It is this challenging of concepts that may inspire them to make permanent changes in their lives.

FAMILY THERAPY

Tawa Witko, in her work with Indian families, has found it helpful to use what Martin Topper has referred to as *multimodal therapy* (Topper, 1992). This type of therapy evaluates an individual child from the perspective of the four basic dimensions of human existence: medical, psychological, socioeconomic, and cultural historical. Viewing the adolescent from each of these areas develops a clear assessment of what is needed. For example, I worked with one family in which the adolescent was having difficulties in school; he was often truant and did not appear to be achieving up to his potential. His mother was frustrated and often angry with him. One of the first steps in this situation was to determine if the child had any neurological difficulties, such as fetal alcohol syndrome, fetal alcohol effects (FAE), or attention deficit hyperactivity disorder. It was determined that the adolescent did have some of the symptomatology of FAE, which helped explain some of his difficulties in school. This also allowed me to work with the mother to educate her about some of the symptoms of FAE and what she could do to help her child. Next, we reviewed his psychological makeup, including how he felt about himself and his family and his relationships with friends. We then examined the resources available to him in his environment. How easy was it for him to receive services? Were there other areas of difficulty in the home that contributed to the problems (poverty, lack of transportation, etc.)? Finally, we addressed how he felt about his ethnic identity. How did he perceive himself as an Indian person? How comfortable was he participating in ceremonies and other Indian activities? Once all four of these areas were evaluated, we were able to develop a comprehensive treatment plan that addressed all of them. In this case, the mother worked with a case manager to assist her in environmental and social areas, the adolescent worked with a therapist to address some of his issues related to self-esteem and self-concept, the mother and child began family therapy to help them communicate more effectively with each other, and the child was able to participate in cultural activities with other Indian adolescents.

The preceding discussion does not necessarily mean that the multi-modal therapeutic approach should be required of all American Indian families in therapy. However, clinical experience with this approach suggests that it can be an effective strategy in determining treatment plans that address the many dynamics within families with children and adolescents.

TRADITIONAL MEDICINE

For Indian adolescents living in urban environments, the concept of self and identity is often a struggle. For many of these youths, participation in cultural activities and events has proven to have a tremendously positive effect on their well-being.

Many urban facilities are supplying Indian youths with opportunities to attend ceremonies such as the sweat lodge. Here they are able to learn about their heritage and participate in a ceremony that offers cleansing, insight, and spiritual growth. For one adolescent boy who struggled with alcohol addiction, attending sweat lodges helped him stay clean. He knew that he could not participate if he had been drinking; therefore, he was motivated not to drink when he knew a sweat was approaching. Although the change was not transferred to all situations, it was a beginning step.

For other Indian youths, learning the traditional dances and stories gives them the connection that they feel they have lost living in the city. They begin to feel that they are a part of the Indian culture and actively participate in its renewal. In addition, many Indian centers bring in tribal elders and healers to talk with the youths about traditional ways and encourage them to walk the "Red Road" (this refers to walking a path that adheres to the traditional norms of a tribe and is often associated with recover and wellness). The youths can then ask questions of these elders and healers and learn about their heritage. Many Indian youths make further connections with the healers who then help them transition into adulthood through traditional rites of passage ceremonies.

Because most Indian centers are now offering these types of traditional activities, Indian adolescents are beginning to heal from the wounds of their ancestors and to find ways to rejuvenate themselves as Indian people. This rejuvenation translates into positive mental health functioning of the adolescents involved.

Conclusion

Today's urban Indian youths lack positive role models, are affected by acculturative stress, lack rites of passage, have a loss of cultural heritage, and must deal with multiple stressors of urban living. Their problems stem from inadequate role models, cultural conflicts, heritage loss, and peer pressure and are exacerbated by the disadvantaged economic position of their families.

Thus, today's Indian youths should be seen as searching desperately for some group or rite of passage to help them negotiate the difficult transition from adolescence to young adulthood. Given the lack of cultural tradition, it is not surprising that a substantial proportion of Indian youths become involved in gangs, substance abuse, and self-defeating activities. At the extreme, the desperation that results can contribute to suicide attempts, a tragic manifestation of mental health problems among Indian children. Other problems that may result are low self-esteem, breakdown of traditional values, acculturative stress, internalized feelings of lack of control over their lives, hopelessness, and dysfunctional families. Underlying these are the fundamentally painful issues of repeated relocation, cultural domination, suppression, and forced assimilation.

All of these factors and all of the trauma can have devastating effects not just on this generation but on the generations that will follow. It has been documented that the effects of trauma can change actual neural functioning, which can lead to severe personality difficulties such as borderline personality disorders, conduct disorders, and impulsivity (Bleiberg, 2001). These are issues that have not been addressed in working with Indian youths yet affect their mental health functioning.

Although their plight seems hopeless, many Indian adolescents are finding ways out of difficulty by turning to their culture and the traditions of their ancestors. It is through this self-discovery and reawakening of the spirit that these youths will become the next generation of Indian nations, a generation strong in culture, strong in pride, and strong in traditions.

References

Beauvais, F., Oetting, E. R., & Edwards, R. (1985). Trends in drug use of Indian adolescents living on reservations: 1975–1983. *American Journal of Drug and Alcohol Abuse, 11*, 209–229.

Beauvais, F., Oetting, E. R., & Edwards, R. (1989). American Indian youth and drugs, 1976–87: A continuing problem. *American Journal of Public Health, 79*, 634–636.

Bechtold, D. W. (1994). Indian adolescent suicide: Clinical and developmental considerations. *American Indian and Alaska Native Mental Health Research Monograph, 4*, 71–80.

Berlin, I. (1987). Effects of changing Native American cultures on child development. *Journal of Community Psychology, 15*, 299–306.

Bleiberg, E. (2001). *Treating personality disorders in children and adolescents: A relational approach.* New York: Guilford Press.

Chamberlin, J. (1999). Indian psychologists support retiring of offensive team mascots. *APA Monitor Online, 30*(4). Retrieved on August, 3, 2004, from http://www.apa.org/monitor/apr99/mascot.html

Champagne, D., Goldberg-Ambrose, C., Machamer, A., Phillips, B., & Evans, T. (1996). *Service delivery for American Indian children in Los Angeles, 1996* (Report No. RC021766). Los Angeles: UCLA American Indian Studies Center. (ERIC Document Reproduction Service No. ED426827)

DeBruyn, L., Chino, M., Serna, P., & Fullerton-Gleason, L. (2001). Child maltreatment in American Indian and Alaska Native communities: Integrating culture, history, and public health for intervention and prevention. *Child Maltreatment, 6*, 89–102.

DeBruyn, L., Lujan, C., & May, P. (1992). A comparative study of abused and neglected American Indian children in the Southwest. *Social Sciences and Medicine, 35*, 305–315.

Edwards, E. D., & Egbert-Edwards, M. (1990). American Indian adolescents: Combating problems of substance use and abuse through a community model. In A. R. Stiffman & L. E. Davis (Eds.), *Ethnic issues in adolescent mental health* (pp. 285–302). Newbury Park, CA: Sage.

Flynn, K., Clark, R., Aragon, M., Stanzell, S., & Evans-Campbell, T. (1998). *The mental health status of at risk American Indian and Alaska Native youth in Los Angeles County.* Los Angeles: Indian Health Services.

Geffner, R., Jaffe, P., & Sudermann, M. (2000). *Children exposed to domestic violence: Current issues in research, intervention, prevention, and policy development.* Binghamton, NY: Haworth Maltreatment & Trauma Press.

Gelles, R. (1987). What to learn from cross-cultural and historical research on child abuse and neglect: An overview. In R. J. Gelles & J. B. Lancaster (Eds.), *Child abuse and neglect: Biosocial dimensions* (pp. 15–30). New York: Aldine.

Hauswald, E. (1987). External pressure/internal change: Child neglect on the Navajo reservation. In N. Schepter-Hughes (Ed.), *Child survival* (pp. 145–164). Boston: Reidel.

Indian Health Service. (1997). *Trends in Indian health, 1996.* Rockville, MD: U.S. Department of Health and Human Services, Public Health Service, Indian Health Service, Office of Planning, Evaluation, and Legislation, Division of Program Statistics.

LaFromboise, T. D. (1988). American Indian mental health policy. *American Psychologist, 43,* 388–397.

Los Angeles County Department of Mental Health. (1999). *Planning files percent distribution of primary diagnosis for each age and race/ethnic group* [Data file]. Los Angeles: Author.

Lujan, C., DeBruyn, L., & May, P. (1989). Profile of abused and neglected American Indian children in the Southwest. *Child Abuse and Neglect: The International Journal, 13,* 449–461.

Morrissette, P. J. (1994). The holocaust of First Nation People: Residual effects on parenting and treatment implications. *Contemporary Family Therapy, 16,* 381–392.

Nighthorse-Campbell, B. (2000). Challenges facing American Indian youth: On the front lines with Senator Ben Nighthorse-Campbell. *Juvenile Justice Journal, 7*(2), 3–7.

Piasecki, J., Manson, S., Biernoff, M., Hiat, A., Taylor, S., & Bechtold, D. (1989). Abuse and neglect of American Indian children: Findings from a survey of federal providers. *American Indian and Alaska Native Mental Health Research, 3,* 43–62.

Sanchez-Way, R., & Johnson, S. (2000). Cultural practices in American Indian prevention programs. *Juvenile Justice Journal, 7*(2), 20–32.

Staurowsky, E. (1999). American Indian imagery and the miseducation of America. *Quest, 51,* 382–392.

Substance Abuse and Mental Health Services Administration. (1993). *National Household Survey on Drug Abuse 1991–1993.* Rockville, MD: National Clearinghouse for Alcohol and Drug Information.

Topper, M. (1992). Multidimensional therapy: A case study of a Navajo adolescent with multiple problems. In L. A. Vargas & J. D. Koss-Chioino (Eds.), *Working with culture: Psychotherapeutic interventions with ethnic minority children and adolescents* (pp. 225–245). San Francisco: Jossey-Bass.

U.S. Bureau of Indian Affairs. (1997). *Youth risk behavior survey of high school students who attended Bureau-funded schools.* Washington, DC: Author.

Witko, T. (2002). Providing culturally competent services to American Indians. *California Psychologist, 35*(4), 25, 29.

Witko, T. (2005). Understanding the psychological implications of Native American mascots and symbols. *California Psychologist, 38*(1), 18–19.

Carrie Lee Johnson

An Innovative Healing Model: Empowering Urban Native Americans

10

U rban Native Americans today are faced with many challenges and difficulties that have a tremendous effect on the individual and family. Because of the high rates of substance abuse and mental health problems, I developed a community healing model to work with Native Americans. These difficulties and challenges that many Native Americans are faced with today may be attributed to historical trauma that has been passed down from generation to generation. This model was designed to assist Native American children, families, and communities with healing from multigenerational trauma. The model focuses on the individual, family, and community through the use of the medicine wheel, which enables examination of the healing process from the context of the four directions and focuses on the importance of traditional values and healing to create harmony and balance (see Figure 10.1).

The Impact of Historical Factors: Colonization, Residential Schools, and Value Conflicts

Historical events, beginning with colonization and continuing with the dominant culture's treatment of Native peoples

FIGURE 10.1

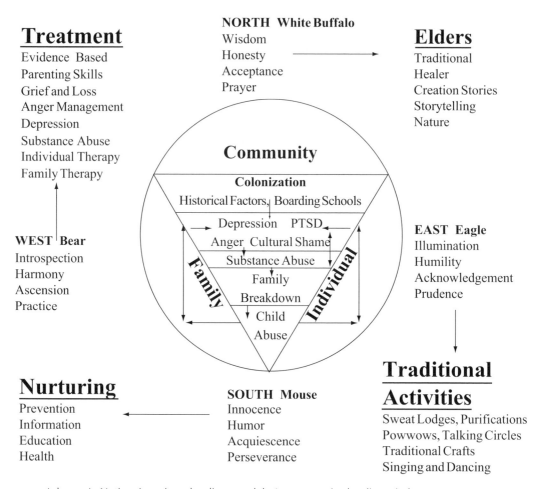

Treatment
Evidence Based
Parenting Skills
Grief and Loss
Anger Management
Depression
Substance Abuse
Individual Therapy
Family Therapy

WEST Bear
Introspection
Harmony
Ascension
Practice

Nurturing
Prevention
Information
Education
Health

NORTH White Buffalo
Wisdom
Honesty
Acceptance
Prayer

Community

Colonization
Historical Factors, Boarding Schools

Depression   PTSD
Anger Cultural Shame
Substance Abuse
Family
Breakdown
Child
Abuse

Family

Individual

SOUTH Mouse
Innocence
Humor
Acquiescence
Perseverance

Elders
Traditional
Healer
Creation Stories
Storytelling
Nature

EAST Eagle
Illumination
Humility
Acknowledgement
Prudence

Traditional Activities
Sweat Lodges, Purifications
Powwows, Talking Circles
Traditional Crafts
Singing and Dancing

Johnson's Native American healing model: A community healing circle.
PTSD = posttraumatic stress disorder.

to the present day, have had a major impact on the well-being of Native Americans.

COLONIZATION

The model first examines the effects of colonization on Native American individuals, families, and communities. As is discussed in the introduction to this volume, colonization has resulted in the systematic destruction of culture and life ways of indigenous people around the world. Prior to colonization of America, the individual, family, and community were intact and spiritually connected to their surroundings. Child abuse was not common in the culture. Children were considered sacred and were valued. Native Americans were free of the many influences that have so greatly impacted their lives. Colonization brought destruction of traditional cultural values, practices, and beliefs as well as disease, epidemics, massacres, slavery, destructive federal policies, and broken treaties.

BOARDING SCHOOLS

Boarding schools were set up to assimilate Native American children, ostensibly to educate them but in reality to keep them from practicing their traditions, language, and culture. The boarding schools were major agents in the loss of Indian languages, which are prime carriers of culture. In addition, children were often subjected to physical, emotional, and sexual abuse. Another consequence of the residential schools was that Native American children did not learn traditional parenting skills; often, what they learned was harsh punishment and abuse, and this in turn, affected their ability to parent later in life. A more thorough discussion on American Indian parenting is provided by Tawa Witko (see chap. 8, this volume).

VALUE CONFLICTS

Another effect of colonization and the residential schools is the conflict of Native Americans' traditional values with mainstream values. Native Americans lost their land, way of life, self-esteem, and identity, and traditional cultural values, practices, and behaviors were destroyed. Even so, many of these values and behaviors have been retained, and a large number of Native Americans have not been able to acculturate fully into dominant society. This has led to their being caught between two conflicting cultures.

The values, attitudes, and behaviors of Native Americans conflict with those of the dominant society (see Aragon, chap. 1, Table 1.1, this volume). Anthropologists and sociologists have studied these values and behaviors, and psychologists have begun to examine them in terms of the counseling process (Lazarus, 1982). Research on conflicts between Native and non-Native cultures is cited in the paragraphs that follow. It is important to recognize that the values are comparative differences. In addition, Native Americans represent over 500 different tribes, and there are many differences between the tribes; therefore, some of these value conflicts may be different depending on tribe of origin. Lastly, depending on his or her acculturation level, an individual may hold onto some of the values and not others or show elements of the values and, depending on the situation or setting, evoke different values. Some common value conflicts between Native and non-Native culture are described below.

First, Native people show more of a tendency to share, cooperate, and work successfully in groups than competitive non-Native individuals. For Native people, the value of cooperation in a group is so strong that being better than other children is extremely uncomfortable (Mitchum, 1989).

Second, Native children are not encouraged at home to ask questions. They are expected to learn by observation and to be patient, in contrast to non-Native children who are expected to be curious and ask a lot of questions (Mitchum, 1989).

Third, during personal interactions in non-Native culture, one is generally expected to look directly at the other individual, but when a Native individual interacts with someone, he or she will look down, avoiding eye contact. This glancing away in Native culture is a sign of respect and compliance (Trimble, 1976).

Fourth, one's status in Western society is based on one's job, how much money one makes, the car one drives, and the part of the city in which one lives. However, in the Native culture, status is based on who you are rather than what you have (Mitchum, 1989).

Fifth, traditional Natives do not live by time; time is viewed as a continuum with no beginning and no end. In contrast, Western society places great value on punctuality. The Native's world is "now" oriented, and Native individuals may have difficulty relating to future goals and the concept of goal setting (Trimble, 1976).

Mental Health, Substance Abuse, and Other Psychosocial Problems as a Part of the Multigenerational Trauma Cycle

Mental health problems and alcohol and drug abuse are often seen as comorbid in the Native American population. These serious concerns have also been related to other psychosocial problems, such as family violence and child abuse. The underlying causes are discussed below.

MENTAL HEALTH PROBLEMS

The influences of boarding schools and historical factors have contributed to many problems within American Indian communities, both rural and urban. These problems include depression, anxiety, posttraumatic stress disorder, and other mental health problems. As a result of the historical trauma, Native Americans are at higher risk for mental health problems than any other cultural group (Nelson, McCoy, Stetter, & Vanderwagen, 1992).

Manson, Walker, and Kivlahan (1987) reported that the prevalence rates for mental illnesses may be higher in Native Americans than in the general population. Neligh (1988) stated that considering the lack of community-based data about the incidence and prevalence of major mental disorders on reservations, the lack of diagnostic instruments that have been developed and standardized for different Indian cultures, and the limitations of service use data, it can only be concluded that very little is actually known about patterns of major mental illnesses among American Indian and Alaska Native peoples. However, the research that has been conducted on mental health in Native Americans often shows that alcoholism is the most common problem, followed by depression (Beauvais, 1992; Neligh, 1988).

SUBSTANCE ABUSE

The high rates of substance abuse among Native Americans may be due to self-medication to alleviate the emotional pain caused by mental health problems. Substance abuse may also be a factor in coping with other stressors associated with their loss of dignity; negative self-perception; discrimination; racism; estrangement; and economic, social, and cultural stress. There is a high level of comorbidity in Native American communities, and it is often difficult to determine which was the precursor, the mental illness or the alcohol or drug problem. There is sufficient research showing the high rates of substance abuse among Native Americans. Often substance abuse is combined with a psychiatric disorder, mainly depression and anxiety. These may be a result of cumulative trauma and unresolved grief among Native Americans (Brave Heart, 2003; Brave Heart & DeBruyn, 1998; Robin, Chester, & Goldman, 1996). Clark (see chap. 4, this volume) provides a more thorough discussion on the impact that alcoholism and drug addiction have had on Indian communities.

FAMILY VIOLENCE AND CHILD ABUSE

The effect of substance abuse on the Native American family has been devastating. Family and community closeness deteriorated, and this resulted in a breakdown of the family structure and networks. The stressors in the family and negative experiences in boarding schools also impinge on parenting abilities.

Native American children growing up in a stressful family situation and with parents who lack parenting abilities are at high risk for child abuse and other serious behavioral and emotional health problems. Child abuse and neglect as well as domestic violence in Native Americans are serious problems. According to the National Child Abuse and Neglect Data System (U.S. Department of Health and Human Services, Administration for Children and Families, 1997), there was one substantiated report of a child victim of abuse or neglect for every 30 Native American children ages 14 or younger compared with one report for every 58 children of any race. Native Americans and Asians were the only racial groups to experience an increase in the rate of child abuse and neglect from 1992 to 1995. Much of the data suggest that child abuse and neglect are underreported in American Indian and Alaska Native children. Evans-Campbell (see chap. 2, this volume) provides more information on child abuse and neglect in Indian country.

Substance abuse has also been associated with child abuse and domestic violence. One study attributed chaotic family situations and other problems such as alcoholism and depression to child abuse and neglect (Piasecki et al., 1989). Another study found that the most frequently indicated offender in neglect cases was the child's mother (62.9%), in physical abuse cases the father (36.3%), and in sexual abuse cases other biological relatives (55.3%). This study showed that substance abuse was a factor in most cases, except for sexual abuse (Chino, Melton, & Fullerton, 1992). Witko, Marinez, and Milda (see chap. 5, this volume) provide a more in-depth look at family violence. According to the U.S. Department of Justice (2004), American Indian victims of violence (62%) were more likely than any other racial group (42%) to report an offender under the influence of alcohol or drugs at the time of the offense.

The Multigenerational Trauma Cycle

Native American children who were victims of child abuse and stressful family situations continue to be impacted by the multigenerational trauma. If the symptoms are left untreated and the grief unresolved, then the trauma may be passed down to subsequent generations, becoming a multigenerational trauma cycle.

The literature supports problems in adulthood as a result of being a victim of child abuse. In a Southwestern American Indian tribe, a study found that a history of childhood sexual abuse was a risk factor for psychiatric problems in adulthood (Robin, Chester, Rasmussen, Jaranson, & Goldman, 1997). Among Native Canadian women who were sexually abused as children, there were significantly higher levels of symptomatology, such as sleep disorders and somatic complaints, compared with Caucasian women who were sexually abused as children (Barker-Collo, 1999). Another study found that child abuse and both physical and sexual abuse were risk factors for conduct disorders and that both child abuse and conduct disorders were risk factors for alcohol dependence. Alcohol dependence was a risk factor for physical intimate partner violence. However, just a history of physical abuse in childhood was a significant predictor of being a victim and a perpetrator of physical partner violence (Kunitz, Levy, McCloskey, & Gabriel, 1998).

The Native American multigenerational trauma cycle impacts the individual, family, and community. Many Native Americans have not healed from this trauma, so as a result, it is passed on from generation to generation. Nelson et al. (1992) reported that a combination of poverty, poor opportunity in jobs and education, frustration, and substance abuse have led to an overabundance of depression in both adolescents and adults. By adolescence, Native Americans show higher rates of suicide, alcoholism, drug abuse delinquency, and out-of-home placement compared with the non-Native population. If these problems are left untreated and unresolved, these adolescents may one day have children of their own and the cycle is most likely to continue. The multigenerational trauma cycle shows that Native Americans are often faced with multiple traumas throughout their lives.

Disharmony and imbalance are created by the multigenerational trauma cycle. When harmony and balance are broken, the spiritual self is weak, and one is more vulnerable to the effects of the cycle. Restoration of harmony and balance is needed to break out of the multigenerational trauma cycle so that it does not continue to be passed to future generations. Psychologists and mental health practitioners must continue attempts to restore the harmony and balance that was lost in so many Native American individuals, families, and communities.

The Use of the Medicine Wheel and the Healing Model

The context of the medicine wheel is used to integrate Native American culture into treatment. Integration of traditional practices into established Western evidence-based treatments or adapting evidence-based treatments to Native Americans may be more successful in healing this population than use of Western treatments alone.

THE MEDICINE WHEEL

The medicine wheel is an ancient symbol for many Native Americans, and the way it is taught and understood differs from tribe to tribe. It is divided into four quadrants, and the quadrants are expressed in many different ways. Some of these include the four directions (north, south, east, and west); the four elements (fire, earth, air, and water); and the four parts of the self (physical, mental and cognitive, spiritual, and social). The quadrants also include other concepts that can be talked about in sets of four and again can have different meanings across tribes. The important aspect of the medicine wheel is having the four quadrants in balance. When all the four quadrants are in balance, life continues in an intricately balanced and harmonious way. When in harmony, one is in step with self and the universe.

The Native American multigenerational trauma cycle represents this imbalance and disharmony in the individual, family, and community. This is due to many years of trauma that has not been healed and has been passed from generation to generation. Many Native Americans have *unresolved grief* over the trauma, which is the grief a person experiences when he or she incurs a loss that cannot be openly acknowledged, publicly mourned, or socially supported (Doka, 1989).

In the Native American healing model, the concept of the medicine wheel is used to assist with healing and restoring harmony and balance to Native American individuals, families, and communities. Each of the four directions connects to different aspects of healing. Healing focuses not only on Western evidence-based treatments but also on Native American culture, traditions, elders, and traditional healing. This focus of treatment is needed to break out of the multigenerational trauma cycle.

NORTH: ELDERS AND TRADITIONAL HEALING

North on the medicine wheel is located at the top of the wheel. Movement around the medicine wheel flows in a clockwise or counterclockwise direction depending on the tribe. North is connected with the white buffalo, emphasizing wisdom, honesty, acceptance, and prayer. This is further connected to elders and traditional healers (see Figure 10.1). Elders have a lifetime of wisdom and as a result are honored and respected. Before colonization, elders played a significant role in Native American communities. Elders often told stories and used storytelling as a way to pass on traditions. Elders teach through song, stories, language, and legends. They are the carriers of culture and tradition and play many different roles in their communities: They act as parents, teachers, leaders, and spiritual advisors. The wisdom and knowledge of the elders are an essential part of the healing process.

Traditional healers are also important because of the spiritual focus of Native Americans. The traditional healers often have rituals (again, this will differ depending on the tribe) that serve to prevent illness and treat medical and mental health problems. The traditional healer provides two vital aspects of the healing process: a support system for the person (family, friends, and other significant community members) and some type of ceremony or ritual that helps restore the person to harmony and balance with the environment (Garrett & Garrett, 1994).

An individual may choose traditional healing as the preferred treatment; therefore, it is important for a therapist to collaborate with the traditional healer. Even if Western approaches are the treatment of choice for the client, supplementing a traditional counterpart will likely improve therapist and treatment credibility, treatment compliance, and outcome and may enhance prevention efforts (Renfrey, 1992). Elders, traditional healers, and traditional practices assist with the fulfillment of the spiritual self.

EAST: CULTURE AND TRADITIONS

East on the medicine wheel recognizes the eagle, which emphasizes the spirit and is connected with illumination, humility, acknowledgement, and prudence. This, in turn, is connected to traditional activities and culture (see Figure 10.1).

Native Americans have suffered many losses as a result of colonization, boarding schools, relocation, and other historical and ongoing traumas. These losses have included the loss of lives, land, culture and traditional practices, traditional healing practices, language, and traditional family systems and values. All of these losses have had a significant impact on cultural identity. A positive cultural identity is important in restoring harmony and balance. Learning about culture and traditions may causes individuals to feel connected and involved, which increases pride in self as a Native American. This builds cultural identity.

In discussing cultural activities, it is important to recognize differences across tribal communities; therefore, just as in the case of elders and traditional healers, the cultural activities used would depend on the individual's tribe. Some Native American cultural activities are dances, powwows, songs, crafts, and different ceremonies. One significant cultural ceremony for some tribes is the sweat lodge ceremony, which is used as a healing practice. It involves the connection with mother earth and community. Other cultural practices include purification, the talking circle, and prayer. The talking circle is similar to a support group in which members can express their feelings and concerns. The individual who facilitates the group starts the circle; sage, sweetgrass, or other blessing herbs may be passed around for smudging. Smudging involves directing the smoke from the herbs toward oneself or one's surroundings, which is thought to have a purifying effect and bring physical, spiritual, and emotional balance. A rock, feather, or some other sacred object is passed around the circle; the person to whom the object is passed can share thoughts or concerns or pray. Again, this will vary among tribal communities. Participating in these cultural activities may assist an individual in identifying and feeling more connected with their Native American culture, which further restores harmony and balance in the self.

SOUTH: PREVENTION AND EDUCATION

South on the medicine wheel recognizes the mouse and represents peace. It is connected with innocence, humor, acquiescence, and perseverance. In the model (see Figure 10.1), the south is further connected with nurturing, prevention, and education. Prevention and education are an important part of Native American healing. Understanding of the risk and protective factors relevant to prevention is essential. Examination of the multigenerational trauma cycle and the relevant research provides a clear view of risk factors, which include alcoholism, family violence, mental health problems, behavioral problems, poverty, and isolation from family and community. It is also important to consider the protective factors, such as family support and cultural identity.

Preventive programs can be focused on many areas, such as Alcoholics Anonymous; Al-Anon; Head Start; and information on effects of smoking, effects of alcohol and drugs on the fetus, and HIV/AIDS. The type of preventive program or educational material used will depend on the needs of the community. Cultural sensitivity in prevention is thought of as being composed of two dimensions: surface and deep structure. Surface structure involves matching interventions to observable characteristics of target populations, such as food and location. Deep structure involves incorporating cultural, social, historical, environmental, and psychological aspects of the target population. When developing preventive programs or educational materials for Native Americans, therapists should be aware that it is important to incorporate cultural, social, and historical factors. It is also important to recognize that these will differ depending on the tribe and acculturation levels.

WEST: WESTERN AND EVIDENCE-BASED TREATMENTS

West on the medicine wheel can represents introspection, harmony, ascension, and practice. It is connected with Western evidence-based treatments in the model (see Figure 10.1). There is little research on the success of Western conventional treatment approaches when working with Native Americans. However, research has shown that Native Americans tend to drop out of treatment earlier than non-Native clients and are likely to terminate after the initial session (Sue, Allen, & Conaway, 1978). This may be due to the therapist's lack of cultural competence and sensitivity to Native Americans. The historical experience of Native Americans has engendered an extreme amount of mistrust of non-Native or Western approaches. Trimble and Fleming (1989) found that flexibility and trustworthiness are the most important characteristics of a counselor for an American Indian client. Therefore, it is important to create a safe therapeutic culturally sensitive environment. In addition, some traditional Western evidence-based treatments (cognitive–behavioral, psychoanalytic, etc.) do not fit with the culture and traditions of many Native Americans. The focus is more on the individual and less on the family, extended family, and community, all of which are all important for Native Americans.

The demonstrated success and the preference for different types of Western evidence-based treatment approaches on Native Americans have not been well documented. Among different types of Western treatment choices, group therapy has been shown to be a popular intervention among American Indian communities. The incorporation of Indian traditions and values, like a talking circle, has been an important part of the success of this type of treatment (Edwards & Edwards, 1984).

Therefore, what is crucial is the integration or adaptation of Western evidence-based approaches with Native American values and traditions and incorporating the cultural context of the individual, family, and community. It is also essential to consider other aspects of the client, such as tribal identification, differences in values, and level of acculturation.

When working with Native Americans, therapists must be culturally sensitive and assess for these differences to obtain a clear picture of the client's worldview and needs. The therapist will then be able to determine which approach to use with the client. Therefore, the individual's problem must be understood in the context of the culture.

Using the Healing Model to Empower Native Americans

As Native Americans begin to understand, grieve over, and heal from the multigenerational trauma, they will be empowered to break its cycle and restore harmony and balance.

BREAKING THE CYCLE

The multigenerational trauma cycle has affected and continues to affect many Native individuals, families, and communities. To break out of the multigenerational trauma cycle, Native Americans first need to understand and be aware of the impact that multigenerational trauma has had on them, their families, and their communities. They then need to deal with their unresolved grief from this trauma. As mentioned earlier, unresolved grief is the grief a person experiences when he or she experiences a loss that cannot be openly acknowledged, publicly mourned, or socially supported (Doka, 1989). Healing from the multi-generational trauma and restoring balance and harmony can be achieved by different facets of healing, depending on the needs of the individual, family, and community. All of these different facets of healing, however, must take into consideration culture and traditions of the individual, family, and community.

RESILIENCY AND EMPOWERMENT AMONG NATIVE AMERICANS

Native Americans have endured significant losses throughout history, yet they have shown tremendous strength and resiliency in survival and holding onto their culture and traditions. Therapists working with Native Americans need to consider and respect these strengths and resiliencies. The expectation was that Native American would lose their culture and way of life and assimilate into the majority culture. This has not happened, and in fact, Native Americans are growing in population, particularly urban Native Americans. However, the majority of Native Americans now live in urban areas and not on reservations.

Data from Census 2000 indicate that of the estimated 2.5 million American Indians in the United States, approximately 1.4 million live in urban areas (U.S. Census Bureau, 2000). This has led to many other problems for urban Native Americans, such as unemployment, poverty, oppression, racism, loss of family and community support, and mental health problems and substance abuse. In urban areas, Native Americans may not have as much access to traditional healers, family and cultural supports, or culturally competent mental health providers. Therefore, it is important to train more mental health providers to work with Native Americans as well as to work with the client from his or her cultural context. Urban Native Americans are extremely diverse; they come from many different tribes and speak different languages. Some of them have never lived on a reservation, some go back and forth, some are very traditional, and some are assimilated and do not hold onto many Native traditions and values. When working with urban Native Americans, therapists must not stereotype; rather, they must accurately assess the cultural context and worldview of the individual. This will assist in determining what facet of treatment the individual would like to work from.

It is essential to involve Native Americans in examining the experience of multigenerational trauma to themselves, their families, and their communities; this will empower them to break out of the cycle. It is also necessary to involve Native Americans in their treatment and to create a system of care that is determined by the individual. Cultural competency is important when working with Native Americans because it will allow the individual to gain more trust in treatment and feel more empowered. As Native Americans break out of the multigenerational trauma cycle, they will continue to grow in areas important to Native people. These include family, education, love and trust, self-identity, cultural pride, and spirituality. The model in Figure 10.1 shows the medicine wheel placed around all other factors because of its importance in keeping harmony and balance for Native Americans.

THE NATIVE AMERICAN HEALING MODEL AND A SYSTEM OF CARE APPROACH

When working with Native Americans, one should focus not only on Western evidence-based treatments but also on either adapting these treatments to be more culturally appropriate or incorporating the culture and traditions into treatment. In terms of diagnosing Native Americans, it is also important to consider the cultural and value differences and not to limit diagnosis, because often an array of symptoms and problems is seen in these clients. A diagnosis such as posttraumatic stress disorder does not always capture the multiple historical and other traumas or the systemic problems. In addition, because of the high rates of comorbidity among Native Americans, treatment services for substance abuse and mental health problems need to be more integrated. The array of symptoms, problems, and traumas and the effects not only on individuals but on their families and communities calls for a system of care approach as an essential part of the health process. The Native American healing model focuses on a system of care and healing by using the context of the medicine wheel and the four directions. These four directions are can also be connected with spiritual, physical, social, and cognitive needs of the individual. In a system of care for Native Americans, all of these needs should be in balance and harmony, and the involvement and preferences of the individual, family, and community should be honored.

The Native American system of care focuses on involving key people in the individual's life. Because extended family is significant to many Native Americans, it is important to find out who is significant in the person's life and who he or she feels should be involved in the treatment. These individuals can come from various elements of the community. They can be friends, teachers, elders, traditional healers, nurses, case workers, and so on. These individuals can play an important role in coordinating the best system of care and healing for the individual, care and healing that the individual agrees to. Those involved in planning these services should not simply put in place a system of care that they feel would best benefit the individual; rather, the individual should choose the different aspects of care from the four directions and different facets of treatment that he or she feels will work best.

Conclusion

The Native American community healing model examines foremost the multigenerational trauma cycle and discusses the unresolved grief, the multiple traumas, and the importance of healing. For Native Americans to grieve and heal, it is necessary to integrate culture and traditions as well as foster an awareness of the impact the multigenerational trauma has had on that individual, family, or community. The model examines healing from different facets; is multigenerational, spiritual, and community focused; and takes into consideration an array of symptoms and traumas. This interaction is important in the healing process.

Healing from child abuse, domestic violence, substance abuse, or mental health problems in Native Americans cannot fully be addressed without acknowledging and understanding the historical factors and traumas that continue to impact native Americans today. These historical traumas must be understood and integrated into these current symptoms and problems to begin the healing and great out of the multigenerational trauma cycle. I use the concept of the medicine wheel to incorporate the importance of culture and traditions into treatment to restore harmony and balance. However, it is up to the individuals to choose which direction or aspects of healing they wish to focus their energy on and that will help them achieve harmony and balance. This community healing model can be applied to urban, reservation, or rural American Indians and Alaskan Natives to help them restore the harmony and balance that was lost as a result of the impact of multi-generational trauma on the Native American communities.

References

Barker-Collo, S. L. (1999). Reported symptomatology of Native Canadian and Caucasian females sexually abused in childhood: A comparison. *Journal of Interpersonal Violence, 14*, 747–760.

Beauvais, F. (1992). An integrated model of prevention and treatment of drug abuse among American Indian youth. *Journal of Addictive Diseases, 11*, 63–80.

Brave Heart, M. Y. H. (2003). The Historical Trauma response among Natives and its relationship with substance abuse: A Lakota illustration. *Journal of Psychoactive Drugs, 35*, 7–13.

Brave Heart, M. Y. H., & DeBruyn, L. M. (1998). The American Indian holocaust: Healing historical unresolved grief. *American Indian and Alaska Native Mental Health Research, 8*, 56–78.

Chino, M., Melton, A., & Fullerton, L. (1992). *Child abuse and neglect in American Indian/Alaska Native communities and the role of the Indian Health Service: Final report.* Rockville, MD: U.S. Department of Health and Human Services, Public Health Service, Indian Health Service, Office of Planning, Evaluation, and Legislation.

Doka, K. J. (1989). *Disenfranchised grief: Recognizing hidden sorrow.* New York: Lexington Books.

Edwards, E., & Edwards, M. (1984). Group work practice with American Indians. *Social Work With Groups, 7*, 7–21.

Garrett, J., & Garrett, M. (1994). The path of good medicine: Understanding and counseling Native American Indians. *Journal of Multicultural Counseling and Development, 22*, 134–144.

Kunitz, S. J., Levy, J. G., McCloskey, J., & Gabriel, K. R. (1998). Alcohol dependence and domestic violence as sequalae of abuse and conduct disorder in childhood. *Child Abuse & Neglect, 22*, 1079–1091.

Lazarus, P. (1982). Counseling the Native American child: A question of values. *Elementary School Guidance and Counseling, 17*, 83–88.

Manson, S., Walker, R., & Kivlahan, D. (1987). Psychiatric assessment and treatment of American Indians and Alaska Natives. *Home and Community Psychiatry, 38*, 165–173.

Mitchum, N. T. (1989). Increasing self-esteem in Native American children. *Elementary School Guidance and Counseling, 23,* 266–271.

Neligh, G. (1988). Major mental disorders and behavior among American Indians and Alaska Natives [Monograph]. *American Indian and Alaska Native Mental Health Research, 1,* 116–159.

Nelson, S., McCoy, G., Stetter, M., & Vanderwagen, W. (1992). An overview of mental health services for American Indians and Alaska Natives in the 1900s. *Hospital and Community Psychiatry, 43,* 257–261.

Piasecki, J., Manson, S., Biernoff, M., Hiat, A., Taylor, S., & Bechtold, D. (1989). Abuse and neglect of American Indian children: Findings from a survey of federal providers. *American Indian and Alaska Native Mental Health Research, 3,* 43–62.

Robin, R. W., Chester, B., & Goldman, D. (1996). Cumulative trauma and PTSD in American Indian communities. In A. J. Marsella, M. J. Friedman, E. T. Gerrity, & R. M. Scurfield (Eds.), *Ethnocultural aspects of posttraumatic stress disorder: Issues, research, and clinical applications* (pp. 239–253). Washington, DC: American Psychological Association.

Robin, R. W., Chester, B., Rasmussen, J., Jaranson, J., & Goldman, D. (1997). Prevalence, characteristics, and impact of childhood sexual abuse in a southwestern American Indian tribe. *Child Abuse & Neglect, 21,* 769–787.

Renfrey, G. (1992). Cognitive–behavior therapy and the Native American client. *Behavior Therapy, 23,* 321–340.

Sue, S., Allen, D. B., & Conaway, L. (1978). The responsiveness and equality of mental health care to Chicanos and Native Americans. *American Journal of Community Psychology, 6,* 137–146.

Trimble, J. E. (1976). Value differences among American Indians: Concerns for the concerned counselor. In P. Pederson, J. Draguns, W. Lonner, & J. E. Trimble (Eds.), *Counseling across cultures* (pp. 84–100). Honolulu: University of Hawaii Press.

Trimble, J. E., & Fleming, C. (1989). Providing counseling service for Native American Indians: Client, counselor, and community characteristics. In P. Pedersen, J. Draguns, W. Lonner, & J. E. Trimble (Eds.), *Counseling across cultures* (3rd ed., pp. 177–204). Honolulu: University of Hawaii Press.

U.S. Census Bureau. (2000). *U.S. Census 2000.* Washington, DC: U.S. Government Printing Office.

U.S. Department of Health and Human Services, Administration for Children and Families. (1997). *Child maltreatment 1995: Reports from the states to the National Child Abuse and Neglect Data System.* Washington, DC: U.S. Government Printing Office.

U.S. Department of Justice. (2004). *American Indians and crime.* Washington, DC: U.S. Government Printing Office.

Tawa M. Witko

Conclusion: What Psychologists Have Learned and Where They Need to Go

T his is a time of growth in regard to Indian research and understanding. The chapters in this volume are examples. The authors have considered some of the current research in the field. Readers have learned about historical events such as relocation, residential schools, and colonization as well as how these events impacted parenting and the roles of women and children, created identity confusion, and contributed to the development of serious mental health dysfunction such as substance abuse and complex posttraumatic stress disorder. In addition, readers have learned that through good assessment and understanding, therapists can work with parents, children, and communities to develop a stronger sense of cultural identity and reduce the amount of dysfunction within the community. Therapists have learned how treatment tools based on traditional Native medicine can be successful in helping clients make sense of their losses and regain an understanding of their cultural past.

Historical and Theoretical Background of Urban American Indian Mental Health

In Part I of this volume, the authors explored the historical background of Indian nations pre- and post-Columbus and how this has impacted mental health, family systems, and identity. A. Mike Aragon (see chap. 1, this volume) explored in depth how through colonization Indian people began to hate the Indian in the mirror; how through repeated exposure to bigotry, discrimination, and prejudice, Indian people began to internalize the negative images of themselves; and how because of this mental health functioning, a community that had once thrived began to fall apart. Alcohol became the weapon of choice as a way to hide feelings of loss. The author addressed the serious obstacles that mental health practitioners and the field of psychology must face if they are to make a dent in the "Indian problem." He then addressed clinical approaches that appear to be effective and encouraged therapists to look at and compare the Native value systems with mainstream value systems and how that may impact treatment.

Where Aragon explored historical background as it impacted mental health functioning, Tessa Evans-Campbell (see chap. 2, this volume) explored the struggle Native communities experienced keeping Native children in the community. She discussed the alarming statistics surrounding Native children within the child welfare system and how child maltreatment continues to rise within Native families. She explored the history of the Indian Child Welfare Act, its purpose, its implementation (or lack thereof), and how Native communities are impacted by it. She also offered solutions to those working with Native families on ways to address the cultural differences that may lead to children being removed from the home.

Finally, Joseph P. Gone (see chap. 3, this volume) explored how the complexity of identity is achieved within Native communities. He discussed his struggle in trying to determine how one develops an authentic American Indian identity when one's culture has been dismantled and one's people disillusioned by poverty, racism, and despair. He explored dimensional and discursive models as a means to explore this complex issue and ended with recommendations for improving the lives of urban Indians.

All three chapters in Part I gave readers an understanding of the events that have impacted Indian nations (colonization, relocation, and residential schools) and offered a beginning step to helping Indian communities heal.

Specific Urban American Indian Treatment Considerations

In Part II of this volume, the authors addressed specific urban Indian treatment needs. The chapters provided information on alcohol and drug rehabilitation, violence in the community, and the impact of trauma.

Rose L. Clark (see chap. 4, this volume) focused on alcohol and drug rehabilitation and provided statistics, concrete examples, and treatment methods for addressing alcohol and drug rehabilitation within the American Indian community, paying particular attention to urban communities where access to traditional forms of treatment may not be available. She explored barriers to treatment and how to overcome those barriers as well as limitations to the current research available on this population. Her conclusions offered readers hope in helping communities heal from the devastating effects of addiction.

Tawa M. Witko, Rae Marie Martinez, and Richard Milda (see chap. 5, this volume) focused on violence within Indian communities and the impact colonization has had on the way communities looked at women, and in turn, how views of women changed. The authors explored how the community attitude went from that of respect for women to that of ownership of women. The tactics of power and control were explored using examples of how this may look within urban communities. The authors concluded with solutions for how to break the cycle of violence by examining two treatment programs, one rural and one urban.

Nadine Cole (see chap. 6, this volume) focused on trauma and explored how the destruction of American Indian culture led to a loss of meaning and spirituality within the community. She looked at intergenerational trauma and its effects on subsequent generations and the formation of complex posttraumatic stress disorder. She discussed the treatment of this disorder, in which a physical trauma can affect the soul, mind, and body (described in the chapter as a "soul wound") and how work with Indian communities must be different from work with the mainstream society.

The authors in these three chapters explored areas that are common in mainstream society but have a different impact with Indian populations. Because of this, treatment must be undertaken in ways that coincide with cultural beliefs.

New Directions for Working With Urban American Indians

In Part III of this volume, the authors addressed new clinical models for working with Indian populations including storytelling, parenting, and working with adolescents and communities.

Dolores Subia BigFoot and Megan Dunlap (see chap. 7, this volume) focused on the use of storytelling as a healing tool for Native communities. The authors outlined the historical context of storytelling, its purpose, and results. They explored how storytelling can be used to help treat children with abuse histories and adults with substance abuse issues. They explored various concepts of storytelling, including video storytelling and journaling, as well as future treatment and research considerations.

Tawa M. Witko (see chap. 8, this volume) focused on family systems and how to work effectively with Native parents. She explored three parenting programs, the use of family therapy, the use of couples therapy, and the impact of the community on family functioning. The author discussed various factors that can impact effective parenting, such as lack of cultural parenting and interracial marriages, and ways to help parents regain the parenting knowledge that was lost as a result of relocation and residential schools.

Rose L. Clark and Tawa M. Witko (see chap. 9, this volume) focused on the specific treatment needs of urban Indian adolescents. The authors discussed some of the current problems facing urban Indian teenagers, including substance abuse, child abuse, educational difficulties, and biculturalism. They explored current treatment modalities such as youth camps, group exercises, individual therapy, family therapy models, and the use of traditional Native medicine.

Finally, Carrie Lee Johnson addressed some of the challenges facing urban Native Americans and how the development of her community healing model can help bring back traditional ways of being. She discussed the different sections of the model, their historical context, and the current impact on the community. In addition, she explored how this model can empower Native individuals to break out of the multigenerational trauma cycle and restore harmony and balance to the community.

Policy, Research, and Administrative Implications

Throughout this volume, the authors have had to ask themselves some tough questions related to the current knowledge base and where they and others in the field need to be in terms of policy, research, and administration. They found that psychologists must first acknowledge what some of the difficulties are. Why do Indian people in general have a difficult time receiving services?

One reason is that within urban areas, Indian people are often misclassified, and therefore complete numbers of the Indian population are never obtained. Second, within the therapeutic arena, clinicians often do not obtain a complete history because they do not ask questions about boarding schools or relocation. Clinicians usually look at the individual in front of them and treat that person as if he or she is not Indian, possibly because they are unaware that Indians still exist or because they make a general assumption on what Indians are supposed to look like.

This raises the following question: What makes it difficult for non-Indian clinicians to accept the Indian client? Indian therapists say that it is due to the inherently racist society in which we live and to the schools, which have ignored the Indian experience because Americans are still unable to accept their treatment of Indian nations. Non-Indian therapists also believe that schools are involved; they maintain, how-ever, that they were never made aware of the Indian experience and until hearing scholars' recent thoughts on various matters simply were ignorant of what was going on. This ignorance is important to under-stand. It does not imply that all non-Indians are ignorant because they know nothing of the Indian experience, but it does force a dialogue on this matter. It raises these questions for non-Indians: As you were growing up, what was your experience with American Indians? Did you know any? Did you learn anything about them other than that they were supposedly all alcoholics? Did you know the history of boarding schools and colonization? Did you learn about the mental health needs of Indian people while going to college and graduate school, or did you simply read a chapter here and there? It behooves psychologists to know these things. The internalized feelings of shame go deep in many Indian people; it was not long ago in Indian history that Indian people changed from treating each other with equality to engaging in violence against one another. Indians must understand how this impacts treatment and program development if there is to be effective change.

Indians cannot ignore the problems any longer. They must find a way to bridge the gap between community needs and service use. They must fight the powers that control funding so that programs that serve the Indian community are not ignored. They must also implement policy change both internally and externally to ensure that the needs of the Indian community are being met. It is only then that the mental health functioning within tribal communities will cease to be a problem.

Emerging Trends and Future Directions

How then do psychologists bridge the gaps between knowledge, service use, and community needs? The authors in this volume have done an excellent job at starting a dialogue on this important topic, but there are many areas that were not covered and need to be. There is little to no research on the needs of American Indian children with learning and developmental disabilities, the impact that cancer has on the physical and mental well-being of American Indian people, or how serious mental health disorders such as schizophrenia and bipolar disorder impact American Indian individuals.

There is, however, emerging research on violence within Indian communities. Many people, including some of the authors in this volume, are studying the impact violence has on Indian communities and how to effectively treat both men and women in ways that are culturally sensitive. In addition, authors such as Clark and Stately (2004) and Walters and colleagues (Walters, 1999; Walters & Simoni, 1999) have been at the forefront of exploring what does and does not work in this community with regard to HIV/AIDS within Indian populations.

There are also growing numbers of Native and non-Native scholars who are doing research within urban and rural Indian communities. More schools are actively encouraging students to do research with American Indians, and more authors are publishing their work.

Several current books offer some insight into the urban Indian experience. In particular, *American Indians and the Urban Experience* by

Susan Lobo and K. Peters (2001) is an excellent look at how relocation has impacted Indian communities. In addition, *Healing and Mental Health for Native Americans: Speaking in Red* by E. Nebelkopf and M. Phillips (2004) brings together several new and reproduced articles by Native scholars on such varied topics as historical trauma, HIV/AIDS, traditional ceremonies and healing, and building healthy communities. Also, my own upcoming book *Trauma and Tribal Children: Utilizing Play with American Indian Children* (Witko, in press) integrates current research on the impact of trauma on children's functioning, including the types of trauma that children experience, such as abuse and witnessing violence; how the brain is impacted by exposure to trauma; and how age-specific play therapy techniques can be used to heal.

This, of course, is very promising considering that just 10 years ago one would have been hard-pressed to find any research on the strengths within Indian communities. Now, however, scholars are exploring this and many other areas to help heal the past trauma that has affected Indian nations and are looking to these nations as a way to change the Indian people's future. It is hoped that through this book, readers will be encouraged to ask questions that will lead to further research and, in turn, a better understanding of how psychologists can incorporate the best of psychology with what tribal traditions encourage.

References

Clark, R. L., & Stately, A. (2004). American Indians and HIV/AIDS. In E. Nebelkopf & M. Phillips (Eds.), *Healing and mental health for Native Americans: Speaking in red* (pp. 159–165). Lanham, MD: AltaMira Press.

Lobo, S., & Peters, K. (2001). *American Indians and the urban experience.* Lanham, MD: AltaMira Press.

Nebelkopf, E., & Phillips, M. (2004). *Healing and mental health for Native Americans: Speaking in red.* Lanham, MD: AltaMira Press.

Walters, K. L. (1999). Urban American Indian identity attitudes and acculturation styles. *Journal of Human Behavior in the Social Environment, 21,* 163–167.

Walters, K. L., & Simoni, J. M. (1999). Trauma, substance use, and HIV risk among urban American Indian women. *Cultural Diversity and Ethnic Minority Psychology, 5,* 236–248.

Witko, T. M. (in press). *Trauma and tribal children: Utilizing play with American Indian children.* Yankton, SD: Native Healing Network.

Index

A

AAIA. *See* Association on American Indian Affairs
Access
    to services, 92
    to state records, 42
Accidental deaths, 177
Accidents, 84, 85
Acculturation
    and child maltreatment, 37
    definition of, 159
    issues of, 12–13, 159–160
    recognizing levels of, 45
Acculturation stress, 87
Active listening, 26
Adolescents, 173–185
    alcohol-/substance-abuse-related problems in, 175–177
    and biculturalism, 178–180
    education of, 178
    family therapy with, 182–183
    group exercises with, 180–181
    health needs of, 160
    impact of trauma on, 174–175
    individual therapy for, 181–182
    maltreatment of, 177–178
    and multigenerational trauma, 173–174
    PTSD in, 119–120
    storytelling used with, 135–136
    and traditional medicine, 183–184
    youth camp programs for, 180
Adoption, 40, 41
Adoption Promotion and Stability Act (1996), 44
Advocacy
    for battered women, 110

    for families, 168
    for Indian rights, 7
African American children, 34
Agricultural societies, 5
AIANs. *See* American Indians/Native Americans
AIM (American Indian Movement), xi
Alcohol and substance abuse, 83–96
    by adolescents, 175–177
    barriers to treatment for, 91–93
    and child abuse, 36, 89, 194
    dual diagnosis of, 88–89
    health problems related to, 84–85
    historical background of, 86–88
    and identity issues, 56–57
    and limitations of research, 93
    mortality rates related to, 84–85
    patterns of, 89–90
    and PTSD, 124–125
    rates of, 83–84, 193
    storytelling therapy with, 148–149
    as tool of colonialism, 21–22
    treatment for, 90–91
    and violence, 102, 103
Alcoholism, 84
Alcohol use
    stabilization of, 26
    theories of, 22
Alienation from tribal culture, 45
American Indian foster homes, 48–49
American Indian Movement (AIM), xi
American Indians/Native Americans (AIANs), 33, 36
American Indians
    blood quantum of, 11
    government policies regarding, 22–23

About the Editor

Tawa M. Witko, PsyD, a Sicangu Lakota, received her doctorate in clinical psychology from the California School of Professional Psychology in Los Angeles, California. Dr. Witko has worked in Indian country for several years, most recently on the Pine Ridge Indian Reservation in South Dakota for Cangleska, Inc., and in Los Angeles, California, for United American Indian Involvement, Inc. She has provided individual, family, and group counseling; alcohol and drug abuse assessment; parenting assessment and classes; and program development for several Indian communities. She currently works for Heartland Psychological Services in Yankton, South Dakota, providing individual and family counseling to men, women, and children.

Dr. Witko's specialty is mental health treatment of Indian children and their families that incorporates American Indian culture and spirituality with mainstream treatment modalities as well as understanding the impact that violence and substance abuse has on the entire family system. She has been active in programs that support American Indian people, including serving in the American Psychological Association (APA) governance through the Committee on Ethnic Minority Affairs (CEMA) from 2002 to 2005. While serving on CEMA, Dr. Witko worked on issues such as racial profiling and the development of a resolution to the board that would take a stand against Native American mascots.

In addition, Dr. Witko served as the program director of the Diversity Project 2000 and Beyond Summer Institute, a mentoring and leadership program for ethnic minority community college students that encourages them to pursue careers in psychology.

Dr. Witko has also helped in developing the first Diversity Conference for the California School of Professional Psychology, the first convention program for graduate students for the California Psychological Association, and the first American Indian Wellness Conference: Healing Generations for the Department of Mental Health in Los Angeles, all of which are ongoing entities.

Dr. Witko has published articles in the California Psychological Association's Division 7 monograph, *Breaking Barriers: Psychology in the Public Interest* (1998) and in the *California Psychologist* (1999, 2000, 2002, and 2005). In addition, Dr. Witko has developed her own parenting program for urban Indians entitled Honoring the Child, which incorporates mainstream parenting techniques with traditional American Indian parenting approaches; it has been utilized with both urban and reservation Indians.